## DATE DUE

# HYSTERICAL
# PERSONALITY STYLE
# AND THE
# HISTRIONIC PERSONALITY
# DISORDER

# COMMENTARY

"This is one of those few volumes that has the immediate impact of improving one's clinical understanding."

—Allen Frances, M.D.

"*Hysterical Personality and the Histrionic Personality Disorder* provides a creative and jargon-free approach to these disorders. Mardi Horowitz has a clear and original approach to clinical complexity that will allow clinicians to rework their formulations of even their most familiar patients in fresh and helpful directions."

—George E. Vaillant, M.D.

"This is a comprehensive, theoretical, and practical presentation of the subject with emphasis on the clinical and technical handling of the particular facets of the hysterical personality style and dynamics. It is a major contribution to understanding and treatment of the spectrum of hysterical phenomena, and required reading for all mental health practitioners."

—Leon Salzman, M.D.

"[This is] clear, well written, easily understandable, and comprehensive in scope. . . . It is a compendium of our knowledge of hysteria and the hysterical personality."

—Edward Adelson, M.D.

"Hysteria has outlived its obituaries, as Sir Aubrey Lewis predicted, and is alive and well and living in the University of California. [This book's] authors, mostly analysts at that university, define hysterical personality broadly, combining description (the APA definition), dynamics (repression and denial), and cognitive style (following Shapiro's view that hysterical personalities have a global perceptual manner and poor memory)."

—I. M. Ingram, M.D.

# HYSTERICAL PERSONALITY STYLE AND THE HISTRIONIC PERSONALITY DISORDER

Revised Edition

edited by
MARDI J. HOROWITZ, M.D.

JASON ARONSON, INC.
*Northvale, New Jersey*
*London*

*Jason Aronson Inc. gratefully acknowledges permission from Plenum Publishing Corporation to publish Table 1-1 by Gedo and Goldberg from* Models of Mind *(1973).*

**Library of Congress Cataloging-in-Publication Data**

Hysterical personality style and the histrionic personality disorder /
    edited by Mardi J. Horowitz.—Rev. ed.
        p.   cm.
    Rev. ed. of: Hysterical personality. c1977.
    Includes bibliographical references and index.
    ISBN 0-87668-546-7
    1. Hysteria.   2. Personality disorders.   I. Horowitz, Mardi Jon,
1934–    .   II. Hysterical personality.
    [DNLM: 1. Histrionic Personality Disorder.   WM 173 H9995]
RC532.H97   1991
616.85′24—dc20
DNLM/DLC
for Library of Congress                                                     91-4552

Manufactured in the United States of America. Jason Aronson Inc. offers books and cassettes. For information and catalog write to Jason Aronson Inc., 230 Livingston Street, Northvale, New Jersey 07647.

The contributors dedicate this work to the
ideal of the University of California:
*fiat lux.*
This is not pure nostalgic love of institution:
the motto is central to the treatment of
hysterical personality disorders.

# Contents

# Preface to the Revised Edition

The first edition of this work, *Hysterical Personality*, was published in 1977, before the issuance of *DSM-III*, the official nomenclature of the American Psychiatric Association. In *DSM-III*, *hysterical personality disorder* was labeled as *histrionic personality disorder*. We considered changing terminology for the second edition, but as such, *hysterical* has a long and well-known history, and our own work on the topic has become known by its original title.

The term *hysterical*, directly related to women in its etymology (from the Greek word for *womb* or *uterus*), is often pejorative in common usage (e.g., "Don't get hysterical about it"). Unfortunately, all terms can be used pejoratively; no one wants to be diagnosed as having borderline, antisocial, compulsive, or dependent traits. *Histrionic* (from the Late Latin word for *actor*) is not much better. Some people with the core set of maladaptive traits under consideration may not present with conspicuous theatricality but, rather, with shyness and inhibition. Perhaps having warded-off states of attention-seeking that only rarely emerge, they still meet the prototype because of the presence of the other characteristics.

Thus, our present title is a compromise. In the text the term *hysterical* is used more frequently but, as in the *DSM* systems, we mean *hysterical* and *histrionic* to be interchangeable.

This edition begins with a new chapter, introducing the core characteristics of this personality disorder and providing the reader with an introductory framework that will change and be enlarged

ix

with each successive chapter. The second chapter deals with the fundamental diagnostic and formulative issues. The third chapter considers the development of the disorder in terms of childhood and adolescent antecedents. Basic treatment principles are presented in the fourth chapter, and the change process in reschematizing psychological treatment is addressed in the fifth chapter. This last chapter presents a case in detail, indicating development of schemas of self and others, and shows how core aspects of personality (person schemas and habitual self control processes) may change as a consequence of new forms of relationship and new uses of conscious thought.

A chapter in the first edition that dealt with the history of hysteria has been omitted. (The reader is referred to that author's major work, *Hysteria: The History of a Disease* [Veith 1965].) The epidemiological chapter had become too outdated and has also been omitted. All other chapters have been updated by their authors. They still bear the imprint of the fine editing of Nancy Wilner from the first edition; we were fortunate to have Amy Wilner for the editing of this edition. The support of the Program on Conscious and Unconscious Mental Processes by the John D. and Catherine MacArthur Foundation has led to work on person schemas and control processes that permitted changes in my own chapters.

Mardi J. Horowitz, M.D.
San Francisco
March 1991

## REFERENCES

Veith, I. (1965). *Hysteria: The History of a Disease*. Chicago: University of Chicago Press.

# Contributors

David W. Allen, M.D.
Clinical professor emeritus of psychiatry, University of California, San Francisco; past faculty, San Francisco Psychoanalytic Institute.

Kay H. Blacker, M.D.
Professor and Chairman, Department of Psychiatry, University of California School of Medicine, Davis; training and supervising analyst, San Francisco Psychoanalytic Institute.

Mardi J. Horowitz, M.D.
Professor of psychiatry and Director, John D. and Catherine T. MacArthur Foundation Program on Conscious and Unconscious Mental Processes, University of California, San Francisco; faculty, San Francisco Psychoanalytic Institute; training and supervising analyst, SFIPPP.

Aubrey W. Metcalf, M.D.
Clinical professor of psychiatry, senior supervising child and adolescent psychiatrist, University of California, San Francisco.

Joe P. Tupin, M.D.
Medical Director, University of California, Davis Medical Center; professor of psychiatry, University of California School of Medicine, Davis.

# CHAPTER 1

# Core Traits of Hysterical or Histrionic Personality Disorders

MARDI J. HOROWITZ, M.D.

This chapter aims to provide a rapid overview of key diagnostic features of these disorders of personality. Clinical examples that enrich understanding, and explanations, will be found in other chapters.

Personality classification, and classification of disorders of personality, have been human activities throughout history. A paradox haunts the effort: personality typology groups persons together by the very attributes that highlight their individual differences. One may generalize on the traits of a hysterical personality, but no particular person will ever precisely fit the description. The study of any individual must formulate those traits that differ from type as well as those that conform to a typology.

A general framework for understanding the core traits of hysterical personality disorder can be obtained by considering common (1) signs and symptoms, (2) states of mind, (3) self schemas and role-relationship models, and (4) styles of information processing and control. Person schemas and control processes, and so the emergent signs and symptoms, may vary from state to state. Surprising state transition patterns may occur and may vary according to the person's (5) level of self development. This chapter covers each of these five topics in sequence.

## SIGNS AND SYMPTOMS

Patients complain of symptoms; clinicians observe psychiatric signs. Together, clusters of signs and symptoms indicate a syndrome. In personality disorders the signs and symptoms are often traits in that signs and symptoms recur.

Patients who seek treatment for a hysterical personality disorder may complain of recurrent and uncontrolled episodes of emotional flooding of conscious experience. Feelings emerge involuntarily and then are hard to dispel. Thought is sometimes jumbled but seldom grossly irrational or delusional. Such patients complain that their interpersonal relationships are unsatisfactory.

Aims at satisfying long-term relationships are periodically frustrated. There may be a sense of desperation and inability to "wait" for new relationships to develop gradually. The insistent need for attention can alienate others. Values may fluctuate according to the interests of current companions rather than the self. Naiveté may be maintained, leading to poor interpersonal decisions and, eventually, to plummeting self-esteem.

Productive work is sometimes impaired by mood variation, impulsive shifts in direction, and social friction. An intolerance for frustration may be manifested by insistence on immediate gratification. Patience is rare. Alcohol or other self-prescribed drugs may be used to quickly stop states of negative feeling, with a variety of secondary effects from addiction and impaired mind-brain functioning.

Labile change in emotionality may occur. The person may go from gaiety to tears, and the reasons may be obscure to companions. Somatic preoccupations and suddenly enraged, despairing, or fearful states may occur. Intrusive traumatic memories, suicidal thoughts, impaired sensory, motor, or memory function, or clouded consciousness may occur.

## STATES OF MIND

Signs and symptoms are often intermittent rather than constant. This is especially true when personality traits are the elements of psychopathology. Signs and symptoms occur in clusters and with features that are relevant but neither complained of nor labeled as psychopathology. The overall configuration can be regarded as a state of mind, and contrasted with other states of mind in the repertoire of the person (Horowitz 1979/1987).

States of mind are recognized by clinicians in terms of their relational-emotionality and qualities of apparent self regulation. Over- and undermodulated states appearing to have either too much or too little in the way of voluntary self-control are the most salient to diagnostic formulations. Issues of which states are desired, dreaded, or used defensively are also important.

The term *histrionic* has become the contemporary label for these personality disorders because observers are often struck by a dramatic state of mind. What observers note as "theatrical" is the intensity of attention-seeking display during this state and also the suddenness of state transitions from a duller state into this striking one. Emotional expressions during such histrionic states of mind appear oriented to whatever may arouse the interest of others (Millon and Everly 1985).

The body, as erotic or ill, is often used to attract the attention of others. The actual sensual arousal may be low; the real illness or handicap may be less than displayed. The person is then accused of being manipulative and of feigning attitudes. But the person with a hysterical personality is not consciously aiming to deceive and is unaware of any fabrication. The accusations are unfair and may, in the case of real illness, prevent the patient from getting optimum medical or psychiatric treatment (Slavney et al. 1989). The person may be hurt at being treated as inauthentic.

The dramatic state of mind is an animated one and it stands in contrast to depressed states of mind, which it may reciprocally inhibit. In other words, while the dramatically animated state may have maladaptive consequences, it is nonetheless relatively more desired than dreaded. The states of being flooded with uncontrolled negative affects are the most dreaded, especially frightened–depressed states dwelling on fears of being left alone and angry states that may drive others away from companionship. In this sense, the dramatic states are adaptive.

The histrionic or dramatic state of mind has the hallmark of inappropriateness. In the wrong setting, the person presents the body as sexually attractive, dressing seductively for a business meeting, for example. Or the person presents needs or handicaps in the wrong context, asking for sympathy when there are other pressing issues that require working cooperation. A state transition to sullen, hurt pouting may occur when the attention sought is not given. Shy, inhibited states of mind may also be used as a compromise, avoiding the dangers of self display. The person wants to gain attention rather than giving up to despair but fears that when he or she does get the desired attention it will be too exciting and lead towards undermodulated states of mind in which self-control is lost.

## SELF SCHEMAS AND ROLE-RELATIONSHIP MODELS

States of mind recurr and seem the same, then, because the same schematizations are used to organize conscious experience and action. The most relevant of these forms of schematized knowledge involve self as related to others. Person schemas theory describes how each person functions with a repertoire of such schemas of self and others, including schemas for controlling other schemas (Horowitz 1987, 1989, 1991).

The traits and attributes of each person in a relationship, as well as a script of interactions, may be schematized as a role-relationship model.

During the histrionic or dramatic state of mind the role-relationship model that is used to organize experience and action may schematize the self in a role such as a sexy star, a distressed or wounded hero, a worthy invalid, or an appealing but neglected waif. Display of the attributes of this role attracts attention from a desired other. Roles of other are complementary, such as an interested suitor, a devoted rescuer, or a rueful and now responsible caretaker. The responsive activity of the other is, in a schema of script sequence, to provide the desired attention. The self, having gained interest, then feels restored, grateful, and loving.

A real transaction may not fit such schematized scripts for a desired sequence of transactions. Also, the schematic script may have a sequence derailed from wish to fear. In a dreaded form of role-relationship models of the theme of desire, the other, once interested by displays, may then misuse the self. In sequence, the self may become angry or fearful about the misuse. The other may abandon the self. The result of enactment of such scripts is a transition from states of dramatic display through ones of accusatory rage and then despair. The cycle of states resumes by once again soliciting interest from others in order to relieve despair.

In actual interpersonal patterns, the result may be that the self feels exploited by the other person, while the other feels manipulated because the initial display was insubstantial (for example, shallowness or coldness lay beneath the surface of apparent warmth or depth). The result is a variety of scenarios in which victim, aggressor, and rescuer roles are enacted with little in the way of deep satisfaction or true intimacy. These scenarios will be clarified in the clinical examples of the ensuing chapters.

Memories of such scenarios may emphasize a passive self that was exploited, poorly cared for, or abandoned. Others held the active, and hence blameful, roles. The person's conscious sense of self, and the stories related to clinicians, may not contain an acknowledgment of his or her active use of charm, vivacity, sex appeal, brilliance, creativity, childlikeness, need, or infirmity to gain and maintain attention from others. In addition, awareness of the intentions and feelings of others is often shallow or colored by erroneous beliefs (Standage et al. 1984). In other words, dramatic repetitions of victim–aggressor–rescuer scenarios may be enacted without clear conscious awareness of what is happening and without self-reflection on how and why it is happening.

To recapitulate, the person may display him- or herself to solicit interest without consciously realizing the likely consequences. He or she may then get too enthralled or enmeshed in a relationship in which he or she is exploited or harmed. The person then "wakes up" into a context of threat. States of animation from being the center of attention may shift to severe fear of sadistic assault or despair at being abandoned. He or she may angrily depict the other person as one who broke rules of what was supposed to happen, with the self perceived consciously as innocent, injured victim. Usually, however, there is also unconscious self criticism and self-punitive impulses.

In stories about relationships, both self and other(s) may be described in a way that seems caricatured. The tales may have a cardboard, melodramatic quality. The person may live through many dramatic events, but he or she may still experience life as somehow unreal. Relationships are established too quickly and with the wrong kind of person. Commitments do not last. With aging, the person may feel that he or she has wasted life by drifting through it (Pilkonis and Frank 1988, Pfohl et al. 1984). The result can be a depression.

Neurotic cogwheeling may occur in establishing relationships. Sadomasochistic unions are not uncommon. The person with a hysterical style may make a kind of masochistic prepayment on the assumption that after causing hurt the aggressor will feel remorse and so provide compensatory love and attention. In other unions, there may be a chronic dependency on a person who has to feel strong in relation to a the self as a fragile companion. Unfortunately, there may also be a tendency to seek attention from new companions, which can provoke unwise separations from a long-standing partner.

Countertransference reactions may also be observed by clinicians and used as a sign in recognizing these disorders of personality. On first meetings, the person with a hysterical personality disorder, with his or her stories and eager interest, may activate a sense in the clinician of being quite special, unusually likely to be of help. A period of enthusiasm may follow. Later the patient may be seen as shallow or distant. Hostile rejecting impulses may then occur. The patient may be abandoned just when he or she is most in need of help.

## CONTROL OF INFORMATION PROCESSING

Many persons with this form of personality disorder have maladaptive forms of information processing that have been well described by Shapiro (1965). They may deploy attention globally and diffusely. But they may also rivet attention on a singular focus of whether another is paying attention to and wanting to get closer to them. There may be a gifted attunement to gaze, facial expression, and voice inflections. Yet, this attention remains on the surface; the deeper intentions of the other person are not consciously considered. Attention to understanding the past and planning the future may be diffuse and excessively brief rather than organized and sustained.

Because of their vivacious emotionality, such persons may be quite interesting to listen to. But on closer attention to the stories they relate about maladaptive interpersonal patterns, it will be hard to know what happened and in what sequence. Who really instigated which course of action will be difficult to determine. In part, as already mentioned, this will be found to be due to a tendency to avoid blame by taking passive roles either at the time or in retrospect.

Attention may shift rapidly and may be focused less on a shared topic of dialogue and more on whether or not the companion is attuned to the self in whatever manner is most desired. Dialogue on a topic is nonlinear in terms of how one concept is linked to another in developing a rational sequence of ideas. Associations are unusually free, to the point that the linkages made may actually derail thought. Images in auditory or visual modes, or bodily gestures and positionings, are poorly translated into words; nonverbal modes of representation may contain meanings that contradict the concepts presented verbally. These characteristics are more prominent in states of high emotional arousal.

Instead of staying with problems in order to consider alternative solutions, the person with this personality style characteristically may tend to short-circuit to quick, impulsive conclusions. This looks to them like a decision, but the results are often maladaptive due to wishful thinking.

## LEVEL OF SELF DEVELOPMENT: SELF AND OBJECT SCHEMATIZATION

Many normal persons are buoyant, emotional, dramatically expressive, given somewhat more to impulsive action than is conventional, and vivacious in interpersonal transactions. They possess traits of flamboyance, flair, and drama. They command interest. *This is a normal style, not a personality disorder.*

The hysterical personality disorder is not a normal style. It occurs in a range of neurotic, narcissistically vulnerable, borderline, and even psychotically fragmented disturbances (Horowitz 1987, 1988, 1991, Horowitz and Zilberg 1983, Kernberg 1988, Stone 1981). A formulation about level of development of self is indicated. Using person schemas theory, a person with a hysterical personality disorder might be formulated as being at Modes 1–4 in organizational level of self and object schematization, as defined in Table 1–1 (derived from Gedo and Goldberg 1973, Horowitz 1987).

The person with a *neurotic level* (Mode 4 in Table 1–1) of hysterical personality may have a superficial relationship style that leads to overinvolvement with and then separations from others.

## Table 1–1

### Organizational Level of Self and Object Schematization (OLSOS)*

| Mode | Description |
|------|-------------|
| Mode 5 normal | Such persons have a well-developed supra-ordinate self (a schema of several self-schemas) and function from a relatively unitary position of self as agent, and have values about long-standing issues. They have conflicts and negative moods and own these as "of the self." Conflicts are between various realistic pros and cons or limitations of real relationships. Conflicts tend to be consciously handled well through the use of well-modulated restraints, renunciations, sublimations, choices, wisdom, humor, or even resignation. The person is able to achieve intersubjectivity or "we-ness" and to empathically know that another is separate with equivalent characteristics to his or her own, also experiencing wishes, fears, emotional reactions, conflicts, memories, and fantasies. |
| Mode 4 neurotic | Such persons have self schemas of a realistic nature. Yet, in some situations, these persons experience contradictory aims of self as agent of action and self as critic that are not resolved in a reasonable time by rational choices. For example, they may see themselves continually as both intending to express some aim in behavior and opposing such expression on moral grounds, with indecisive repetitive rumination on the theme or repetitive doing and undoing actions. Enduring, unresolved enactments of conflicts about sexuality, love, attention, responsibility, and power indicate this mode. |

| Mode | Description |
|---|---|
| Mode 3 narcissistically vulnerable | These persons are often able to maintain a cohesive and relatively realistic self schema, but there are states of exception; in these situations, they are vulnerable to a sense of self-impoverishment, a loss of a sense of self-cohesion, to grandiosity, or to externalization and internalization of characteristics of self and other at an unrealistic level. For example, a person with enduring grandiose delusions confined to a sphere of creativity or sexuality might be assigned this mode, as would a person who consistently disowned personal aggressive behavior, although it was flagrantly obvious to others. Some others are viewed irrationally as if extensions of self (selfobjects). |
| Mode 2 borderline | These persons are not able to stabilize self-cohesion that includes positive and negative self schemas in a supraordinate schema of schemas. Rather, they have various self schemas that are each only part of the actual self and various schemas of others that include only part of the actual behavior of others. Composites that are all-good may be dissociated from composites that are all-bad. |
| Mode 1 fragmented | These persons have a self and other differentiation that is only partial and transitory. At times they display or experience a significant level of confusion of self with other, or they regard self and other as merged or interchangeable. Parts of the bodily self may be disowned or dissociated. |

*Modes derived and revised from Gedo and Goldberg (1973) and Horowitz (1979/1987).

11

The pattern may include a tendency to develop envy and rivalry in triangular situations. The person will recurrently desire the kind of bond seen in pairs of other people, and then enact or inhibit overtures to occupy an intimate role in that relationship by displacing the person seen as a rival for attention.

The person with a *narcissistic level* of hysterical personality disorder (Mode 3 in Table 1–1) may use other persons as selfobjects (Kohut 1971, 1977) and seem self-centered to the point of lacking concern for the needs and sensitivities of others. Demands for praise from mirroring selfobjects, obsequious sidling up to idealized figures, or inappropriate twining with complementary others may characterize their recurrent maladaptive relationship patterns.

The person with *borderline level* of hysterical personality disorder (Mode 2 in Table 1–1) may dissociate views of self as related to others into all-good and all-bad variants (Gunderson and Singer 1975, Kernberg 1975). Explosive shifts in state of mind can occur with rage reactions when a lapse in attention from another is noted. If a frustrating or insulting response comes from a desired person, the view of self may change from worthwhile to worthless, the view of the other from well-intentioned to malevolent. Short-term "hysterical psychotic states" or "reactive psychoses" may occur. Functioning may even reach the fragmented organizational level (Mode 1 in Table 1–1).

## REFERENCES

Gedo, J., and Goldberg, A. (1973). *Models of the Mind*. Chicago: University of Chicago Press.

Gunderson, J. G., and Singer, M. T. (1975). *Defining Borderline Patients: An Overview*. New York: International Universities Press.

Horowitz, M. J. (1979/1987). *States of Mind*. 1st and 2nd eds. New York: Plenum.

———(1988). *Introduction to Psychodynamics*. New York: Basic Books.

———(1989). Relationship schema formulation: role-relationship models and intrapsychic conflict. *Psychiatry* 52:260–274.

———(1991). Person schemas. In *Person Schemas and Maladaptive Interpersonal Patterns*, ed. M. J. Horowitz, Chicago: University of Chicago Press.

Horowitz, M. J., and Zilberg, N. (1983). Regressive alterations in the self-concept. *American Journal of Psychiatry* 140:284–289.

Kernberg, O. (1975). *Borderline Conditions and Pathological Narcissism.* Northvale, NJ: Jason Aronson.

———(1988). Hysterical and histrionic personality disorders. In *Psychiatry,* ed. R. Michels et al. Philadelphia: Lippincott.

Kohut, H. (1971). *The Analysis of the Self.* New York: International Universities Press.

———(1977). *Restoration of the Self.* New York: International Universities Press.

Millon, T., and Everly, Jr., G. S. (1985). *Personality and Its Disorders: A Biosocial Learning Approach.* New York: Wiley.

Pfohl, B., Stangl, D., and Zimmerman, M. (1984). The implications of *DSM-III* personality disorders for patients with major depression. *Journal of Affective Disorders* 7:309–318.

Pilkonis, P., and Frank, E. (1988). Personality pathology in recurrent depression: nature, prevalence, and relationship to treatment response. *American Journal of Psychiatry* 145:435–441.

Shapiro, D. (1965). *Neurotic Styles.* New York: Basic Books.

Slavney, P., Teitelbaum, M., and Chase, G. (1989). Referral for medically unexplained somatic complaints: the role of histrionic traits. *Psychosomatics* 26:103–109.

Standage, K., Bilsburg, C., Subhash, J., and Smith, D. (1984). An investigation of role-taking in histrionic personalities. *Canadian Journal of Psychiatry* 29:407–411.

Stone, M. (1981). Borderline syndromes: a consideration of subtypes and an overview. *Psychiatric Clinic of North America* 4:3–24.

CHAPTER 2

# Hysteria and Hysterical Structures: Developmental and Social Theories

KAY H. BLACKER, M.D., AND
JOE P. TUPIN, M.D.

We will trace the main concepts of hysterical character structure and hysterical symptoms throughout the twentieth century. To begin this review of the modern era, we look to the origins of psychoanalysis. Hysteria's more ancient origins have been summarized elsewhere by Veith (1965).

## PSYCHOANALYTIC THEORIES

The psychoanalytic understanding of hysterical behavior began with Breuer's observation of his patient, Anna O. Since hysterical behaviors cannot be understood outside the context in which they occur, it is helpful to understand the physician who made the observations, as well as the young woman who produced the phenomena.

Joseph Breuer was a highly respected, 40-year-old physician at the time Anna's family contacted him to aid their daughter. He was a "doctor's doctor" whose diagnostic skills and medical acumen were so well recognized and acknowledged by his colleagues that he was a physician to many of them. His career had been distinguished. As a young man at 26 and again at 32, he had made important scientific observations regarding human physiology that are acknowledged as basic contributions even today. He was described by colleagues and family as a gentle, sensitive man with an inquiring, scientific spirit.

Breuer's scientific training with his teacher, Brücke, gave him a thorough grounding in empirical observation. He was caught up in

17

the philosophical zeitgeist of his time, that is, the attempt to explain all phenomena on physical grounds. His extensive and clear descriptions of Anna O. reflected his attempt to apply strict scientific principles to the bewildering phenomena—the complicated montage—of symptoms that unfolded before him.

In his famous study of respiratory physiology, which he published when he was 26, Breuer (Schlessinger et al. 1967)

> conceived the idea of self-regulatory process—a hypothesis of feedback control mechanisms which proved to have wide, general applicability . . . [he] devised novel techniques which permitted observation of the natural excitatory processes occurring in pulmonary tissue during expansion and contraction of the lungs. [p. 408]

Previous investigators had either stimulated or severed the vagus nerve, which had precluded observation of the normal physiological state and prevented the identification of a feedback control mechanism. Breuer's subsequent physiological investigation of the semicircular canals follows the same pattern. Again, meticulous dissection and a patient approach enabled him to make observations that were not possible when utilizing the blunt methods of his predecessors.

Breuer's work with Anna shows the same dedication and meticulous attention to detail he had used in making his earlier physiological discoveries. His approach enabled him to discover psychological processes that had not been observable when utilizing the medical treatments of his day. He was with this young woman almost daily for two years, and his descriptions are a model of Germanic scientific exactitude. Paradoxically, while his intense, focused attention enabled him to make the crucial observations, his attention also unknowingly encouraged a proliferation of symptoms and intensification of the illness (see Gedo et al. 1964).

Anna was the second of four children of an Orthodox Jewish, wealthy mercantile family. Two younger sisters died in early childhood. She had a brother two years her senior. Although there is little mention of her mother in the famous case report, material from Anna's later life suggests they were close. Her difficulties began after her father developed symptoms of a pulmonary illness that continued in an unremitting fashion, resulting in his death nine months later (see Pollock 1968, 1973).

Breuer saw this young woman as bubbling over with intellectual vitality and smothered by the monotonous existence in her puritanically minded family. He felt she gained relief by "indulging in systematic daydreaming, which she described as her 'private theatre'. . . . She pursued this activity almost continuously while engaged in her household duties, which she discharged unexceptionally" (Breuer and Freud 1893–1895, p. 22). Breuer felt that this habitual daydreaming played an important role in the development of her illness.

He described a variegated illness, one filled with symptoms of many types: disturbance of vision, paralysis to the point of contractures, paresthesias, and altered states of consciousness. The form of Anna's difficulties varied in relationship with the course of her father's terminal illness (Breuer and Freud 1893–1895):

> . . . two entirely distinct stages of consciousness were present which alternated very frequently and without warning and which became more and more differentiated in the course of the illness. In one of these states she recognized her surroundings; she was melancholy and anxious but relatively normal. In the other state she hallucinated and was naughty—that is to say, she was abusive, used to throw cushions at people, so far as the contractures at various times allowed, tore buttons off her bed clothes and linen with those of her fingers which she could move, and so on. [p. 24]

Gradually the doctor and the patient became aware of variations in her disorders and both began to sense some regularity in these variations (Breuer and Freud 1893–1895):

> And now for the first time the psychical mechanism of the disorder became clear. As I knew, she had felt very much offended over something and had determined not to speak of it. When I guessed this and obliged her to talk about it, the inhibition, which had made any other kind of utterance impossible as well, disappeared. [p. 25]

> She aptly described this procedure, speaking seriously, as a talking cure, while she referred to it jokingly as chimney-sweeping. [p. 30]

Breuer became increasingly attuned to this phenomenon and observed:

This was because every one of the spontaneous products of her imagination and every event which had been assimilated by the pathological part of her mind persisted as a psychical stimulus until it had been narrated in her hypnosis, after which it completely ceased to operate. [p. 32]

These observations prompted Breuer and Freud to advance their now familiar formulation: "hysterics suffer mainly from reminiscences" (Breuer and Freud 1893–1895, p.7).

In 1893, Breuer and Freud hypothesized that hysterical symptoms were caused by intense memories or ideas of events; these they termed *psychic traumas*. They postulated that the recollection of these traumas formed an irritant that resulted in psychical splitting, a process that accomplished the removal of the memory from consciousness and that formed the basis for hysteria. They suggested two reasons why they felt the traumas were not experienced in a normal fashion and why the memory of them failed to wear away or diminish: first, because "it was a question of things which the patient wished to forget, and therefore intentionally repressed from his conscious thought and inhibited and suppressed" (Breuer and Freud 1893–1895, p. 10). Simply stated, the trauma was viewed to be actively isolated by the patient's mind because its content and associated affects posed serious threat to the emotional well-being or self concept of the patient. Second, because the memories "originated during the prevalence of severely paralyzing affects, such as fright, or during positively abnormal psychical states, such as the semihypnotic twilight state of daydreaming, autohypnosis, and so on" (Breuer and Freud 1893–1895, p. 11). Breuer named this state "hypnoid" and felt that the nature of the state made a normal reaction to an event impossible. This postulate is remarkably close to a modern theory developed out of neurophysiological laboratories, which is termed "state dependent learning" (Weingartner and Faillace 1971).

Breuer did not continue with the cathartic method or even his investigation of hysterical symptoms after Anna O. He was frightened off by Anna's outpouring of love for him. Freud, on the other hand, continued his own work and became increasingly impressed that the psychological factor was the cause of the psychic splitting and the formation of hysterical symptoms. In 1894, he stated (Freud 1893–1899),

I was repeatedly able to show that the splitting of the content of consciousness is a result of an *act of will* on the part of the patient; that is to say, *it is initiated by an effort of will whose motive can be specified* [italics mine]. By this I do not, of course, mean that the patient intends to bring about a splitting of consciousness. His intention is a different one; but, instead of attaining its aim, he produces a splitting of consciousness. [p. 46]

Freud specified that this splitting occurred when

an occurrence of incompatibility took place in their ideational life—that is to say . . . the ego was faced with an experience, idea, or feeling which aroused such distressing affect that the subject decided to forget about it because he had no confidence in his power to resolve the contradiction between the incompatible idea and his ego by means of thought—activity. [p. 47]

"In females," Freud further stated, "incompatible ideas of this sort arise chiefly on the soil of sexual experience and sensation" (p. 47). He proposed that the emotions that were pushed away or suppressed were expressed in another form: "But the sum of excitation which has been detached from [the idea] must be put to another use. . . . In hysteria, the incompatible idea is rendered innocuous by its sum of excitation being transformed to something somatic. For this I should like to propose the name of conversion" (1893–1899. p. 49).

Initially, Freud believed his female hysterical patients when they told him they had been sexually molested as children. Only with further clinical experience did he recognize that he was at that period "unable to distinguish with certainty between falsifications made by hysterics in their memories of childhood and traces of real events" (Freud 1901–1905, p. 274). With this added information he revised his theory in the following way: "They [hysterical symptoms] were now no longer to be regarded as direct derivatives of the repressed memories of childhood experiences; but between the symptoms and the childish impressions, there were inserted the patient's fantasies (or imaginary memories)" (Freud 1901–1905, p. 274). Such fantasies were usually unconsciously manufactured attempts to conceal a variety of infantile sexual wishes and activities. It was these wishes and activities Freud now viewed as producing the splitting and conversion symptoms.

The richness of his new theory is readily observable in the famous Dora case (Freud 1901–1905). In this paper, Freud used the case material to illustrate his recent discoveries of childhood sexuality and his more sophisticated knowledge of mental functioning. The case is a complicated tale involving not only the difficulties of a bright and stubborn young woman, but also of a complex relationship between two families, and a series of falsifications on the part of the father. What is crucial to our modern understanding of hysteria, however, is Freud's discussion of the many hysterical symptoms. With Dora, Freud clearly recognized and detailed the multiple determination of a single symptom. Dora both loved and felt betrayed by her father; her father's friend, Herr K.; and the wife of her father's friend, Frau K. Her symptoms seemed to be expressions of both heterosexual and homosexual love, guilt, anger, and rage influenced by a severe repression of early childhood masturbatory activities—activities that Freud had been able to decipher from Dora's dream reports.

This strong-willed young woman broke off treatment after three months. After publishing this case report and a paper on the etiology of hysteria in 1906, Freud left the investigation of hysterical phenomena. He did not proceed further than the explanations he provided in the Dora case, in which he stressed the multidetermined nature of hysterical symptoms and the repression of infantile sexual wishes and activities.

Although Freud did not attempt to organize and integrate his theories, others did. There resulted from these efforts, and the addition of later psychoanalytic concepts, a symmetrical, generally agreed-upon formulation of hysterical symptoms. Freud's theories of libidinal development and of the Oedipus complex were amalgamated into a stereotype. According to this stereotype, hysterical symptoms arise from repressed sexual wishes. These strivings are unable to achieve expression or sublimation because of oedipal fears—that is, because of fear of punishment from the parent of the same sex. According to this formulation, this conflict induces a psychic regression and the production of symptoms. For example, the globus hystericus was felt to represent sexual excitement displaced upwards from the vagina to the throat. Vomiting was interpreted as concern about oral impregnation.

Fenichel (1945), in his encyclopedic summary of psychoanalytic phenomena and theories, felt secure enough to state:

> Conversion hysteria is the classical subject matter of psychoanalysis. As a matter of fact, the psychoanalytic method was discovered, tested, and perfected through the study of hysterical patients . . . the technique of psychoanalysis still remains most easily applicable to cases of hysteria, and it is the psychoanalytic treatment of hysteria that continued to yield the best therapeutic results. [p. 230]

And he continues: "Freud's statement that the oedipal complex is the nuclear complex of the neuroses is particularly valid in hysteria, which remains on the level of the phallic phase of sexual development" (p. 231). Although early analysts were aware of preoedipal conflicts in hysterical patients, they considered these conflicts to represent regressions from oedipal struggles, not fixations at earlier developmental levels:

> And between the original Oedipus fantasies and the latter day-dreams there are inserted infantile masturbatory fantasy, whose Oedipus character is sometimes rather distorted. The conflicts which were originally connected with the Oedipus complex frequently are displaced onto the act of masturbation. That is why so frequently the struggle against masturbation is found as the unconscious content of hysterical symptoms. [p. 231]

This stereotyped formulation held sway for many years until clinical experience demonstrated its fallacies. Many analysts had begun to question the alleged ease with which hysterics were thought to be treated by psychoanalysis and psychotherapy, and in 1953 Marmor brought together much of the analytic experience that raised questions concerning the oedipal formulation of hysteria. Many analysts had found that, although symptom relief might occur early and dramatically in the course of treatment, it was more often a form of transference compliance than of major and enduring personality change. Often this compliance and the associated wish to be loved and protected became the major source of resistance to further maturation. For example, Wittels (1930) as early as the 1920s had noted the difficulty that the hysterical character had in freeing himself from fixation at an infantile level. To Wittels, the hysteric remained as a child confusing fantasy and reality. Reich (1933) formulated his theoretical understanding in terms of conflict at the genital phase of development, but in his descriptions he stressed preoedipal developmental facts: "in as much as pregenital, oral, anal, and urethral strivings form a part of the hysterical character—as is always the case" (p. 206).

Marmor argued that the oral mechanisms and symptoms are always conspicuous in hysteria, for example, globus hystericus, vomiting, anorexia, bulimia, history of prolonged thumb sucking in childhood. He stated the preoedipal conflicts played a greater role in determining the dynamics of hysteria than had been generally assumed. To him, the incestuous dream of the hysteric concealed, behind the symbolic wish to cohabit with the mother (or father), a deeper wish to be loved and protected by her (or him) to the exclusion of the rest of the world. He held, for example, that the phallus in a dream represented, in the deepest sense, the breast. Marmor felt that much of the sexuality of the hysteric was a sham, primarily because it expressed a pregenital oral-receptive wish rather than a genital one.

The distress and surprise of the hysterical woman when her seductiveness leads her to being approached genitally is consequently understandable. She is being approached as a woman when what she really desires is to be taken as a child. Repeatedly, one hears the hysterical woman say, "If only a man would just kiss me and hold me in his arms instead of wanting sex!" This theme of the hysterical woman's wanting to be held—not seduced—was developed further by Hollender (1971).

Marmor maintained that oedipal conflicts played a prominent role in the hysteric's psychopathology. He felt, however, that early oral fixations gave the subsequent Oedipus complex of the hysteric a strong pregenital cast. He felt it was possible to note in the oedipal history of most hysterics either intense frustration of oral-receptive needs as a consequence of early rejection by parents or an excessive gratification of these needs. Either, Marmor postulated, resulted in preoedipal fixations. He also speculated that the greater frequency of hysteria in women as compared to men may be a cultural phenomenon. He felt that the oral receptivity, dependency, and passivity were perhaps more easily expressed by women in our society, since they were acceptable feminine traits. We agree with Marmor's speculation and will have more to say about this later.

An article by Melitta Sperling (1973), describing many years of analytic work with hysterical patients, probably summarizes today's psychoanalytic conceptualization. Sperling described a woman much like Freud's Dora. The symptomatology was remarkably similar, consisting of "frequent attacks of severe difficulty in breathing, associated with rapid heart beat, dizziness, and fainting spells. She also had coughing spells which often lasted for a month, attacks of 'laryngitis' which resulted in her becoming aphonic for days at a time, and migraine headaches" (pp. 745–746). Sperling noted that in her patient, "the whole body and bodily functions were highly sexualized. Vagina and anus, the womb and the rectum, sexual functions and secretions, were mixed up with anal functions and excretions and then displaced from the genital and anal areas to the oral cavity and respiratory system, including the nose" (p. 752). The basic issue in the dynamics of this patient, and the many other hysterics Sperling had worked with during her thirty years of analytic experience, was the fear of attaching herself to the analyst and then being unable to bear losing the analyst. The patient had recurrent dreams in which the outstanding feeling was that of being alone in an empty street. She saw the analyst as a mother whom she feared would disappoint her and leave her.

Sperling stressed the primitive and destructive meanings of hysterical symptoms: "It [the quality of object relations in these patients] is a special form of symbiotic mother–child relationship in which the mother, because of her own pathological needs, does not permit overt expression of aggression, self-assertion, and rebellion against her, but puts a premium on submission and dependence and rewards the child by special care given to him when he is sick. The child early learns to repress aggressive and other impulses and affects objectionable to his mother" (pp. 763–764). According to

Sperling's understanding of hysteria and conversion symptoms, "the concept of the preoedipal mother transference, its role in the production of negative therapeutic reactions, and the technique of recognizing and analyzing it are of utmost importance in the treatment of patients with conversion symptoms" (pp. 766–767). She felt that oedipal conflicts and adult sexual wishes and conflicts can serve as the trigger for the development of hysterical symptomatology. However, in her view the conversion symptoms per se are only understandable in terms of the early relationships between the mothering parent and the child: "It would seem that conversion is possible only in a state of regression to pregenital, symbiotic phases of development. All conversion is therefore pregenital by nature" (p. 769).

Freud's initial theories concerning hysterical symptoms focused on their sexual meaning and the sexual conflicts involved. These concepts in turn were reformulated by other analysts in terms of the Oedipus complex. Sperling's paper is one of a long series of reports detailing the pregenital components of hysterical symptoms. These papers stressed the primitive type of object relationships in hysterical patients resulting from disturbances in early mothering and the importance of the aggressive impulses, as well as the sexual ones, in the formation of hysterical symptoms.

Some of the confusion within psychoanalytic theories was further clarified when, in 1959, Rangell pointed out the error of equating the symptom of conversion with the concept of hysteria: "There lingered on the general automatic association of conversion with hysteria, so the two have been indissolubly linked. Tell an analyst conversion, and he adds hysteria. . . . This automatic associating has long since outlived its usefulness and even longer its accuracy" (p. 633).

Rangell amassed evidence that the conversion process itself "is employed to express forbidden wishes throughout the entire gamut of psychopathological symptomatology" (p. 636) and is not merely limited to the expression of adult genital sexual conflicts in hysterical patients. The conversion mechanism is seen to be a process that can be placed into operation at any or all phases of conflictual pressure. For example, "A stiff neck can, via its hypercathected voluntary musculature, symbolically represent a forbidden erection based upon incestuous wishes" (p. 639). It can also, as in catatonia, symbolically represent an archaic and primitive level of functioning, such as a restraining of an aggressive discharge toward the outer world.

Rangell suggested the term "conversion" be used in the following manner: "Conversion, as we would restrict it, is a sequel to conflicts, mild or severe. It is an act of ego process, in the direction of symptom formulation (p. 645). They (conversion symptoms) are all of the nature of pathological defensive formations in the service of maintaining homeostasis" (p. 646). Indeed, it is uncertain as to whether or not conversion symptoms are more frequently found in connection with other hysterical symptoms. Two investigators, Chodoff and Lyons (1958), state there is no association, while others (see Guze 1975) claim there is a common, although not an invariable, association with hysteria.

Thus, the classic theory of genital libidinal fixation and incestuous yearnings has given way to a broader, richer, and more complex formulation emphasizing pregenital elements and ego functions. This new picture, developing from Marmor's amalgamation of classic libidinal theory with ego psychology, emphasizes oral fixations, the close relation to addiction, depression, and schizophrenia. It appears that within an individual patient there is a heterogeneous mixture of fixations and conflicts. And when we begin to compare hysterical patients to one another, we find they differ greatly and can best be described as existing at points on a continuum of disorders marked by two polarities, the "good genital" and "bad oral hysteric" (Easser and Lesser 1965, Kernberg 1967, Lazare 1971, Zetzel 1968). This spectrum essentially reflects the degree of ego impairment and/or the level of ego development achieved in the course of maturation. The usefulness of the concept of a continuum of disorders relative to the structure of an individual's personality, which in turn is determined by the level of fixations and conflicts, will be further developed below.

## AFFECTIVE THEORY: HYSTEROID DYSPHORIA

Kline and Davis (1969), in a brief passage in their book, describe a patient type that they call *hysteroid dysphoria*. They describe the behavior of these patients as characterized by emotionality, irresponsibility, shallowness, giddy affect, and shortsighted action.

They are further characterized as seductive, manipulative, exploitive, exhibitionistic, egocentric, and narcissistic. Kline and Davis comment that the patients' thinking is determined by emotions and, as a consequence, is illogical. But, they point out,

> Although these patients refer to their dysphoric mood as 'depression' the essential characteristics of the pathologic depressive mood are not salient. They are prone to oversleep and overeat. Although they may express themselves disparagingly, they are activity oriented and successfully strive to engage in new, rewarding situations. . . .
> We view these character traits as secondary to the primary affective disturbance. [p. 185]

Placing an affective disturbance at the base of hysteria is predicated on clinical observation and research reports suggesting that some of these patients improve on monoamine oxidase inhibitors. The authors imply that, since this condition responds to a pharmacologic intervention, biologic factors play an important role in its genesis.

There seems to be little evidence that this formulation is true. More likely, as the hysteric is confronted with heightened intrapsychic or interpersonal conflict, depressive symptoms develop. This has been noted to accompany aging and the loss of youthful attractiveness.

## NEUROBIOLOGICAL THEORY

Ludwig (1972) has postulated that the basic defect in hysteria is biologic, stemming from two distinctive patterns: (1) violent motor reactions and (2) a sham death reflex. Violent motor reaction is described as an "instinctive defense reaction against disturbing or external stimuli" (p. 772). Once a threatening situation is perceived, be it real or fantasy, a person responds with an "overproduction of aimless motions" (p. 773), and should this prove successful, it is then reinforced. The sham death reflex has been noted in a number of animals and is characterized by "partial loss of reaction to other stimuli, and often a well-marked analgesia" (p. 773).

The symptoms arising from these two defects include such things as fugue states, convulsive paroxysms, dreamy states, various fits and spells, blindness, and deafness. Ludwig further suggests that when these are combined with operant conditioning and regressive activity the total picture of hysteria evolves. Unfortunately, he does not clearly differentiate between hysterical personality, conversion, and dissociative symptoms. He further elaborates a concept of "selective depression of awareness of a bodily function brought on by corticofugal inhibition of afferent stimulation at the level of the brain stem reticular formation" (p. 774). This, he concludes, is an attention dysfunction, leading to "a constant state of distraction manifest by dissociation between attention and certain sources of afferent stimulation with a simultaneous diversion of attention to nonsymptom-related areas" (p. 775). Defect in this area may relate to dysfunction of memory, attention, control and field articulation.

This theory is such a radical departure from traditional concepts that full evaluation must await further elaboration of detail and empirical validation or refutation. Although a biological factor is suggested by the work of Guze, and of Kline and Davis, there is no basis to assume that it fits the pattern suggested by Ludwig. Furthermore, the behavioral deficits described, generally familiar to clinicians and typical hysterics, are not a priori a function of a biologic substrate defect as is the apparent case in animals.

## SOCIAL THEORIES

Halleck (1967) points out that the earliest dynamic descriptions of the hysterical personality emphasized unresolved oedipal conflicts as the primary determinant of the disorder and goes on to note the importance of early nurturant problems. In addition to this core psychoanalytic formulation, Halleck adds a social–cultural dimension, a position echoed by other authors. He notes that in our society "a man who feels deprived can deny his needs for others and turn upon and attack those he perceives as having rejected him. Such behavior is usually characterized as a form of sociopathy" (p. 753). He goes on to say that "the American girl, however, is not expected to deny her dependency needs and has little opportunity to express aggression directly. The female child is more likely to adapt to deprivation by seeking to bind people through relationships in which she assumes a highly dependent role" (p. 753).

Sociopathy roles, he points out, are rarely available to women in our society, although it is sometimes possible for lower class and adolescent women. Thus, he postulates that cultural determinants play an active role in personality formation. These roles, however, are perhaps changing as a result of the feminist movement. For example, the rates of crime, of violence, and of suicide are now increasing among women.

Hollender (1971) points out that a hysterical lifestyle is fostered in a society in which female children are encouraged to be "childlike, relatively helpless and a man's plaything" (p. 21). He postulates that the ideal climate for the production of hysterical personalities existed in the "plantation society of the antebellum South" (p. 21). He summarizes by saying hysterical personality as a lifestyle is fostered by social forces in little girls who are attractive in terms of appearance and personality. The individual psychodynamic pattern that "adds oil to the fire is maternal deprivation and turning to father for mothering" (p. 24). Hollender points out that "since many, perhaps most women, show some hysterical traits and no precise quantification is possible, it would be technically correct but cumbersome to say that a person is more or less a hysterical personality" (p. 17). "Furthermore," he states, "some women find it possible to be more flexible because they did not adopt the socially positive hysterical pattern to a marked degree or with deep intensity. In these instances an explanation may be found in the fact that the socially psychodynamic forces did not play into and amplify (or distort) the socially fostered lifestyle" (p. 23). Lastly, he asserts that "beneath the facade of grown women, they are little girls" (p. 26).

Lerner (1974) reviews much of the literature relevant to the question of social determinants as they relate to hysterical personality and subscribes to the point of view that there are many cultural expectations of women's behavior that are captured in the hysteric's personality style. Lastly, Chodoff and Lyons (1958) point out that nearly all of the papers about hysterical personality have been written by men. Luisada, Peele, and Pittard (1974) go a step further in speculating that the literature on hysterical personality written by women might have much more to say about male hysterics, thus emphasizing the last link in the social determinant—the eye of the beholder.

Halleck (1967) presents a convincing although largely anecdotal case for his formulations. His ideas are likely to be accepted with less critical review than are Ludwig's or Kline and Davis's because of their "fit" with current general assumptions about the importance of childrearing practices and cultural patterns on psychopathology. However, as with much of dynamic psychiatry, empirical validation continues to be lacking and unlikely to be immediately forthcoming.

## FAMILIAL THEORY

Purtell, Robins, and Cohen (1951), Perley and Guze (1962), Guze (1975), and several other psychiatrists at Washington University in St. Louis describe a syndrome—Briquet's syndrome—which, they assert, is hysteria. The syndrome is characterized by multiple, varied somatic complaints, an early age of onset, disordered sexual functioning, dysphoric mood, and multiple operations. A more extensive description is given below (p. 116). Investigators (Arkonac and Guze 1963) feel they have found evidence that this syndrome is a familial condition. In addition, they have found an increased incidence of sociopathic behavior in the first degree male relatives of females they have identified as hysteric (Woerner and Guze 1968). They postulate a genetic transmission but do not describe the genetic mechanism nor the biologic aberration that results. The data are based on carefully done epidemiologic studies of family groups. The two significant problems, however, are: first, whether hysteria as they define it is the same as hysteria as usually thought of by today's psychiatrists, and second, whether a positive family tree invariably implies a genetic, biologic linkage for the shared characteristic, or whether the characteristic is the consequence of a shared environment and learned behavior.

Guze's work is careful, statistically sound, and clearly epidemiological in nature. Such descriptive and correlational studies provide the basis for experimental investigation but do not conclusively establish a genetic origin over a psychodynamic one. Studies of adopted children, using large populations, careful sampling, and rigorous diagnostic standards, might clarify the nature–nurture point.

## CULTURAL THEORIES

We know of no attempts that compare the manifestations of hysterical personality among varying cultures. However, individuals with hysterical symptoms are found in all cultures. Indeed, the form that the hysterical symptom assumes seems to be culturally defined. This suggests that the forms are learned and have symbolic meanings. In some cultures, periods of dissociation and symbolic and ritualized behaviors occur only in men, while in others they occur only in women. In addition, these hysterical symptoms and states occur within specific age groups and at predictable times. The variation from culture to culture is in marked contrast to the fixed stereotyped behavior of schizophrenic patients. Schizophrenic patients seem to manifest similar behaviors across cultures, and evidence suggests the severe schizophrenias can be diagnosed without reference to culture. In schizophrenia, of course, the content of delusions will be determined by the beliefs of a culture; but the form of the behavior, such as personal disorganization, withdrawal, and so on, is similar (Crocetti and Lemkau 1967).

Anthropologists have studied hysterical behaviors in many cultures. Langness (1967) found the concept of hysterical psychosis (developed by Hirsch and Hollender in 1964 and further elaborated in 1969) useful in organizing field observations. It is these more blatant and gross hysterical symptoms that have been most clearly described within the cultural studies. Langness's review and discussion may be the most complete. Foulks's work (1972) on Arctic hysteria is the most intensive investigation of a single syndrome. Hysterical behaviors vary from subculture to subculture within the United States. La Barre's 1956 description of the snake-handling cults of Appalachia is a classic (La Barre 1969). Other authors have pointed out that minicultures, such as army basic training camps, increase the incidence and determine the form of hysterical behaviors (Rabkin 1964).

Perhaps a most convincing demonstration that severe dissociative and wildly destructive behavior can be learned and is highly symbolic is illustrated by the history of the "running amok" syndrome in Indonesia. Running amok occurred in males. At a time of stress, a male entered a dissociated state and began killing in an indiscriminate fashion, until he was killed. The Dutch decreased the incidence by changing the rules of the game. The Dutch authorities insisted that when a man ran amok, he was to be captured, not killed. After capture he was sentenced to a lifetime of work on a road gang. Within a few years, the syndrome essentially disappeared.

Ralph Linton (1956) summarizes:

> Hysterical phenomena are everywhere very decidedly culturally patterned. In fact, if one knows a culture, one can predict what form hysterias are going to take in that society—or pretty near so. This is the strongest possible argument in favor of the thesis that, whatever the etiology and dynamics of hysteria may be, its symptoms are extensively and intensively shaped by culture. [p. 132]

## OBSERVATIONS OF CHILDREN

There are no studies of hysterical personalities in children; however, hysterical symptoms including conversion reactions do occur in childhood. Their incidence and distribution according to age are unknown as is their natural history. Although Freud described Little Hans in 1904, reports on hysterical behavior in children in the psychiatric and pediatric literature have been infrequent. Proctor's paper (1958) summarized much of the relevant literature. His interest was stimulated by the high frequency of hysterical symptoms in a clinical population he worked with in North Carolina. Interestingly, 56% of his sample of patients were male. Proctor suggested an explanation for the disparity of the diagnosis of hysterical symptoms in male children as compared with adult males: "Within the framework of social acceptance and approval, hysterical mechanisms could be readily used by the male in childhood, but not in later life. Such traits are more socially and culturally acceptable for women than for men, and thus it would seem that hysteria would be more acceptable to women" (p. 439).

Although the exact incidence of hysterical symptoms in childhood remains unknown, the experience of Rock (1971) suggests that the symptoms are not uncommon. Rock, a child psychiatrist, working in conjunction with the Walter Reed General Hospital in Washington, D.C., and the Tripler General Hospital in Honolulu, diagnosed ten cases of conversion reactions in children in approximately two years. The children's ages ranged from 3 to 13.

In each instance, some threat to the dependence relationship between the parent-child had recently taken place; some minor trauma or illness had fixed the symptom; and the child's consequent inability to function at his appropriate age level appeared as a consequence of depressive feelings based on these areas of psychic trauma. [p. 91]

The highlighting of the dependency relationship between the parent and the child as the primarily dynamic issue involved in the symptom formation in these children is remarkably similar to the formulation derived by Sperling from her analytic studies of conversion symptoms in adults.

The reports by Proctor and Rock suggest that conversion reactions in children are more frequent than our past literature would indicate. Rock's report suggests that the incidence is directly proportional to the alertness and knowledge of the physician. He stresses that the diagnosis should be considered in every case of sensory, motor, or neuromuscular disorder in children, and not be made only by exclusion, for the sooner the diagnosis is made, the better the possibility for preventing permanent physical disabilities and more severe psychological disabilities.

## BEHAVIORAL THEORY

Since hysteria is a traditional psychopathological term developed out of dynamic psychology, behavior therapists have written very little on the concept. Behavioral therapy, however, had been extensively applied to hysterical symptoms. Buss (1966) is a good introduction to the manner in which behaviorists think, whereas Yates surveys the many applications of behavior therapy to patients with hysterical symptoms. Brady's articles demonstrate interesting applications of behavioral techniques to the treatment of hysterical blindness (Brady and Lind 1961) and to a variety of female sexual problems (Brady 1967).

The approach of a behavioral therapist to a patient with hysterical symptoms, determined by a therapist's orientation, is probably changing with innovations in this field. A therapist trained by Wolpe (1969) would proceed with systematic desensitization, that is, the pairing of fearful images with relaxation, whereas one trained to use "implosive therapy" (Stampfl and Lewis 1967) would force a similar patient to confront his fears immediately and directly. On the other hand, a behaviorist influenced by Skinner (1953) would focus on the use of positive and negative reinforcements or rewards to encourage a phobic patient to approach and master a fearful situation.

At this point in the development of behavioral therapy, it appears that most therapists use a variety of behavioral techniques. In addition, as behaviorists have applied their theories to the complicated problems of people, as well as to the behaviors of laboratory animals, some have become impressed by factors described by dynamic psychotherapists, such as the power of the relationship or transference to alter behavior. Some behaviorists have incorporated these understandings into their treatment approaches.

## RECENT DEVELOPMENTS

Currently, the word *hysteria* is used by the public and the lay press to refer to extreme emotionality, for example, "She(he) is acting hysterically." Hysteria often appears as a catchall term designating general emotional upheaval associated with accidents, death, or other trauma. The word also often carries a strong negative connotation.

In these last years of the twentieth century, within general medicine and psychiatry, the term is used loosely to refer to a wide variety of symptoms. Prominent in the descriptions associated with the term are disturbances of the genitourinary, the neurological, and the voluntary muscular systems; the appearance of altered states of consciousness, including the presence of multiple personalities; extreme emotional instability, including transient psychotic states; and a style of thinking and experiencing the world characterized by a massive use of repression and denial.

Hysteria is also found in the current psychiatric and anthropological literature as referring to a type of transient psychotic state called *hysterical psychosis* (Richman and White 1970). This syndrome has a documented existence and can be differentiated from other psychogenic psychoses. It is usually sudden in onset, short-lived, precipitated by actual object loss or other significant stress, and has no long-term sinister prognosis of psychotic deterioration. The psychodynamics of an episode are often blatantly evident. Manifestations may include hallucinations, delusions, depersonalization, bizarre behavior, and labile affect. As noted earlier, variations of this disorder have been described in many cultures.

The fact that physicians have been both attracted and repulsed by hysterical phenomena through the ages may be reflected by the disappearance and reappearance of hysteria as a diagnostic entity in the official nomenclature of the American Psychiatric Association. Although hysteria was a commonly used clinical diagnosis in the middle of this century, there was no such diagnostic entity listed in the first diagnostic manual of the American Psychiatric Association (*DSM-I* 1952).

In *DSM-I*, hysterical symptoms were described as psychoneurotic disorders under the headings of "dissociative reaction" and "conversion reaction." The dissociation reaction was to be "differentiated from schizoid personality, from schizophrenia reaction and from analogous symptoms in some other types of neurotic reactions." The conversion type was "to be differentiated from psychophysiologic, autonomic, and visceral disorders."

In the second edition of the *Diagnostic and Statistical Manual* (*DSM-II*), published in 1968, hysteria was diagnosed under two separate headings. The syndrome *hysterical neurosis*, "characterized by an involuntary psychogenic loss or disorder of function," was further divided into two subtypes: conversion, in which the special senses are affected, causing such symptoms as blindness, deafness, anosmia, anesthesia, paresthesia, paralysis, ataxia, akinesia, and dyskinesia; and dissociative, in which "alternations may occur in the patient's state of consciousness or in his identity to produce such symptoms as amnesia, somnambulism, fugue, and multiple personality."

The second diagnostic heading for hysteria in *DSM-II* was *hysterical personality*, a syndrome characterized by excitability, emotional instability, overreactivity, self-dramatization, attention seeking, immaturity, vanity, and unusual dependence. This diagnosis was to be made from manifest traits.

Soon after the publication of *DSM-II*, a group of investigators from Washington University in St. Louis (Woodruff et al. 1974) reported on their concept of hysteria having at its base the descriptions of the nineteenth-century French physician, Paul Briquet (1859). According to the St. Louis group, Briquet's syndrome has an early onset, almost invariably before age 20. It appears almost exclusively in females and is characterized by multiple chronic physical complaints, many hospitalizations, and multiple surgeries, in addition to sexual symptoms, anxiety, and depression. It should be stressed that "St. Louis hysteria" is a medical syndrome defined in the following manner: "For a diagnosis of hysteria, the patient must have twenty symptoms (medically unexplained) in at least nine of the ten defined symptom groups" (Cadoret and King 1974). The relationship of "St. Louis hysteria" (so narrowly defined in terms of conversion reactions and psychosomatic dysfunction) to the usual clinical concepts of hysteria, which include cognitive style, interpersonal patterns of relating, personality organization, and so on, requires further clarification.

The work of this group at Washington University influenced not only subsequent diagnostic categorizations of hysterical phenomena but all of the new American psychiatric nomenclature. Their emphasis on a descriptive psychiatry based on a theoretically neutral and operationally defined (as best as could be approximated) criteria formed the bases of the next generations of American Psychiatric Association diagnoses.

In the third edition of the *Diagnostic and Statistical Manual (DSM-III)*, published in 1980, the broad clinical concept of hysteria is subdivided into more discrete operationally defined entities. Somatic symptoms are classified within a somatoform category. Some of these diagnoses are defined by the presence of a single symptom. A conversion symptom, for example, is diagnosed as *conversion disorder*, while another diagnostic entity within the same category, *somatization disorder*, is a complex syndrome defined by a group of symptoms and behaviors. Officially, *somatization disorder* is a codification of the previously reported "St. Louis hysteria." Also appearing within the somatoform category are two other single-symptom entities: *psychogenic pain disorder* and *hypochondriasis disorder*, plus a residual category, *atypical somatoform disorder*.

Hysterical alterations in the normal functions of consciousness and identity—amnesia, fugue states, multiple personality, and depersonalization—are diagnosed in *DSM-III* within a category of dissociative disorders as *psychogenic amnesia, psychogenic fugue, multiple personality,* and *depersonalization disorder.* There is also a residual category: *atypical dissociative disorder.* These, again, are essentially single-symptom diagnoses.

In *DSM-III,* personality characteristics associated with the broad clinical concept of hysteria are clustered into a diagnosis, *histrionic personality disorder,* which appears within the category of personality disorders and is described as an inflexible and maladaptive syndrome that causes either "significant impairment in social or occupational functioning or subjective distress." It is defined by the presence of "behavior that is overly dramatic, reactive, and intensely expressed," or by "characteristic disturbances in interpersonal relationships." It is diagnosed by the presence of five of ten listed behaviors or symptoms. Later research (Pfohl 1990) indicated that these criteria overlapped both semantically and empirically with borderline personality disorder.

The revised version of *DSM-III, DSM-III-R,* published in 1987, does not substantially alter the hysterical diagnoses from the prior edition. There are several name changes, but the basic concepts and the three clusters of diagnoses relating to somatic symptoms, disturbances of consciousness, and personality are continued.

Within the somatoform disorder category of *DSM-III-R,* diagnostic entities are renamed. *Psychogenic pain disorder* becomes *somatoform pain disorder,* and *atypical somatoform disorder* is changed to *somatoform disorder not otherwise specified.* Two new somatoform diagnoses are added: *undifferentiated somatoform disorder,* for clinical presentations that do not meet the full symptom picture of *somatization disorder,* and *body dysmorphic disorder.* The *DSM-III* diagnoses *conversion disorder* and *somatization disorder* survive essentially unchanged in the revised version.

The new entity, *body dysmorphic disorder,* differs from all others within the somatoform category as it does not relate historically to hysterical symptoms, but, rather, to phobic or delusional diagnoses. It is defined as preoccupation with some imagined defect in appearance in a normal-appearing person, that is, spots on the skin, shape of nose, and so on.

In *DSM-III-R,* hysterical symptoms relating to disturbances in consciousness, memory, and identity are essentially unchanged from *DSM-III*. They appear as they were initially listed, described, and named. The residual diagnosis within the *DSM-III-R* dissociative disorder category, however, is renamed as *dissociative disorder not otherwise specified*.

In *DSM-III-R*, histrionic personality disorder diagnosis is continued. Two additional criteria are added that represent a return to the historical concept of hysteria: "inappropriately sexually seductive in appearance and behavior" and "speech that is excessively impressionistic and lacking in detail. . . ." In turn, several of the criteria that overlapped with borderline personality disorder are omitted.

At the time of this writing (1990), work groups of the American Psychiatric Association are collating information from clinical field trials and their reviews of the scientific literature. Their reports will be reviewed and edited to establish the diagnostic categories and form the text for the fourth edition of the *Diagnostic and Statistical Manual (DSM-IV)*.

Recent scientific breakthroughs in neurophysiology, epidemiology, and genetics have greatly added to our knowledge of anxiety and obsessive–compulsive symptomatology. However, there have not been similar advancements in clarifying the nature and genesis of hysterical symptoms. Changes in the diagnoses associated with hysteria from *DSM-III-R* to *DSM-IV* are likely to be fairly modest.

In regard to the dissociative disorders diagnoses in *DSM-IV*, a recent review by Spiegel and Cardena (1990) suggested that "major stress and traumatic events (e.g., physical and/or sexual abuse, rape, human-made and natural disasters) are common antecedents of dissociative phenomena including reactive dissociative symptomatology, psychogenic amnesia, atypical dissociative disorders and, most prominently, Multiple Personality Disorder." This information suggests that Breuer and Freud's early theory (1893–1895) that psychic trauma caused hysterical symptoms may have been correct.

In consideration of the newly documented data, it is likely that *DSM-IV* will contain a new diagnosis similar to that of the tenth edition of the *International Classification of Diseases (ICD-10)* "acute stress reaction," to be named *brief reactive dissociative disorder*. This diagnosis will be designed to cover "severe dissociative and anxiety acute reactions to trauma from time of the event to one month afterwards," and will be identified by the presence of operationally defined signs and symptoms.

Within the other dissociative diagnoses, several useful but conceptually minor changes are recommended. For example, Spiegel and Cardena suggest the requirement that an alternate personality take "full" control of consciousness be dropped from the criteria for *multiple personality disorder* because dissociated alters often still affect consciousness. They also recommend the reintroduction of the amnesia criterion deleted in *DSM-III-R*, as its presence can often help differentiate this condition from other phenomena.

Spiegel and Cardena (1990) conclude their unpublished review of dissociative phenomena by stating:

> Further research is needed to document: 1) the temporal and causal relationship between traumatic experience and dissociative symptoms, 2) the extent to which personality traits predispose an individual to manifest a dissociative reaction, and 3) the specific cognitive and emotional mechanism underlying dissociative phenomena.

The *DSM-IV* diagnosis of *hysterical personality disorder* will likely be little changed from its predecessor. While there is little empirical research supporting this diagnostic category, what data are available, ". . . along with the nonsystematized clinical observation of the past several decades, suggest that the concept should not be dismissed" (Pfohl 1990).

One difficulty with the diagnosis as presently construed is that, although its criteria may not be sex-biased, its application may be. Further research is needed to determine whether or not this syndrome has the same meaning when it is diagnosed in women as when it is diagnosed in men.

Although there are suggestions that the diagnosis has fair internal consistency and at least some external validity, its biggest problem is overlapping boundaries with other personality disorders. Pfohl (1990) found in five studies that it overlaps by the following mean levels: "Borderline P.D.—67%, Antisocial P.D.—31%, and Narcissistic P.D.—34%." Most likely some changes will be made in the number of criteria and in their definition in an attempt to obtain greater specificity or discrimination.

It is of interest to note that one of Freud's initial observations in his women patients of an association of hysterical personality features and conversion symptoms has been supported by recent studies. "There is modern evidence that Somatization Disorder and Histrionic Personality Disorder are more frequently comorbid than expected by chance" (Pfohl 1990). There are also reports of a familial link between somatization disorder and antisocial disorder. In these studies, male subjects received antisocial diagnoses, whereas females received somatization diagnoses.

In *DSM-IV*, several of the diagnoses categorized as somatoform may be moved to other locations. Recent work by Salkovskis and colleagues (1990) suggests that hypochondrias disorder may be more closely related to the anxiety disorders, particularly *obsessive–compulsive disorder* and *general anxiety disorder*. Another review by Hollander (1990) suggests that *body dysmorphic disorder* may also be more closely related to *obsessive–compulsive disorder* than to other somatoform diagnoses.

## HYSTERICAL PERSONALITY

We believe there have been refinements in the recent clinical descriptions of patients that now make it possible to better conceptualize the phenomena of hysteria within the concept of hysterical personality. The crucial ideas for this advance arise from two broad streams. The first is the development of the psychoanalytic concept of character. The second is the development of subtypes of hysteria—the "good" and "bad hysterics"—which has arisen out of experience with a wide range of hysterical patients undergoing psychoanalytic treatment.

As you will recall, initial psychoanalytic research into psychopathology focused on the instinctual and symbolic content, on the impulses and fantasies. Later, there gradually developed an interest in the enduring characteristics or typologies of patients. Freud (1908), Abraham (1912), and others began to describe patient types. Their first descriptions were couched in terms of libidinal development and fixations; for example, Abraham's description of the anal character type and Freud's delineation of erotic, obsessional, and narcissistic types.

A further shift occurred when Reich (1933) focused on repetitive patterns of behavior that he felt were caused by a fixation of libidinal energy bound by psychological mechanisms and muscle tone. He called this combination of psychological and somatic factors "character armor." According to Reich, conflict between impulse and defense was fixed into enduring psychological somatic patterns, destined to be repeated over and over. Anna Freud's observations (1936), parallel in time, contributed further to understanding patterns of psychological defenses and the organization of personality.

Hartmann's contributions (1958) stressed the integrative and adaptive capacities of the ego. He postulated that there were enduring capacities within each individual's ego that arose independently of psychological conflict. He termed these independent capacities "autonomous ego functions." Hartmann felt these perceptive and cognitive functions were derived from innate biological givens or potentials. He assumed these functions could remain independent of psychological conflict or could become involved in and influenced by conflict. His suggestions added an important dimension to the psychoanalytic model of personality, for personality structure was now seen as resulting from interactions between conflict-free ego capacities and psychological conflict.

Erikson (1950) added to this personality model through his observations on the contributions of culture to personality. He pointed out how a culture may either reinforce or interfere with the development of a person's emergent use of particular types of psychological defenses. He described the process by which cultures shape the personalities of their members into adaptive personality types for given geographical and social environments.

Shapiro (1965) evolved the concept of neurotic style out of the broader psychoanalytic concept of character by focusing on the question: How does the individual operate? This new concept highlighted the patterns of operation of ego functions, not the forces that motivate these functions. According to Shapiro, these styles were most apparent within controlled observational settings, such as psychoanalytic sessions or psychological test interviews. Shapiro illustrated his concept of neurotic style in the following way:

Suppose we observe an Indian, whose culture is unfamiliar, performing a strange dance with great intensity. As we watch, puzzled, we may notice there is a drought and that this is an agricultural community; we consider the possibility that this is a prayerful dance designed to bring rain and that possibility that it is an expression of apprehension as well. By careful observation, we may be able to decipher certain regular gestures that confirm our guess. There is no doubt that at this point we have achieved a significant measure of understanding. But the limitations of that understanding become apparent if we only consider that nearby, watching, is a non-Indian farmer who also suffers from the drought but who does not join in the dancing. It does not occur to him to perform these gestures; instead he goes home and worries. The Indian dances not only because there is a drought but also because he is an Indian. His dancing follows observed attitudes and ways of thinking—a frame of mind that is likely to be long standing and relatively stable. Knowledge of these stable forms adds another dimension of plausibility, of sense to his behavior. [p. 16]

The concept of neurotic style focuses on the transformations occurring between the push or drive and the particular constellation of defenses employed by an individual. In the preceding quotation, the desire for rain resulted in differing behaviors: the rain dance by the Indian and the fretting by the non-Indian.

The hysterical neurotic style described by Shapiro is based on a pervasive use of repression: "What we mean most often by repression is forgetting . . . the loss not of affect, but of ideational contents from consciousness" (p. 109). Shapiro thus utilized the observations and ideas that Freud postulated in 1896, when Freud suggested that in hysterics ideational content was split from consciousness. Shapiro amplifies Freud's concept as he relates this psychical maneuver not only to the conversion symptom, but to a characteristic ongoing process, an enduring part of an individual's personality. Shapiro supports his thesis by pointing out that when a clinician inquires for a specific description from a hysteric, he is likely to get "not facts but impressions. These impressions may be interesting and communicative, and they are often very vivid, but they remain impressions—not detailed, not quite sharply defined, and certainly not technical" (p. 111). Such responses from hysteric patients indicate that ideas, concepts, and facts are not easily available to them. Shapiro stresses as characteristic features of hysterical cognition: "the relative absence of active concentration, the susceptibility to transient, impressive influences, in a relatively nonfactual subjective world" (p. 116).

Shapiro's description of hysterical neurotic style also stresses the extreme emotionality found in this style. Emotionality, as well as repression, are distinctive of the style. To an observer, a hysteric's emotions seem exaggerated and unconvincing. To others, hysterics do not seem to be sincere. Indeed, hysterics often seem surprised when others do take them seriously, when they find that a logical sequence of their own statements and actions has come to pass. "This attitude becomes apparent, sometimes, in the form of astonishment or incredulity on the part of hysterical people when a consequence of some action of their own or of circumstances of which they were aware comes to pass, a consequence that may have been completely predictable to everyone else" (Shapiro, p. 122). Their extreme variation in emotion also seems to defend against still other emotion. Their subjective world seems to lie at a great distance from an intellectual understanding of their own behavior.

Zetzel (1968) was perhaps the first to describe subtypes of hysterics. She observed wide variation in the character or personality structure among patients who sought psychoanalysis because of hysterical symptoms. She called the polar types in the patient mix she observed the "good hysteric" and the "bad hysteric." "Good" referred to patients who had predominantly genital or oedipal conflicts, relatively mature personality structures, and who did well in psychoanalytic treatment. "Bad" referred to patients who had predominantly preoedipal conflicts, defects in ego and personality structure, and who did poorly in psychoanalytic treatment.

Lazare (1971) further developed Zetzel's concept. He emphasized the developmental, characterological, and behavioral aspects of the hysterical spectrum. The "good hysterics" appear to come from intact families with adequate early mothering, whereas the "bad hysterics" seem to come from chaotic family backgrounds, with mothers who were often absent, seriously depressed, or who offered poor models for identification. The psychopathology is more pervasive throughout the personality of the "bad hysteric," the sexuality more perverse, the behavior more blatant. In the "good hysteric" the symptoms are more isolated, ego alien, the sexual difficulties are at a genital level and secondary to inhibition, and the behaviors are more modulated. The "good hysteric" is usually the more successful in school, at work, socially, and in psychotherapy.

## HYSTERICAL PERSONALITY

We believe it may be advantageous to consider hysterical phenomena within a broad concept of hysterical personality. This approach contrasts with the strategy operationalized within *DSM-III* and *DSM-III-R* diagnoses and those proposed for *DSM-IV*. The *DSM* strategy, as briefly reviewed above, splits hysterical phenomena into subtypes for diagnostic purposes. Somatic symptoms, disturbances of consciousness, and personality symptoms are further divided and are diagnosed as separate entities.

The two perspectives, treating hysterical phenomena, for example, within a broad concept of hysterical personality—a "lumping" approach—or treating hysterical phenomena as discrete subtypes—a "splitting" approach—may both be useful. Often a broad view or a gestalt of a patient is more clinically relevant than an itemization of symptoms that may serve to scatter rather than highlight important nuances of patient behaviors. On the other hand, a discrete subtype approach may increase the possibilities for defining homogeneous populations for empirical investigation.

Conceptualizing hysterical phenomena within hysterical personality is a clinical approach closely based on psychoanalytic psychology. Kernberg (1988) made a similar suggestion. The crucial ideas for such an approach come from two directions. The first is the development of the psychoanalytic concept of character. The second is the observation that there is a continuum of hysterical patients ranging from the "good" hysterics on one end to the "bad" hysterics on the other. This latter suggestion arose out of experience with a wide range of hysterical patients undergoing psychoanalytic treatment.

The concept of neurotic style, coupled with the genetic, characterological, and behavioral features now makes possible a new model. This model is based on an understanding of an individual's character and the contributions to this structure of the relative amounts of preoedipal and oedipal conflicts. The structure is assumed to be derived from the biological and experiential components of an individual's life history, that is, the relative admixtures of intactness of family, physical and emotional health of parents, and richness and type of education and social milieus.

We view symptoms as existing within the matrix of a hysterical character structure. We place emphasis on the matrix, the structure. We view the symptom as an epiphenomenon. This conceptualization constitutes an almost total reversal of the early views in which hysteria was equated with hysterical symptoms.

This new model enables us to emphasize those enduring personality traits that have been associated with the hysterical personality. Chodoff and Lyons (1958), for example, identified with the following: dependence, egocentricity, emotionality, exhibitionism, fear of sexuality, sexual provocativeness, and suggestibility. Lazare and others (1966, 1970), using factor analytic techniques, found aggression, emotionality, oral aggression, obstinacy, exhibitionism, egocentricity, and sexual provocativeness. In contrast to Chodoff and Lyons, they did not find dependence, fear of sexuality, and suggestibility to be striking in their population. In Lazare's studies, however, there was an overlapping of oral, obsessive, and hysterical personality traits in some patients. These findings are in accord with our view that hysterical personality traits occur along a psychosexual continuum of psychosexual development.

Female hysterics have been described as "caricatures of femininity" (Chodoff and Lyons 1958). We have broadened this concept to a "caricature of sexual role." Caricature, of course, means a likeness or imitation that is so distorted or inferior as to seem ludicrous. The phrase "caricature of sexual role" is a convenient notation that allows us to stress two ideas that we see as central to the understanding of hysteria. The first is that a failure of a firm sexual identity is always part of hysterical structure, and the second is that such a failure is central to hysterical difficulties in men as well as women.

It is important to think in symmetrical terms. We believe the male counterpart of the overly feminine female hysteric is the hypermasculine, pseudosociopathic Don Juan male. (Don Juan is used here to refer to the seventeenth-century seducer of women, not to Carlos Castaneda's teacher. We believe that the hypermasculine male hysteric is characterized by all of the essential features found in female hysterics, and thus should be thought of in the same diagnostic, descriptive, prognostic, etiologic, and therapeutic manner. Thus, in both males and females, the behavioral manifestations are a "caricature of sex role."

Abse (1959) has written perceptively of males with hysterical symptoms who attempt to gain a strong male identification through hypermasculine activities, such as daredevil motorcycle riding. It seems to us and to several other authors —Kolb (1973), Malmquist (1971), Halleck (1967), and MacKinnon and Michels (1971)—that there must be two types of male hysterics: the passive, effeminate, often homosexual male; and the assertive, pseudohypermasculine, aggressive hypersexual (Don Juan) male.

Luisada and colleagues (1974) studied twenty-seven men admitted for inpatient treatment who fit the *DSM-II* criteria for hysterical personality. The majority had a history of suicidal gestures or threats. There was a frequent family history of mental illness, usually alcoholism. Fathers were described as being unassertive or as being absent during the patient's childhood. The subjects had poor educational and occupational success. Most were heterosexual, and half had been married. Few, however, had stable marriages. Many of those who were married had older wives, and "all had disturbed sexual relations ranging from fears of inadequacy to unhappy homosexual relationships" (p. 19). The majority abused alcohol or drugs and had criminal records of drunkenness or robbery. Striking effeminacy was noted in four patients and hypermasculinity in two. Antisocial behavior was typical of the group. Physical complaints were common in some patients, but there was no indication of overuse of surgery. Problems in sexual performance did not predominate; social problems were more common.

To restate our hypothesis, the common theme in male and female hysterics is a caricature of sex role; thus, instead of only looking for effeminate characteristics in the male, one should also look for pseudomasculine or hypermasculine characteristics stemming from the same general genetic-dynamic base as the hyperfeminine characteristics in the female. Thus, the conflict, defensive structure, cognition, perception, and interpersonal styles are the same in males and females, but the most common behavioral manifestations are mirror images, pseudofemininity in the female, and pseudomasculinity in the male.

## CHARACTEROLOGICAL PATTERNS

Previous authors have emphasized various attributes of the hysteric, and consequently we find a personality pattern description determined, at least in part, by the perspective of the author. We assert that the following descriptors constitute the core characteristics of a hysterical personality. Some of these behaviors occur more commonly than others and prominence varies among individuals; each behavior may have a range and variety of expression. These descriptors are a synthesis of the literature and our clinical experience. (Additional descriptions of hysterical style are provided by Horowitz in Chapter 1 of this volume under the sections on self schemas and role-relationship models and control of information processing.)

The core descriptors are aggressive behavior, emotionality, sexual problems, obstinacy, exhibitionism, egocentricity, and sexual provocativeness and dependency. These behaviors express sexual confusion, pseudomasculine and pseudofeminine adaptation, and a false maturity. Unique perceptual, cognitive, and communicative styles complete the descriptive picture.

Core determinants of the personality style are two: (1) early maternal deprivation and (2) distorted resolution of the oedipal situation and of the emergent sexual role identification. Psychosocial, psychosexual, and ego function perspectives will be related to this developmental model. Zetzel's good–bad (oral–genital) polarity is in actuality a continuum that reflects the two predominant developmental stages in which significant conflicts begin. Not only is there a make-believe quality to the sexual identity of hysterics but there is also a similar "as if" quality in other aspects of their behavior. Thus, maturity is more apparent than real—a pseudoadult facade as is suggested by the term *child-woman*, which some authors have applied to the female hysteric. There is both a distortion of gender role and a false maturity. The "little girl" quality of some female hysterics is well recognized. A similar "little boy" quality in the male hysteric is frequently seen when illness or injury intervenes, and a break occurs in the shell of the counter-phobic bravado.

Table 2–1 at the end of this chapter gives examples of the manifestations of the diagnostic descriptors for pseudofeminine and pseudomasculine adaptations. Looking down the list of descriptors, some are more culturally consistent with a pseudomasculine adaptation, whereas others are more consistent with direct expression by the pseudofeminine individual. For example, aggression is more commonly directly expressed by males, while emotionality and dependency are more culturally consistent with the feminine role. Obstinacy, exhibitionism, egocentricity, and sexual provocativeness seem to be directly expressed by both males and females. Table 2–1 shows these expressions for both males and females as well as the relevant diagnostic descriptors.

The better integrated (genital or "good") hysteric may adapt reasonably well, particularly in aggressive or creative pursuits. Some males may act out aggressively and antisocially; they may be gang or group leaders and may develop strong, although somewhat superficial, relationships. There is some capacity for closeness in the family and outside, but she or he usually continues to be somewhat irresponsible and egocentric. Vanity and bravado characterize the pseudofeminine and the pseudomasculine individual. Turbulent interpersonal affairs, particularly those with sexual relationships, are common.

The more genitally fixated, less oral, less narcissistically vulnerable hysteric may be ambitious and successful with fairly good employment and educational records. However, under stress there may be a development of either depressive or psychosomatic complaints. This may come at the time of growing older with the loss of physical attractiveness and virility, or in association with rejection from a sexual partner. Repression is the central mechanism and is reflected in the cognitive and perceptual style of the hysteric.

The more pregenitally fixated or more narcissistically vulnerable hysteric is characterized by ego weakness with poor integration of personality elements and poor differentiation of internal and external reality. The diffuseness of cognition and affect is more pronounced and, under stress, quickly regresses to a passive, depressed, or psychotic role with a serious risk of suicide. They have few problem-solving techniques—acting out, regression, or sickness frequently being their only resource. Negative self concepts and poor self-esteem are common. There is poor adaptation with an unstable, unpredictable, and lonely adjustment. Relationships may be intense but quite chaotic and unpredictable with primitive aggressive outbursts, intense jealousy, and possessiveness. There may be grandiose beliefs in self. A variety of sexual behaviors may be attempted with little investment or satisfaction. Often, there is an abuse of drugs or alcohol. The caricature of femininity or masculinity is often more bizarre.

In the infantile hysteric with a pseudomasculine adjustment, aggressiveness and sexual exploitation may be common, whereas in the hysteric with pseudofeminine adjustment, promiscuous and jealous behavior, characterized by strong emotional outbursts, are common. There is a poor vocational and educational record, and often behavior, particularly in the pseudomasculine hysteric, leads to arrest. Sex partners are seen only as temporarily relieving sexual needs and providing marginal nurturance. Although relationships may be confused and primitive, they are of vast importance as a buffer for poor self-esteem. Nurturance is eagerly sought, but it is also inevitably distrusted. This combination, of course, produces chaotic relationships with others. The person may be inconsistent, irresponsible, sadistic, or masochistic, rarely integrating into group or gang behavior. He is, at best, a follower on the periphery of a group. With distress, he may act with impulsive aggressive behavior. Depression or psychosis may be associated with violence or suicide attempts. Physical complaints are very common.

Both the biologic male and female have the potential for developing a pseudomasculine or pseudofeminine adjustment. The pseudomasculine adaptation in the male is the supermale, Don Juan, he-man. He may be attracted to physically active, risk-taking kinds of activities and jobs. He is frequently pushed to demonstrate his power and strength. This may be effected through a variety of extralegal maneuvers that may get him into recurrent trouble with legal authorities. This sociopath-like behavior may be confused with the true sociopath; however, the hysteric will show splitting of his personality. The underlying dependency in many of his antisocial acts will seem exaggerated, often grotesque and bizarre, in contrast to the true sociopath, whose actions and personality are more integrated and, in one sense, more mature.

The pseudosociopathic Don Juan represents one end of a continuum. At the other end is pseudofemininity in its most extreme form: the dependent, passive, coy, exhibitionistic, manipulative, Southern belle type. Between these polarities, both for males and females, lies a range of sexual and characterological adaptations that may have a mixture of both feminine and masculine elements, all the while maintaining many of the core descriptors noted previously. Pseudofeminine adjustment in males has been recognized for some time and may be associated with homosexuality. In biologic females, pseudomasculine adjustment seems to be less well described and recognized, and most likely would represent the "butch" adaptation of the lesbian.

## SUMMARY OF BEHAVIORAL DESCRIPTORS
## BY AGE AND SEX

The prototypical descriptions given below may aid in evaluating individuals for diagnostic and therapeutic purposes. We have chosen to describe three ages: teenage, adulthood, and middle age.

### Men

*Teenage.* The more primitive, oral, pseudomasculine male hysteric may seek membership in gangs or small socially deviant groups. He will tend to remain distant and unintegrated and may drift away as he grows older. His behavior may be so bizarre and impulsive as to make him an outcast even within a subculture of social deviancy. Thus, he may become a loner with bouts of alcohol or drug abuse and aggressive and other impulsive exhibitionistic acts. He may develop an intense, although very dependent-dominant relationship with a girl, a relationship that will be turbulent and unstable. He will achieve little in educational or vocational success; exhibitionism and egocentricity will be manifest through demanding, impulsive, risk-taking behavior with insistence on loyalty from associates. He will use sexuality to satisfy dependency and nurturant needs.

The more integrated, oedipal male hysteric will have many of the same elements but with a higher probability of "success" and satisfying outcomes. Thus, friendships will be more stable and less exploitive. Gang membership may occur but central, even leadership, roles may be achieved. Impulsivity and risk-taking will be less bizarre and self-destructive. Heterosexual relationships will develop but may be more stable with some give and take. Success may be achieved in athletic, selective academic, or vocational areas. Exhibitionistic, vain behavior will be reflected in clothes and manner. He may sustain and attract prolonged loyalties and will often be found to be likeable and attractive to others. Aggression and fighting will occur, but that, like sexuality, will be less compulsively and exploitively pursued.

*Adult*. At this stage, the oral, primitive, male hysteric will have developed a very lonely lifestyle, often characterized by overt criminal behavior and alcohol and drug abuse. He may have experienced jail terms or other brushes with the law. Regular aggressive behavior may be centered around alcohol use or automobiles. Drug-taking may have become a serious problem. Interpersonal relationships will have deteriorated, and sexual behavior will be more clearly a compulsive act serving nurturant needs. Heterosexual relationships will be turbulent. There will be little academic or vocational success, and the individual will drift from one impulsive, risk-taking, exhibitionistic act to the next. Emergent egodystonic feelings will be dealt with by drinking and compulsive sexuality.

The more successful, integrated hysteric may well achieve a reasonably satisfying and socially acceptable kind of behavior. He may be attracted to educational and vocational opportunities that reward egocentric and exhibitionistic needs. Long-range goals may be formulated and sought and occasionally achieved. Aggressive behavior may be channeled into leadership activities or into competitive behaviors necessary to success in certain kinds of business. Vanity is reflected in clothes, automobiles, and choice of sexual partners. Marriage may develop but will be unstable and unrewarding with frequent extramarital liaisons and alcohol abuse.

*Middle age*. The primitive male hysteric by this time will have had a heavy involvement in alcohol or socially deviant behavior. He may have experienced long periods of incarceration or serious physical damage from alcohol abuse. His risk-taking behavior may have led to accidents, causing serious injury or even death. Industrial accidents with chronic disability are common. A lifestyle characterized by aimless drifting, transient interpersonal relationships, and marginal sexual adjustment is present. Exhibitionism and egocentricity are lessened by the development of depression, social isolation, and the appearance of chronic physical complaints. Overreaction to injury and illness and excessive complaints of pain or other physical problems will be visible. Exploitation of others through dependency will become prominent; overt aggression will take a more verbal form.

The better integrated, middle-aged male hysteric may persist much as he did through early adulthood, with some stability of vocational interest and even a large measure of financial success. Exhibitionism and egocentricity continue and may be manifest in interpersonal relationships, dress, excesses, and "flashy" use of money. Fighting is only manifest through verbal exchanges. Vanity and egocentricity may lead to poor business decisions. Communication may be poor with family and co-workers, and increasingly autocratic behaviors may develop.

### Women

*Teenage.* The oral female hysteric will follow a pattern much like her male counterpart. After early attempts to integrate herself into a gang or some socially deviant or outcast subgroup of peers, she will gradually drift away, developing a lonely lifestyle marked with a lack of success in academic, interpersonal, or vocational pursuits. Impulsivity is more likely to be reflected in sexual rather than in aggressive behavior. Exhibitionism will center around seductive behavior that will depend heavily on clothes and behavioral mannerisms. This exhibitionism may at times be perceived as bizarre. She will be seen as being "too available." Clinging dependence may alternate with aggressive, angry behavior toward others. Interpersonal relationships are chaotic and unstable, leaving those around her puzzled, angry, and hurt. Sex serves to achieve her nurturant and dependent needs.

The more integrated teenager may effectively participate in group activities or gangs. She may be sought after in a variety of social situations. Occasionally tomboyish, her athletic abilities may be useful entrees to social acceptance. Coy and seductive behavior make her attractive to males and "popular" in high school and college. Aggression may be channeled into improved social relationships and academic and extracurricular activities. She will feel more comfortable in the company of men and may develop skills that will be useful for career goals. She may be attracted to drama or similar pursuits in which her exhibitionistic needs can be satisfied. Interpersonal relationships may remain stable, although fluctuated with frequent flights, separations, and reunions.

*Adult*. The more primitive hysteric may marry early to an insecure, dependent male who perceives her aggression as a sign of independence and capability. She, in turn, may develop a dependent, destructive role with her husband. They very quickly develop an isolated "parallel play" type of relationship in which sexuality may be the major activity of common interest. However, their sexuality is usually unsatisfying and serves only a need for nurturance. The relationship often deteriorates, and as a consequence, the woman may develop psychosomatic complaints or depression, or begin extramarital affairs. Alcohol or drug abuse may increase. The woman may either turn to her husband with increasing dependence or passivity or may look outside the marriage to other men or, occasionally, to interests in club activities as a means of satisfying her dependent needs. She will achieve little in the way of academic or vocational success. She is viewed as emotionally unstable, demanding, and impulsive by her husband. Her relationship with children will be difficult and she will see them as demanding and nonrewarding.

The well-integrated hysteric, on the other hand, may develop considerable success in career goals and continue through to some academic success. Sexual contacts will persist as a way of achieving nurturance and attracting partners. Sexual satisfaction will be limited, however. Marriage may depend on her dependent–aggressive relationship with men, which may become prominent. She may look outside the marriage for more satisfaction, using either sexual or career avenues to achieve this. Clothes and cosmetics will become important ways to sustain physical attractiveness and achieve her exhibitionistic, egocentric goals. She may often be perceived as castrating and competitive by men. Exhibitionistic needs may be served by community organizations and work. Physical complaints and psychosomatic problems may occur.

*Middle age*. The oral hysteric will develop more problems with alcohol or drug abuse, psychosomatic complaints, and depression as her sexual attractiveness fails. Chaotic relationships with men will continue in the same way. She may look older than her years. Exhibitionism and egocentricity tend to diminish as depression and other new psychopathology may appear. Chronic drug abuse, chronic depression, and suicide are not uncommon.

Better integrated hysterics will keenly feel the loss of beauty and sexual attractiveness. Exhibitionism, egocentricity, and aggressiveness may be served through success in career or volunteer work. Excessive use of cosmetics and redoubled energy in achieving attractiveness may occur. She may look outside the marriage for sexual contact or may find some satisfaction in her career. She and her husband may dimly recognize the distant, superficial relationship they have. She will experience difficulty with teenage children and may alternate between indulging and encouraging their sexual and aggressive behavior or becoming extremely moralistic, disciplining in a rigid arbitrary fashion. Depression and psychosomatic problems may emerge, and alcohol may be heavily used.

## POSTULATED DYNAMICS

The hysteric experiences a period of early maternal deprivation. The more severe this is, the more the adult personality is seen as oral, dependent, infantile, pregenital, or reactive to the threat of narcissistic injury. Each potential hysteric is thus left with the need to generate additional nurturant sources throughout his or her subsequent development. This need becomes the mainspring for further developments and conflicts and is central to the adult personality. In the family, the availability of nurturance is often tied to sexual provocativeness, sickness, or childlike behavior alternating with adultlike behavior. Exhibitionism and manipulation are useful techniques to further satisfaction of these needs.

For the female child, the mothering person, having been unable to deliver sufficient nurturance during infancy, continues to be found wanting as the child grows older, and the little girl turns to the parent of the opposite sex. Hollender (1971) notes: "The crucial point developmentally is that young girls who become hysterical personalities turn to their fathers or mother's father as substitute mothers" (p. 22). A young girl then looks to father to supply the missing nurturance and can only extract it on the basis of her coy, seductive, flirtatious behavior, which is, of course, rewarded with superficially focused interest—hardly an answer to her needs but better than nothing. As genital, sexual feelings and thoughts emerge, these must be repressed; however, the associated actions—for example, coy, seductive, flirtatious behavior—persist and are rewarded. This results in the split between behavior and feelings and thoughts—a characteristic that will continue and is critical.

The little girl wants mothering at two levels: in infancy as a nurturant source and again during the genital period as an identification model. Without a stable maternal resource for identification, the personality becomes that patchwork of behaviors rewarded by father, through sexualized interaction, and those acquired through mimicry of cultural stereotypes. Thus, a superficial, rigid, compartmentalized and incomplete identity or self-concept evolves. There is no integration or flexibility. The repertoire of behavior that is acquired is generated from the child's observation of social stereotypes and rewarded behaviors. Hollender (1971) suggests that the jet-set and movie colonies may provide the models. Subsequently, outside the home, such behaviors are reinforced by peers, fantasy, and further exposure to cultural stereotypes and cultural sources, for example, television, movies, and novels. Thus, the social arena in some measure acts as a surrogate family providing models and reinforcements.

The male is faced with a somewhat similar situation. He also experiences the relative maternal deprivation during infancy, leaving him with the same felt need for nurturant sources. At the time of the oedipal struggle, he finds his father absent or unavailable as a role model. Consequently, this leaves him with only his mother to relate to. She can now provide limited nurturance as a part of an eroticized overindulgent relationship.

Although mother has been unable to control and sustain a relationship with father, she now has a captive respondent in the child-man. She can reinforce those behaviors that she desires and extinguish those that are not needed. Again, since the boy has no adequate masculine role model to identify with, behaviors that develop are the results of the reinforcement from mother and mimicry of cultural stereotypes. They are a superficial patchwork of unrelated, poorly integrated actions, and, since genital sexual feeling and thought must be repressed while sustaining the behaviors, affective and cognitive splitting results. Impulsive, pseudomasculine, hedonistic, manipulative behavior patterns may result depending on what behaviors mother rewards. Self-concept develops through the reinforced behavior patterns and interaction with mother, and the borrowed, romanticized behavior found among peers, gangs, and folk heroes on television and in movies. Such social stereotypes provide the basis then for a caricature of masculinity, with emphasis on the hypermasculine pattern, in an effort to deny the lack of firm masculine foundation and the early deprivation leading to dependency.

The child may either model his behavior after the parent of the opposite sex, producing a pseudomasculine female or pseudofeminine male, or may develop a biologically appropriate but exaggerated pseudoadult behavior that is a caricature of the cultural norm for his or her biologic sex. As the child turns to the parent of the opposite sex for both nurturance and as a source of identification formation, a series of rather complex forces begins to operate. The male child, with no suitable father available, continues to relate to the mother, not only to capture the missed nurturance but also as a potential object for sex-role identity. The child is faced with an ever-increasing ambivalence: On the one hand, he wishes to reestablish the passivity suitable for nurturance; on the other, he needs increasingly to deny passivity, particularly in the case of the male child, and to develop the assertive gender role consistent with social dictates. Reaction formation converts passivity to aggressivity as a mimicry of activity as well as an expression of frustration.

The female child, in contrast, has to give up the hope for nurturance from the mother and turn to her father; then, in attempts to create a mothering individual out of father, she is constrained to develop a variety of attention-getting and seductive devices that largely assume the dimension of the "cute little girl."

The child finds herself in an ambivalent relationship: on the one hand, she hopes to resurrect a relationship that will supply the nurturance so sorely missed earlier; on the other hand, she is catapulted to a pseudoadult role. Passivity must be denied through the use of reaction formation, and the opposite, aggressive behavior, is the outcome. The use of obsessive defenses at this stage is primarily related to dealing with feelings of passivity, and it generates aggressive and, at times, obstinate behavior patterns in the adult.

This latter stage of working through with the parent of the opposite sex, dealing with the ambivalence through reaction formations, and constructing an aggressive stance represents the best solution for the hysteric. Necessary for this resolution is the capacity for forming fairly solid object relations. Zetzel (1968) has pointed out that the true hysteric has sustained the capacity to form good honest relations with parents. This model can then be carried into therapy where it serves as the basis for the analytic process. To the extent the child falls short of this resolution, that is, never develops stable object relationships with the parent of either sex, oral issues dominate and the behavior is, at best, a mimicry of adult sexual role behavior. These individuals, the immature hysterics, do not have the capabilities necessary to greatly profit from insight-oriented psychotherapy or analysis.

## CONCLUSIONS

To summarize briefly, early psychoanalysts focused on the primitive urges and psychic conflicts that produced hysterical symptoms. They stressed the sexual rivalries and the fear of punishments associated with the oedipal complex. Later psychoanalysts pointed out the lack of adequate early mothering in individuals who develop hysterical symptoms. They placed additional emphasis on the importance of preoedipal issues and also stressed that aggressive urges, as well as sexual urges, can produce hysterical symptoms.

Modern psychoanalysts broadened the earlier ideas of their colleagues as they further developed the concepts of character and ego psychology, and began to delineate the relationship between personality structure and symptom formation. Shapiro (1965) gave added depth to this perspective with his concept of neurotic style. Zetzel (1968) and Lazare (1971) identified important developmental and social forces involved in the formation of mature or infantile personality structures.

Keeping in mind the many theories regarding hysterical symptoms—social, affective, neurological, familial, and so on—it is our thesis that the concept of hysterical structure or hysterical personality provides us with the firmest clinical and conceptual basis. We understand hysterical personality to be a specific type of personality organization that utilizes repression of internal information and denial of external information as its major defenses, tends to experience the world in a strongly emotional and biased way, and is not concerned with precise logic or clarity of thinking. We visualize hysterical structures as ranging from relatively mature, intact, and functional patterns to grossly immature structures with major deficits and limited ranges of function. We consider symptoms to be more or less epiphenomena existing within the personality structure. The course of a symptom and its possible amelioration by psychoanalysis or psychotherapy is, as we see it, more dependent on the underlying structure than upon the crisis that precipitated it.

Our review leads us to propose the following model and dynamics: Hysterical personality is associated with characteristics arising from both pregenital and genital psychosexual levels. The more infantile personality organization arises as a result of inadequate mothering, sexual and physical abuse, and deprivation during infancy and results in chaotic, extreme, and unstable behavior as an adult that is highly resistant to psychotherapeutic, psychoanalytic intervention. This is contrasted with the genital, or mature, hysterical personality organization, which has experienced less early deprivation, exhibits more intact object relationships, has experienced more success in vocational, educational, and social areas, and has symptoms amenable to the present armament of psychotherapeutic intervention.

We suggest that the central issue for the individual with a hysterical personality is the resolution of gender identity. We also suggest that this conflict is expressed through the lens of a personality structure that has been significantly cast and tinted by the relative amounts of early maternal deprivation and trauma experienced. The particular tinting of the lens may give a different coloration or manifestation to the adult behaviors, but the same central issues will identify the hysteric: aggression, emotionality, sexual problems, obstinacy, exhibitionism, egocentricity, sexual provocativeness, and dependency.

Early maternal deprivation and trauma place the child in a vulnerable position at the time of the oedipal struggle. The female child often seeks out the father as a substitute mother and may either identify with him (a pseudomasculine solution) or develop a culturally stereotyped feminine identity, drawing on cultural elements that are then reinforced in an eroticized relationship with the father (a pseudofeminine solution). The male has essentially the same problems. Upon entering the oedipal solution, he has already experienced moderate to severe early deprivation and, in addition, often finds his father unavailable or distant. He then again turns to the mother, who finds it easier to relate to the older child, and he may either identify with her (a pseudofeminine or effeminate homosexual solution) or he may draw from cultural stereotypes, the elements of which are reinforced by the mother, to develop a shaky, pseudomasculine identity. For both the male and the female child, these identities are more a mimicry of cultural stereotypes, shaped through reinforcements by parents, than true identities obtained through the usual processes of introjection and identification. Thus, the succeeding personality is often rigid, fixed, and superficial and serves as a defense against the inner and earlier deprivation.

The common manifestations of the hysterical personality in the biologic male and female are related as mirror images, that is, exaggeration of feminine or masculine characteristics. In the female, we see as a common solution the prototype of the Southern belle, and in the male we often see the prototype of the exhibitionist gang member who is frequently, we feel, mistakenly diagnosed as sociopathic rather than hysterical.

Our hypotheses and speculations need to be explored and tested by further clinical observation and research. It would be important, for example, to correlate familial studies of Briquet's syndrome with the dynamics and psychological attributes observed by psychoanalysts. Further perceptual and personality research by those interested in cognitive styles would be most helpful. While it is certain that hysterical symptoms will continue, it is less certain, but hopeful, that we may be able to better understand and treat them. At this time, we suggest that the concept of hysterical personality, as we have proposed, is a useful platform from which to proceed.

### Table 2–1

### Masculine and Feminine Hysterical or Histrionic Behaviors

| Pseudofeminine Expression | Diagnostic Descriptors | Pseudomasculine Expression | Proposed DSM-IV Descriptors of Histrionic Personality Disorder |
|---|---|---|---|
| Subtle indirect manipulation, competitive with males, dominant, easily angered, argues, sarcastic, pouts but controlled, provokes guilt in others | Aggression | Direct, threatens others with verbal or physical fights, fights to prove self, bombastic, resists dependency | |
| Poor emotional control, sentimental, romantic, cries easily, behavioral and emotional overreaction, intense emotional response, calms quickly, diffuse, shallow, labile | Emotionality | Impulsive, transient, superficial affect, may deny feelings or be sentimental | Inappropriate emotional expression, speech is excessively impressionistic and lacks detail, shifting and shallow emotionality |
| Frigid, avoids sexual encounters, surprise at men's response to sexual provocativeness | Sexual problems | Sexual exploitation, Don Juanism, hypermasculine | |

## Table 2–1 (continued)

| Pseudofeminine Expression | Diagnostic Descriptors | Pseudomasculine Expression | Proposed DSM-IV Descriptors of Histrionic Personality Disorder |
|---|---|---|---|
| Stubborn, will not give in on "rights," feminine prerogatives | Obstinacy | Stubborn on masculine issues, for example, independence and nondominance by females | |
| Dress, cosmetics, posture and gait, or any attribute including defects or needs used to attract attention | Exhibitionism | Show of strength, bravery or tolerance of pain, dress attracts attention, flashy cars or gadgets | Center of attention, physical attractiveness |
| Own needs first, sensitive to critical remarks, vulnerable to slights | Egocentricity | Self-interest first, body image very important, uses others, vulnerable to slights | Intolerant of delayed gratification |
| Flirtatious cat-and-mouse games with men, romantic, coy, coquettish | Sexual provocativeness | Flirtatious, frequent affairs in fact or fantasy, conquest important | Inappropriately sexually seductive |
| Protests for independence but rarely acts, may abuse drugs or alcohol | Dependency | Pseudo hypermasculinity, disabled with relatively minor illnesses and injuries | |

## REFERENCES

Abraham, K. (1912). Selected Papers on Psychoanalysis. New York: Basic Books.

Abse, W. D. (1959). Hysteria. In American Handbook of Psychiatry, ed. S. Arieti. New York: Basic Books.

American Psychiatric Association (1952). Diagnostic and Statistical Manual of Mental Disorders (DSM-I). Washington, DC.

——(1968). Diagnostic and Statistical Manual of Mental Disorders (DSM-II). Washington, DC.

American Psychiatric Association (1980). Diagnostic and Statistical Manual of Mental Disorders (DSM-III). Washington, DC.

American Psychiatric Association (1987). Diagnostic and Statistical Manual of Mental Disorders (DSM-III-R). Washington, DC.

Arkonac, O., and Guze, S. (1963). A family study of hysteria. New England Journal of Medicine 268:239–242.

Brady, J. P. (1967). Psychotherapy, learning theory and insight. Archives of General Psychiatry 16:304.

Brady, J. P., and Lind, D. (1961). Experimental analysis of hysterical blindness. Archives of General Psychiatry 4:331–339.

Breuer, J., and Freud, S. (1893–1895). Studies on hysteria. Standard Edition 2.

Briquét, P. (1859). Traité Clinique et Thérapeutique de l'Hysterie. Paris: Balliere.

Buss, A. (1966). Psychopathology. New York: Wiley.

Cadoret, R. J., and King, L. J. (1974). Psychiatry in Primary Care. St. Louis: Mosby.

Chodoff, P., and Lyons, H. (1958). Hysteria, the hysterical personality, and "hysterical" conversion. American Journal of Psychiatry 114:734–740.

Crocetti, G. M., and Lemkau, P. V. (1967). Schizophrenia II: epidemiology. In Comprehensive Textbook of Psychiatry, ed. A. M. Freedman and H. I. Kaplan. Baltimore: Williams & Wilkins.

Easser, B. R., and Lesser, S. R. (1965). Hysterical personality—a reevaluation. Psychoanalytic Quarterly 34:389–405.

Erikson, E. H. (1950). Childhood and Society. New York: Norton.

Fenichel, O. (1945). The Psychoanalytic Theory of Neurosis. New York: Norton.

Foulks, E. F. (1972). The Arctic Hysterias. Washington, DC: American Anthropological Association.

Freeman, L. (1972). The Story of Anna O. New York: Walker.

Freud, A. (1936). *The Ego and the Mechanisms of Defense*. London: Hogarth Press.

Freud, S. (1893–1899). Early psycho-analytic publications. *Standard Edition* 3.

———(1888). Hysteria. *Standard Edition* 1:39–60.

———(1901–1905). A case of hysteria, three essays on sexuality, and other works. *Standard Edition* 7.

———(1908). Character and anal eroticism. *Standard Edition* 9:167–176.

Gedo, J. E., Sabshin, M., Sadow L., and Schlessing, N. (1964). "Studies on hysteria": a methodological evaluation. *Journal of the American Psychoanalytic Association* 12:734.

Guze, S. (1975). The validity and significance of the clinical diagnosis of hysteria (Briquet's syndrome). *American Journal of Psychiatry* 132:138–141.

Halleck, S. L. (1967). Hysterical personality—psychological, social and iatrogenic determinants. *Archives of General Psychiatry* 16:750–757.

Hartmann, H. (1958). *Ego Psychology and the Problem of Adaptation*. New York: International Universities Press.

Hirsch, S. J., and Hollender, M. H. (1969). Hysterical psychoses: clarification of the concept. *American Journal of Psychiatry* 125:909.

Hollander, E. (1990). *Body dysmorphic disorder and its relationship to obsessive–compulsive disorder: position paper for DSM-IV workgroup on OCD*.Unpublished paper.

Hollender, M. H. (1971). Hysterical personality. *Comments on Contemporary Psychiatry* 1:17–24.

Kernberg, O. (1967). Borderline personality organization. *Journal of the American Psychoanalytic Association* 15:641–685.

———(1988). Hysterical and histrionic personality disorders. In *Psychiatry*, ed. R. Michels et al. Philadelphia: Lippincott.

Kline, D. F., and Davis, J. M. (1969). *Diagnosis and Drug Treatment of Psychiatric Disorders*. Baltimore: Waverly.

Kolb, L. C. (1973). *Noyes' Modern Clinical Psychiatry*. 8th ed. Philadelphia: Saunders.

LaBarre, W. (1969). *They Shall Take Up Serpents: Psychology of the Southern Snake Handling Cult*. New York: Schocken.

Langness, L. L. (1967). Hysterical psychosis—the cross-cultural evidence. *American Journal of Psychiatry* 124:47–56.

Lazare, A. (1971). The hysterical character in psychoanalytic theory—evolution and confusion. *Archives of General Psychiatry* 25:131–137.

Lazare, A., Klerman, G. L., and Armor, D. J. (1966). Oral, obsessive and hysterical personality patterns: an investigation of psycho-analytic concepts by means of factor analysis. *Archives of General Psychiatry* 14:624–630.

————(1970). Oral, obsessive and hysterical personality patterns. *Journal of Psychiatric Research* 7:275–290.

Lerner, H. E. (1974). The hysterical personality: a "woman's disease." *Comprehensive Psychiatry* 15:157–164.

Linton, R. (1956). *Culture and Mental Disorders*. Springfield, IL: Charles C Thomas.

Ludwig, A. M. (1972). Hysteria: a neurobiologic theory. *Archives of General Psychiatry* 27:771–786.

Luisada, P. V., Peele, R., and Pittard, E. A. (1974). The hysterical personality in men. *American Journal of Psychiatry* 131:518–521.

MacKinnon, R. A., and Michels, R. R. (1971). *Psychiatric Interview in Clinical Practice*. Philadelphia: W.B. Saunders.

Malmquist, C. P. (1971). Hysteria in childhood. *Postgraduate Medicine* 50:112–117.

Marmor, J. (1953). Orality in the hysterical personality. *Journal of the American Psychoanalytic Association* 1:656–671.

Perley, J. M., and Guze, S. B. (1962). Hysteria—the stability and usefulness of clinical criteria. *New England Journal of Medicine* 266:421–426.

Pfohl, B. (1990). *Histrionic personality disorder: a review of available data and recommendations for DSM-IV*. Unpublished paper.

Pollock, G. H. (1968). Bertha Pappenheim: addenda to her case history. *Journal of the American Psychoanalytic Association* 12:734.

————(1973). The possible significance of childhood object loss in the Joseph Breuer-Bertha Pappenheim (Anna O.)-Sigmund Freud relationship: I, Josef Breuer. *Journal of the American Psychoanalytic Association* 16:711.

Proctor, J. T. (1958). Hysteria in childhood. *American Journal of Orthopsychiatry* 28:394–403.

Purtell, J. J., Robins, E., and Cohen, M. E. (1951). Observations on clinical aspects of hysteria—a quantitative study of fifty patients and one hundred and fifty-six control subjects. *Journal of the American Medical Association* 146:902–909.

Rabkin, R. (1964). Conversion hysteria as social maladaptation. *Psychiatry* 27:349–363.

Rangell, L. (1959). The nature of conversion. *Journal of the American Psychoanalytic Association* 17:632–662.

Reich, W. (1933). *Character Analysis*. New York: Farrar, Straus, & Giroux.

Richman, J., and White, H. (1970). The family view of hysterical psychosis. *American Journal of Psychiatry* 127:280–285.

Rock, N. (1971). Conversion reactors in childhood: a clinical study on childhood neuroses. *Journal of the American Academy of Child Psychiatry* 10:65–93.

Salkovskis, P. M., Warwick, H. M. C., and Clark, D. M. (1990). *Hypochondriasis, illness phobia, and other anxiety disorders*. Unpublished paper.

Schlessinger, N., Gedo, J. E., Miller, J., Pollock, G. H., Sabshin, M., and Sadow, L. (1967). The scientific style of Breuer and Freud in the origins of psychoanalysis. *Journal of the American Psychoanalytic Association* 15:404.

Shapiro, D. (1965). *Neurotic Styles*. New York: Basic Books.

Skinner, B. F. (1953). *Science and Human Behavior*. New York: Macmillan.

Sperling, M. (1973). Conversion hysteria and conversion symptoms: a revision of classification and concepts. *Journal of the American Psychoanalytic Association* 21:745–772.

Spiegel, D., and Cardena, E. (1990). *Disintegrated experience: dissociative disorders redefined*. Unpublished paper.

Stampfl, T. G., and Lewis, P. J. (1967). Essentials of implosive therapy: a learning-theory-based psychodynamic behavioral therapy. *Journal of Abnormal Psychology* 72:496–503.

Veith, I. (1965). *Hysteria: History of a Disease*. Chicago: University of Chicago Press.

Weingartner, H., and Faillace, L. A. (1971). Alcohol state-dependent learning in man. *The Journal of Nervous and Mental Diseases* 153:365–406.

Wittels, F. (1930). The hysterical character. *Medical Review of Reviews* 36:186.

Woerner, P. I., and Guze, S. B. (1968). A family and marital study of hysteria. *British Journal of Psychiatry* 114:161–168.

Wolpe, J. (1969). *The Practice of Behavior Therapy*. New York: Pergamon.

Woodruff, R. A., Jr., Goodwin, D. W., and Guze, S. B. (1974). *Psychiatric Diagnosis*. New York: Oxford University Press.

Yates, A. J. (1970). *Behavior Therapy*. New York: Wiley.

Zetzel, E. R. (1968). So-called good hysteric. *International Journal of Psycho-Analysis* 49:256.

CHAPTER 3

# Childhood: From Process to Structure

**AUBREY W. METCALF, M.D.**

One avenue toward understanding the problems of adults is the study of similar conditions in childhood, where the antecedents of later disorder can sometimes be found. With matters hysterical, of course, there are plenty of examples of conversion phenomena in childhood and some of what appears to be hysteria proper. These are the discrete and often striking symptom complexes and behaviors that make the hysterical disorders so attention-provoking in both children and adults. But is there a personality type, a style of thinking and acting, that underlies and gives rise to these symptoms in children as in adults? And if there is such a thing as hysterical personality or character disorder in childhood, does it always or ever precede the adult variety?

First, a clarification is in order. In some psychoanalytic works, an important distinction is made between character disorder and personality disorder. In the psychiatric literature, however, the two terms are most often used interchangeably. For the remainder of this discussion, both concepts will be referred to under the term *personality disorder*.

Second, it seems appropriate to say from the outset that what is ordinarily meant by personality disorder does not occur in children. That is, the stable and predictable configuration of inadequate or pathological thought and behavior, which is the hallmark of the disorder in the adult, cannot ordinarily be ascribed to the child of preschool and grammar school age. Indeed, many of the traits associated with hysterical personality are a part of normal development in children.

Yet the issue is by no means so easily set aside. Everyone knows that even small children have characteristic ways of responding that are predictable. Many children have "styles" that can be recognized through their series of developmental stages, even if the manifest behavior is different in the successive phases of psychological development. The question persists, then, in modified form: can a hysterical style of behavior be identified in childhood, and, if so, how might it predispose to hysterical character later in life?

In attempting to review the concomitants—intrapsychic, interpersonal, and cultural—from which a child develops a hysterical disorder or lays the groundwork for it to emerge in later life, the laws that govern the formation of all personality will be involved. Since so little work has been done that would illuminate the specific roots of hysterical disorder in childhood, we must rely heavily on what is known about the development of personality in general, and of personality disorder in particular.

## THE ORIGINS OF ADULT PERSONALITY DISORDER

It is inevitable in the beginning of psychotherapy with many adults for the therapist to become aware that the patient has a characteristic manner of thinking, feeling, and behaving, which, although inefficient and sometimes downright destructive, seems relatively free from intrapsychic conflict in the usual sense. It is as if the patient has no conflict or has effectively become inured to it. These ways of feeling and behaving seem to the observer to have an enduring, almost automatic feel, as if whatever interpersonal or internal conflict or pathologic learning that originally produced them has resulted in a smoothly functioning set of behavioral systems, a solid psychic structure, which is much less susceptible to insight and change than more current neurotic problems. This is especially true for many of those patients who are finally classed, somewhat despairingly at times, as hysterical characters.

We make the assumption that the rather inflexible personality structure we see in such an adult patient was once more supple, more apparently conflictful and ambivalent, and thus more amenable to resolution than it appears to be in the present. Projecting backward through our patient's life, we infer that there was a time when the patient had the potential to develop alternative routes of behavior and feeling. We may even isolate, through meticulous and repeated recollections and insights in therapy, those periods in the patient's life when specific environmental conditions interacted with specific intrapsychic states to produce these specific sequelae. Dynamic theories of psychopathology have been built on such retrospective reconstructions, and in therapy there are few alternative ways to uncover meaningful data. But when we use these theories for anterospective prediction, the result is much less convincing. Freud (1920) was alive to this problem when he wrote:

> So long as we trace development from its final outcome backwards, the chain of events appears continuous, and we feel we have gained an insight which is completely satisfactory or even exhaustive. But if we proceed the reverse way, if we start from the premises inferred from the analysis and try to follow these up to the final result, then we no longer get the impression of an inevitable sequence of events which could not have been otherwise determined. We notice at once that there might have been another result , and that we might have been just as well able to understand and explain the latter. . . . Hence the chain of causation can always be recognized with certainty if we follow the line of analysis, whereas to predict . . . is impossible. [pp. 167–168]

Almost everyone believes that early interpersonal experience is of the greatest importance in development, but data on causality is difficult to gather. The most glaring lack in the scientific testing of theoretical formulations about the hysterical personality is a first-hand study of the biological, cultural, and especially the interpersonal, relationships of the yet-to-become-hysterical patient while he or she is still a child. Aside from gross neglect and abuse, from which we know many of the more severe disorders of childhood and adult life emerge, there are other, more subtle, factors that we suspect to underlie many less severe psychological maldevelopments. Behaviors reflecting unconscious ambivalence toward the child, narcissistic projections onto the child, symbiosis with the child, and so forth are often not obvious to superficial examination and checklist questioning, but most certainly have their effects. Nothing in cumulative therapeutic work with children and their parents is more secure than the fact that unconscious parental attitudes are effectively communicated to the child (including the necessity that they remain unconscious) and that, through thousands of interactions, the child is inaugurated as a family participant with his or her unique role to play in the interactions and specific style of the family. The hypothesized causal connections are, nevertheless, hard to prove. Since these roles and styles are beyond the conscious recognition of the persons involved they are unlikely to be reported if the examiners do not know what they are looking for, and distorted if they do. Unless the interactions are witnessed in person and recorded, direct retrieval of the matrix that brings about the development is lost.

In the treatment of adults, we usually understand the antecedents of personality as deriving from complicated emotional events in childhood that are represented by the memory residues of the patient twenty or thirty years later. This assumption is, of course, open to the gravest scientific criticism (Garmezy 1974), and yet it has been and continues to be the main source of internal data illuminating the formation of personality, healthy and pathological. It is certainly a frequent experience in long-term psychotherapy and psychoanalysis that, as emotional conflict recedes with treatment, events and persons from the patient's past become more clearly dimensional and humanly understandable to both patient and therapist. One might imagine that in the most serious disorders of childhood, studied while the patient is still a child, reconstruction of the etiological conditions might be clearer. This seems not to be the case. Walker and Szurek (1973) concluded that prolonged therapeutic work prepared only *some* parents for remembering painful events, feelings, and conflict states of possible significance in the evolution of their child's disorder.

What has been lacking are well designed *prospective* studies that include sufficient objective observations of the child and family on the one hand and internal, clinical data from each on the other. From this, valid correlations could be made of the intrapsychic and the interpersonal roots of personality and pathology and their interrelationships. Until such time as these studies are completed, explanations of the origins of psychopathology must remain tentative.

## Progress in Theoretical Formulations

As far as the origins of adult hysterical personality are concerned, things have become more complex as time has gone on; issues once apparently settled simply and elegantly by early writers, such as the relationship between hysteria and conversion, seem now to be much more complicated. In working backward from adult patients with hysterical disorders, Freud, Reich, and Fenechel held that the condition was brought about by an incomplete oedipal resolution in otherwise relatively well-developed persons. They felt the manifestations of the illness indicated that the patients' personalities were fixated at the phallic stage. This formulation held sway for many years.

Beginning with a paper by Marmor (1953), the literature reflected the common experience that the preoedipal history of most patients with hysterical symptoms revealed intense frustration of oral needs and that there was a marked tendency for oral features to predominate in these complaints. Adding weight to the argument, Marmor pointed to the relationship of hysteria to addiction and to schizophrenia, both of which seem associated with early oral pathology. It became clear that, for many patients with hysterical symptoms, problems originating in a phase of development much earlier than the oedipal must play a part. In the ensuing debate, conversion was recognized as a symptom that could occur at almost any age or period of development and in almost any personality configuration or diagnosis. It provided a way to express forbidden wishes in symbolic form, or via body language, as a means to escape life-threatening stress and other dynamics (Rangell 1959, Ludwig 1972).

Lazare (1971) reviewed the psychoanalytic theory of these conditions and found a number of writers in agreement that the group of patients with hysterical traits and symptoms include a broad spectrum ranging from those with serious pregenital problems to those with conflicts only at the phallic level. Their dynamics differ in regard to object relations, mechanisms of defense, levels of fixation and integration, and maturity of the synthetic functions of the ego. These patients share traits in common, but they are more apt to be exaggerated in the "sicker," that is, the more immature, orally fixated group (who show more blatant and infantile hysterical symptoms than do the healthier ones).

Baumbacher and Amini (1981), building on this agreement, attempted to clarify the definition of adult hysterical personality in a developmental context. They deplored the use of descriptions of behavior and other nondynamic features in making the diagnosis, and presented a strong case for reserving the word "hysterical" to describe those difficulties arising predominantly in the phallic phase, in which the ego is relatively well formed and the conflict is between intrapsychic structures. They held that it is a hysterical *character* disorder if the patient has achieved an oedipal resolution and then regresses to phallic–oedipal conflicts. It is a hysterical *personality* disorder if the patient has not yet achieved the oedipal stage. The influence of issues left over from previous phases of development may play some part in the overt behavior, but these earlier phases do not predominate in the internal structure. When they do, deficiencies of ego and object relationship are clearly in evidence and constitute an entirely different intrapsychic matrix. They felt it is misleading to describe both situations as *hysterical* because it implies similar underlying conditions, and they concurred with Krohn (1978) who cautions that mistaking the neurotic symptoms in hysterical personality for preoedipal conditions may lead to errors in psychotherapy that reinforce the hysterical (phallic) defenses rather than relieve them. Anthony (1982) agreed that this was a sound approach for understanding childhood conditions as well. Addressing the same issue from the other direction, Zisook and DeVaul (1978) pointed out that the "healthy hysteric," in Lazare's (1971) or Zetzel's (1968) sense, does not show sufficient deviation from the general population to qualify as disordered and must be considered within the normal spectrum of personality.

Horowitz (1987) deals with this issue by formulating the level of the adult patient's development of the self through the use of person schemas theory. He views an individual with maladaptive hysterical traits as having a personality disorder at one of four successively less organized and unitary levels of self and object schematization: neurotic, narcissistically vulnerable, borderline, and fragmented. (For an overview see Chapter 1 of this volume and Table 1–1 on pp. 10–11.) Viewed in this way, hysterical signs and symptoms can be understood, not as defining a diagnosis or specific psychosexual level of development, but as manifestations of a spectrum of personality disorders that are qualitatively different and vary from mild to severe. Understanding the level and characteristics of such maldevelopment can suggest etiology and proper treatment directions.

Recently, Mueller and Aniskiewicz (1986) have discussed in detail the psychotherapy of hysterical conditions and the many patterns of their mothers' and fathers' personality that emerge from the memory of such adults in treatment. They summarize these patterns by saying that the parents, because of that own immaturity, are unable to behave in ways appropriate for each successive level of their child's development. They hold that variations in the parents' manifest and latent characteristics shape the particular defensive patterns in the child. They add to the earlier warnings against paying too much attention to the dramatic behaviors to the detriment of a clear dynamic (that is to say, diagnostic) understanding of the form of the patient's psyche, which can then guide treatment. They feel that the hysterical personality is a *relationship syndrome* at the phallic–oedipal level, even if this structure is screened from view; the patient appears to have only dyadic relationships because she or he was forced to negotiate separate alliances with the parents. This relatively advanced development level sets the hysteric apart from the borderline patient and requires different treatment.

## Regression and Fixation
When adults present with symptoms of borderline or hysterical personality problems, the convention is to assume they are regressed to, or fixated at, immature psychosexual stages, preoedipal or phallic. This is not to say that they are behaving as normal children do at that age, but only that they lack the skills and integration customarily achieved by that age. Anyone familiar with children can easily observe that average 3-year-olds, in a "good enough" environment, have unimpeded access to parents and other caregivers to whom they signal their needs, which are met in easy reciprocity. Adequate and appropriate emotional expression is achieved, and personal relationships are satisfying and supportive; within this context the children function quite well and are happy.

Whatever the theory suggests about the internal conflicts of this normal stage, the observable facts are that preoedipal children do not behave like borderline adults. Presumably, if we projected the relationship abilities of a 3-year-old into an adult, the result would not resemble the feelings and behavior of the adult patient with preoedipal problems. The child-adult would, unambivalently if naively, seek and find the appropriate relationship figures that are available, including the therapist. On the other hand, borderline adult patients attempting to function in an adult context fail to elicit appropriate and satisfying relationships and are unhappy. They may have developed well in other areas (intelligence, for example), but interpersonal relationships, so crucial to most human socialization, have gone awry. Further, there is no data to show that recovering borderline adults go through a narcissistic and then a neurotic phase before they become normal. Nor does a borderline child trace these steps in recovery. We think of these levels as hierarchical, but they may be only characteristic deviations related to the age and developmental level of the child when inadequacies in the caregiving environment, losses or chronic traumas supervene. The point is, if adult personality problems are related to childhood at all, the maldevelopment seems to be more a *deviation* from the normal pathway of self and other schematization than a fixation at, or a regression to, an as-yet-unresolved stage of normal functioning.

Research on the fate of insecure attachments assessed at the age of 1 year (discussed later in this chapter) suggests that children with relationship problems in nursery school and kindergarten have been developing the disability from the earliest times at home. It can be expected that, among the growing cohorts of children evaluated for security of relationships in infancy and childhood, some cases of childhood "preoedipal" problems will be found, and even that some of these well-studied children will develop such disorders as adults. This is one way this theory of etiology can and will be tested.

With grownups, we proceed in the other direction. We trace the difficulty back to childhood and infer that our disturbed patient felt and acted in this maladaptive way between the ages of 2 and 4, in the case of borderline pathology, and 3½ to 6 with phallic or oedipal problems, *and would have been diagnosable as already disordered during those periods*. We don't know yet whether this is true. Nor do we know the proportion of children who, accurately diagnosed with these problems in childhood, will show up with hysterical personality disorders in adult life. Still, with the study of these issues in its present state, it is helpful to bear in mind the distinctions made by these students of the adult conditions when considering childhood personality as well. The use of such guidelines is made easier by virtue of the fact that the life experience of the latency child does not provide for the development of the skill or the complexity of repertoire that an adult would possess in seeking the very same immature goals. For this reason, children are more direct and simple in their behavior and more transparent in their aims than an adult would ordinarily be. A child seeking an oedipal-level relationship with an adult through sexualized behavior will act in a strikingly different manner from a child sexualizing attempts to elicit more regressive satisfactions. For example, a sensitive adult observer might be shocked by his or her own beginning erotic response to a seductive advance by a child who had achieved the phallic stage of libidinal development. That same observer is not likely to be moved in this way by the blatant sexual provocations of a youngster whose behavior stems from maladapted earlier phases. This distinction usually is not so easily seen in the two types of adult hysteric. The more immature adult still may command rather sophisticated behavior that initially belies its disordered source.

The idea of oral neediness as the basis of hysterical symptoms is natural to our understanding that more primitive patterns of behavior are learned first and most thoroughly, especially those that arise in relation to the first attachment figure. Such behavior is automatically resorted to later when more mature behavior is opposed or otherwise fails to achieve its goal. The level of personality development may be more apparent in children. The normal child, in contradistinction to the normal adult, quickly retreats to these earlier behavioral systems on being stressed or disappointed. The firmly put-to-bed toddler may comfort him- or herself by thumb-sucking after mother leaves. He or she may throw a tantrum when a toy is snatched away by another child. Above all, the child is egocentric and naturally sees the world strictly as it relates to the self. This tendency does not make the child an oral character. Such classification only makes sense when immature traits in an older child or adult predominate where the stage of physical and social interaction calls for more adaptive abilities. The critical feature is the phase-appropriateness and effectiveness of ego functions and the mechanisms of defense.

## CULTURE AND PERSONALITY PATHOLOGY

The diagnosis of personality pathology is always a relative matter in which culture plays a very prominent part. The description of the influence of culture on the formation of character is a whole discipline in itself and cannot be attempted here. It rests, however, on the same hypothesis that underlies our grasp of how the mother, and later the family, influence the developing infant. The early cultural anthropologists, guided by psychoanalytic theory, found that Freud's thesis that sexual development determined personality was inadequate; their data required an interpersonal theory in addition. Just as it seemed evident that the varieties of maternal response affected the direction taken by the drive derivatives in infancy, so it seemed to Fromm and Horney that cultural influences, brought to the child by the family and the subgroup, guided the development of behavior in all parts of personality, including the sexual. Opler (1969) points out that the struggle that produces character is not just between libidinal wishes and some sort of internal ego-control principle, but between actual living persons, the child and his or her models—mother, family, and subgroup. Erikson (1963) has attempted an elaborate extrapolation of the psychosexual theory of development to take into account the influences of culture.

That culture may incline toward hysterical traits and even symptomatology seems evident from the study of some social structures. An example of this is the style of the male children in some Latin cultures in which both fathers and mothers dote on the son's machismo. What may serve well enough in a Central American hamlet or an ethnic subgroup in the barrio may not be sufficient for the interpersonal requirements of a modern large city. What works on the playground or in certain families may not be up to the complications met with later in life. Youngsters developing the hysterical role in such environments do not often become patients because they are either acting like their parents or acting out for their parents and conforming to their culture, and are thus not seen as disordered. Indeed, they are not disordered from a cultural point of view unless their symptoms are too discordant with the social group or for their own functioning. For example, LaBarre and LaBarre (1965) report a well-studied and followed case of cultural conditioning in a 12-year-old prepubertal child raised in the Bible Belt of the South. In this case, the conditioning eventually led to hysterical blindness. Examples could be multiplied (Pierloot and Ngoma 1988). Here the matter must be left in favor of pursuing a further inquiry into the development of hysterical pathology in more familiar circumstances.

## A GENERIC DEFINITION OF PERSONALITY PATHOLOGY

Psychologists and those responsible for the three most recent *DSM* classifications (see pp. 35–41 of this volume) view traits, styles, and personality in terms of dimensionality, in which the boundary between the normal range of adaptations and maladaptive traits of symptoms with similar cast is arbitrary (Widiger and Frances 1985). The *DSM-III* and *IV* criteria are based on individual behavioral characteristics calculated to produce agreement on the phenomenological findings. Development in early life consists of lawful changes across time, however, and what may be normal behavior in one phase is deviant in another. For this reason, the descriptive categories of the present diagnostic nosology are inadequate for the study of childhood disorders. They indicate neither the cause of the disorder nor the avenue for cure.

Psychoanalytic developmental theory, on the other hand, does describe successive stages of growth, with differing behavioral characteristics that are affected by factors such as traumas and disturbances in object relationships. But the focus is on the changing constellation of the three psychic entities that are relatively inaccessible to study in the first 3 or 4 years of life. In addition, these inner constellations are primarily seen to be determined by constitutional givens and for this reason a property of the child alone.

In defining personality pathology, psychoanalysts and physicians in general have been reluctant to abandon the etiologic model of diagnosis, which leads to categories implying causation. They are accustomed to seeing the illness as residing in the patient, who is basically different from the healthy person. It is plain that a developmental psychopathology that resolves these differences is called for. What is as yet unclear is whether the conditions recognized as personality disorder in adulthood have always been within the individual, just insufficiently expressed to be diagnosed, or whether they come to be out of otherwise normal functioning, and if so, how and when.

Aside from any possible genomic or constitutional vulnerabilities, which will be discussed later, and bearing in mind the influence of the family and of culture, a generic definition may be attempted. Personality pathology exists when the individual, who is not otherwise brought to it by biologic deficiency or internal conflict, has failed to develop consistent, mutually satisfying personal relationships *in a milieu where these are not prevented by the social environment*. It exists where resilience of interpersonal functioning appropriate to the age of the individual is lacking, especially where the patterns of adaptation are themselves sources of conflict with the environment. These patterns must be enduring and interfere with the person's life satisfactions and social acceptance.

A personality disorder can be inferred only when maladaptive or disordered behavior consistently occurs where the interpersonal and social situation calls for—and would permit—more effective and mature behavior. This situation can be much less frequently the case in childhood than in adult life because of the impressive effect of the personal relationships the child has with caregivers. That is, the caregivers (the "personal relationships") constrain the alternatives available to the child. The appearance is given that the disorder is within the child when actually it often resides in the context of the child's relationships. This is one reason why diagnosing personality pathology in children is problematic.

Consider how such a definition might fit a common situation in development. When a frustrated child strikes another child, the behavior of the adults is definitive in bringing about reinforcement, suppression, or evolution of alternatives to this form of action. If the parent encourages or demands that the child fight, there will be a strong impetus for this social response to occur and persist even when the situation calls for and would permit more sophisticated arbitration. The development of more mature behavior is hampered by the general unsatisfactory nature of an aggressive response, which itself brings on further regression and a sense of ineffectuality. If, on the other hand, suppression of the self-assertive impulse is required, without indication of how the situation could be better handled, and especially when there is the strong implication that to assert oneself is bad, then the stage is set for submissive behavior with internalization of a conflictual and guilty self-attitude about a natural response. In either case, the child is effectively held back from the elaboration of conflict-free behavioral systems that bring satisfaction; and if the situation goes on long enough beyond those epigenetic phases of childhood where opportunities for learning more adaptive behavior are abundant and relapses are benign, then it becomes more and more difficult to change and will appear more and more like the personality pathology described in adults.

At this point, it is well to remember that the impression of the presence of character disorder in childhood is sometimes gained through the reports of the parents and other caregivers who often are unaware of how their own attitudes and behaviors have constrained the child. Many children brought to evaluation for behavior disorders are seen by the adults with whom they live as incorrigibly maladapted and set in their ways, free from remorse or anxiety, and, in short, evidencing a personality disorder. Yet many of these same children, when provided with a group or foster home environment where there is strong, unconflicted (therapeutic) encouragement to behave more appropriately, will rapidly resume their forward development. Since only a small percentage of children are removed from their home environment, and those that are represent the most seriously disturbed cases, and since fewer still go to such ideal caregiving situations, the potential resilience of childhood is not often so clearly demonstrated. But the fact that it does happen is strong evidence that the inflexible character disorders seen in adult life do not often have their counterpart before adolescence. This underscores the nascency of the personality traits common to childhood and implies that the whole understanding of the child's personality must include the consideration of the intercurrent, as-yet-not-crystallized ego struc-

tures and the as-yet-not-internalized parental and cultural influences. When such intractability as seen in adults does occur in
childhood, as with autism and childhood schizophrenia, we cannot
escape the conviction that these are youngsters who, in addition to
or because of their constitutional vulnerability, have sustained
more serious or prolonged injury or deficiency of attachment in the
early phases of life. Their treatment presents the same difficulties
as does the treatment of the "sick" or oral hysterical personalities in
adult life. The symptomatology of these youngsters may be tinged
with pseudosexuality, but the basic problems appear to rest on
faulty and inadequate early object relations and social learning. The
question of whether a child under 12 could qualify for the diagnosis of
severe personality disorder has been challenged here, but the debate
still warms the child psychiatry journals (see Kernberg vs. Shapiro
1990).

## Longitudinal Research on Diagnostic Continuities

Most longitudinal research on the adult outcome of childhood
psychiatric disorders has concerned itself with deficiency, illness,
or conduct serious enough to bring the family to clinics and
hospitals: major developmental disorders, schizophrenia, and de-
linquency. These conditions tend to remain in the mental health
system and can be followed up. Among those families attending
clinics, there is, of course, a high percentage of less disturbed
children. They receive diagnoses of anxiety states, disturbances of
behavior, depressions, and other "emotional" disorders and are
typically treated on an outpatient basis. The question naturally
arises as to how all these children fare in adulthood. Is there
continuity of disorder in the serious group? In the less serious
group? Beginning with Robins's classic study (1966), follow-ups in
adulthood have indicated that serious psychiatric problems in
childhood have a relatively poor prognosis, although they are not
necessarily predictive of the same type of pathology. The exception
to this lack of predictability of similar pathology is that virtually all
adult antisocial behavior is preceded by a history of childhood
conduct disorder and poor parenting. The same is not true,
however, for the "internalizing" neurotic reactions under which
childhood hysterical problems or incipient hysterical personality
would fall. These conditions correlate weakly, or even negatively,

with the type, or even the presence of disorder in later life, and the children's difficulties as adults do not exceed those of the control groups that did not have a diagnosis in childhood (Cass and Thomas 1979, Robins and Rutter 1990, Zeitlin 1986).

In their own way, all of these authors consider that meaningful continuities exist in the lesser forms of disorder. but, because of differing behavior in different contextual or developmental settings from childhood to adult life, they have not been discovered by the methods used for follow-up. Although a great deal has been written about the matrix out of which hysterical personality grows, from the perspective of the adult disorder (this book, for example), studies confirming these hypotheses are nowhere in evidence. It is clear that for the childhood roots of personality disorder, as for the study of normal personality formation, anterospective research on nonpatient populations is necessary to establish how continuity is effected. This is likely to be observed best in social settings. "The personality variables most suited for understanding people in the life course, across time and in diverse circumstances, are interactional styles that evoke supporting, maintaining and validation support from others" (Caspi et al. 1990, p. 15).

## THE SOCIAL BOND BETWEEN MOTHER AND CHILD

The research discussed in the preceding paragraph points to the association of serious psychopathology in childhood or adult life with traumas and deficiencies in the mother–child attachment in the first year of life. Such inadequacies seem to be able to distort or even prevent normal development, although they do not always do so despite what seem to be hopeless odds. Early oral deprivations, that is, deprivations of adequate social attachment to mother or caregiver, are associated with the functional psychoses of childhood and with sociopathy, addiction, and schizophrenia in later life. The implication of current research on normal children is that the quality of care and attachment relationships and their disturbances also contribute to personality and psychopathology; it is to this subject that we now turn.

It has been the special province of psychoanalytic theory to explain the origins of behavior and the unfolding of personality on the basis of inferred instinctual drives and their derivatives. Insofar as the drives represent biological forces finding psychological representation in the psychic apparatus, they are constitutional. Ethological theory, in approaching the same issue, holds that the behavioral systems that culminate in the focused attachment of the infant to its primary caregiver around the age of 6 months begin as discrete, fixed-action patterns that are present at birth and are constitutional. In physical ontogeny, we see that the organism unfolds properly only if timely and appropriate environmental conditions, nutriments, and stimulations are present, especially during the sensitive periods of rapid growth. In psychological ontogeny, an analogous situation obtains. Innate patterns of perception, fixed-action behaviors, and affectual predispositions are provided in the germ plasm and are mature at birth. They achieve their ordinary potential for development when they are met with phase-specific interactional and emotional experiences, as would be expectable in the environment within which the species evolved. For mankind, these experiences are exceedingly complicated after the first 2 or 3 months of life, when the interaction between the growing child and its caregiver becomes predominantly a social event.

All during this process the infant experiences its social interactions with the caregiver through its physical sensibilities (those visual, tactile, auditory modalities that have a predominantly intaking vector), and its focus is on bodily parts and vague internal satisfactions. Thus, the drives achieve psychic representation in terms of the physical interactions through which they are experienced. The inner picture of what one is grows, apparently *de novo*, in each child as the precipitate of physical and emotional experiences with the social partner. Since the infant in the first few months is ignorant of the survival necessity for the relationship with its caregiver or even of its essentially "social" nature, its psychic representations will be of the physical and emotional needs and their satisfactions. This is the hallmark of the primary process. That the productions of children, psychotic experiences, and the recollections of adults in psychoanalytic treatment so often are rendered in terms of these bodily satisfactions or frustrations is testimony to the fact that the psychic representation of these early impressions colors the experience of subsequent development throughout life.

Despite Freud's famous quote about the infant's relationship with its mother as the prototype of love for a whole lifetime, the influence of this and other personal relationships on development has until recently remained subordinated in psychoanalytic theory to the fate of the drives, the stages of libidinal and ego development, the effect of traumas, and the overriding influence of fantasy. Although emphasizing the importance of early development for the adequacy of later functioning, the data of most psychoanalytic examinations have remained where Freud located them, in the nuclear oedipal complex, a function of the fourth and fifth years of life. This is understandable in light of the fact that reconstructions from adult analyses are mostly built on the patient's memory of the oedipal period of life rather than the less accessible events of earlier stages. It is a rare child who enters analysis while in the throes of the conflicts imputed to be the cause of hysterical personality. The idea of stages of development, in both self-organization and self and object schematization, implies a certain irreversibility in the increasing complexity of the personality. There should be a discernible difference in the subjective and projective features of a playroom child who has mastered at least the first step of the oedipal resolution and is now, due to some stressful hitch, thrown back to an earlier organization of defenses, and a child still in that earlier stage and having trouble with it. This is how the several theorists discussed here differentiate between preoedipal hysteroid conditions, hysterical personality, and hysterical character in their adult patients (Baumbacher and Amini 1981, Blacker and Tupin [this volume, Chapter 2], Krohn 1978, Mueller and Aniskiewicz 1986). There is an enormous amount of clinical detail available from adult therapy that prompts complex theories of the origin of hysterical styles, but alas, when observing for the putative illness *in statu nascendi*, we are perplexed. There is no indication that such conditions, present at ages 3–5 (and they have been reported), go on to be diagnosed as hysterical personality, neurosis, or style in latency or in adult life. We also do not know what these children, undiagnosed but affected in childhood, report about their past when in their analyses 20 or 30 years later. Freud believed all adult neuroses were preceded by such in childhood, but Anna Freud (1965) declared, as the result of her child observation and longitudinal study, that "there is no certainty that a particular type of infantile neurosis will prove to be the forerunner of the same type of adult neurosis" (p. 151). In her concept of developmental lines (1963) she held that healthy progression through the psychosexual stages is dependent on the formation of adequate object relationships appropriate to each stage of development. The quality of these relationships will determine the trust, optimism, and other parameters of the preoedipal period, for good or ill. She considered object relations as only one of a number of developmental lines and gave it no special preeminence. Since then, however, and before the avalanche of new research on attachment, analysts have been giving increasing attention to enduring characteristics of individual children (the "vertical" dimension of development, so to speak, as compared with the "horizontal" succession of stages) and to a focus on the importance of the child–caregiver relationship in their theorizing. Silverman and colleagues (1975) studied a group of forty-five normal boys followed from age 4 to puberty. They reported on the emergence of a core psychic constellation observable in these youngsters during the preoedipal period. They held that, although development proceeds via a process of sequential organization and reorganization, there are ". . . periodic regroupings, leading to new levels of psychic equilibrium, deriv[ing] only partly from the appearance of new ego structures. In part they derive from shifts in coordination of patterning of already existing structures" (p. 147). They deemphasized the oedipal complex as a cause of neurosis and considered it as a dynamically central feature of a developmental process that may or may not predispose to neurotic solutions. Thus, unresolved oedipal conflict appears among the primary manifestations of the neurotic processes rather than their source. Cramer (1975), another member of this same research group, described the development of the three boys from their study with the most outstanding progress through the oedipal phase. The team was tempted to explain this excellence on the basis of genetic determinants:

> Yet, our observations indicated that continuing *external* influence played an important role in determining the continuous progressive push in these children. The parents provided many gratifications at

higher levels of development, and they were sufficiently sensitive to allow the children to regress when needed. [p. 42]

More recently, child analysts and developmental researchers have also been looking at the early years in a more vertical way, that is, following continuities of behavior and affect linearly upward from birth, across transformations, in the manner of developmental lines or pathways. Stern (1985) concentrated on the sense of self, beginning at birth, that accrues qualities as the infant grows, an emergent self, a core self, a subjective self and, finally, a verbal self, all in the context of the interrelatedness with the caregivers. Greenspan (1989) has been elaborating a model of ego development that describes four essential, cumulative processes that characterize infancy and that also emphasize the social bonds. "Shared attention and engagement" start at birth. Then between the 4th and 8th months "two-way communication" is added. "Shared meanings," from 18 to 24 months follows. Lastly, "emotional thinking," from 2½ to 3 years emerges. Greenspan holds that disorders of each of these processes may arise at any time after they have come into being, and this may affect other lines, with which they are related. Inadequate development of any of these emerging ego skills can distort what comes after, but development in the other lines may go on relatively well. Greenspan's scheme does not depend on a stage theory. He relates psychopathology to these successive new complexities and their effect on other parts of the developing ego.

Developmental research is focusing on the origins of internal representations of the self and others, which are paramount in the generation of self-esteem. A sense of well-being is brought about when the child is active, controlling, and competent in the face of adaptive demands (Stern 1985). The infant is equipped with the ability to establish and maintain a coherent sense of self as active and in control (narcissistic regulation) and able to maintain sustained connections with others (attachment). These two systems have great overlap and reinforce each other for good or ill (Mitchell 1988). But an infant can only be competent in the context of a "good enough" caregiver, through which this self-esteem is established. If this is thwarted, a variety of results are possible.

One child might fail to evolve empathy, withdraw, and incline to psychopathy. Another might develop a schizotypal or borderline compromise (Petti and Vela 1990). And a third might continue to seek help in a distorted and self-defeating way and develop hysterical personality traits (Bleiberg 1987). Other routes are possible.

Utilizing psychoanalytic play sessions as the investigative format, Donald Cohen's group at the Yale Child Study Center is assessing normal oedipal-age children to study the dominant ways they communicate to the analyst the tasks that are uppermost in their minds during this phase. This is development *in statu nascendi*. Preliminary results indicate the common destructive and aggressive fantasies and play of the sessions are negotiations between the protective/loving and attacking impulses in the context of mastery of object relations and construction of the self (Cohen et al. 1987).

From a number of sources other than psychoanalytic, it is becoming clearer that at an early time in infancy a child needs one, or at most a few human figures on which to focus an attachment, a social bond; it's through this relationship that the early forms of integrated behavior evolve. The subsequent stages of psychological development are then nurtured, and in part elicited and determined, by this interpersonal experience. In the absence or serious distortion of this essential relationship, severe malformations or arrest of psychic development can occur—even death. But if a minimally adequate attachment is formed, personality development goes ahead, rooted in the biological inclination of the child which is the result of 60 million years of mammalian evolution. Behaviors ready at birth—crying, clasping, sucking, looking— express themselves in fragments and then systems, prompted by intrinsic patterns common to the species and met by the reciprocal encouragement of the caregiving figures. From these interactions, patterns of behavior emerge and are shaped by the interpersonal responses. The child's experience, coupled with his ability to conceptualize reality, will characterize how he perceives the world and deals with what he perceives. These patterns, the beginnings of personality, are also labile and regress easily; above all, they are dependent on the reciprocal reinforcement continuously available from the attachment figures.

Speculation about how the influence of the attachment bond

affects future personality is irresistible, even though scientific data are only now accumulating. There has been an explosion of work on the attachment bond by developmental psychologists friendly to dynamic thinking in the 14 years since this volume first appeared and the evidence is having an extraordinarily important effect on theories of personality and psychopathology.

## Attachment

The findings on attachment are so compelling that a brief review of them is in order here. The theoretical impetus for these researches on the mother–infant bond was orginated by John Bowlby, out of the object relations school of psychoanalysis in London during the 1950s. From an evolutionary–ethological study of animals and observation of children from birth he evolved two hypotheses: that the quality of the infant's tie to its mother is a function of the early care, and that the internalization of this model of caring determines much of the child's later relationships. These ideas stimulated Mary Ainsworth's pioneering experimental work in the 1960s, and since then the effects of maternal behavior on the attachment bond have had a great deal of attention.

## The Strange Situation

Ainsworth and her colleagues summarized their work in 1978. They employed a naturalistic design to study the quality of mother–infant interactions. A group of trained observers made detailed notes about the behavior of mother–infant pairs in the home over a total of 15 hours during each quarter of the infant's first year. At 12 months, Ainsworth administered a short, structured laboratory procedure that was calculated to elicit attachment behavior by introducing mild separation stress. This instrument was called the Strange Situation (referred to here as SS).

Mother and infant enter a pleasant room and there follow eight 3-minute periods during which the mother twice leaves the room and twice returns. At first, Ainsworth thought the quality of the attachment could be assessed by how the infant behaved at separation. She found this response could be illuminating, but it was the behavior in the two *reunion* episodes that reliably differentiated among the children in her normal sample.

Some of Ainsworth's infants greeted their returning mothers by looking at them, smiling, and approaching with positive behavior. If they were overtly upset by the departure, they sought bodily contact. They all showed some combination of these four major criteria: looking, smiling, approaching positively, and seeking contact. These children were the "B" group in their research protocol and were later characterized as "secure" in comparison to the other two groups that emerged. Other children avoided their mothers on reunion. They essentially ignored or moved away from them, even if the mothers sought contact. These children, the "A" group, Ainsworth designated as "insecure–avoidant." Yet others, the "C" group, showed some combination of anxiety, anger, and clinging; they were ambivalent. Ainsworth called this group "insecure–resistant."

The B category was given the classification "secure" because it conformed to the clinically derived and common-sense assumption that its main features, positive affect and the inclination to seek and benefit from reassurance in communication and bodily contact, indicated the infants' ability to use the parents as a secure base for relief of distress and/or for effective play and exploration. In addition, there was absence of the contrary behavior: resistance, negativity, and turning away. Ainsworth found that raters could blindly predict, with a high degree of accuracy, an infant's response in the SS by observing the quality of care given by the mother during the preceding year. The significant variables were two: mother's alertness to and alacrity in meeting the infant's needs, and the contingent sensitivity of the care, that is, effective care that took the child's current needs into account, as opposed to perfunctory or intrusive care. Here, maternal sensitivity depended more on appropriate responses to the infant's signals than to self-initiated actions toward the baby. These findings exactly corroborated Bowlby's first hypothesis, that the quality of attachment is a function of the quality of early care, and have since been replicated many times. In the United States about one-half to two-thirds of normal samples have shown the secure, group B response; one-fifth to one-third have been classified avoidant, or group A. The rest, about one in six to eight, were ambivalent, or group C. There were also a few unclassifiable infants. In recent work, Mary Main has identified a fourth group, which she calls "insecure–disorganized/disoriented," or the D group. These children were drawn from the 15 percent of her large sample that were "forced classified" or unclassifiable as A, B, or C. In some ways, these children proved to be even more maladapted than the A group at age 6 (Main and Solomon 1986).

If the infants behave in this way in the mildly stressful lab challenge of the SS, how do they behave at home or elsewhere? Main (1977) found that avoidant toddlers who had not shown anger in the SS, but rather aloofness, demonstrated a great deal of angry crying, hitting, and petulance in other, more stress-free settings, such as at home, or in familiar care. There, these children did not show the "independent" behavior of the SS but were hostile and negative about being left or put down after holding. Often, this hostility was spontaneous and out of context. In daycare, they were likely to threaten and actually attack both peers and adults. At home, the same unprovoked hostility was evident, together with odd actions such as hand-flapping, inexplicable fears, and other unusual behavior.

Different maternal caretaking patterns were found to be associated with the different categories of infant response in the SS. Avoidance in the SS was highly correlated with mother's anger at the child and her rejection and aversion to physical contact with it in the home during the first year of life. Consistently abused children are highly likely to show the avoidance response.

Ambivalence in the SS, however, correlated with mother's intermittent, ambivalent, or inadequate care and her simple physical neglect of the infant, as opposed to rejection, aversion, abuse, or total withdrawal. Thus, emotional unavailability and hostile aversion lead to the avoidant response in the SS. Inconsistency of nurturance without active aversion leads to the ambivalent response.

Although the insecure children's behavior at home can be seen to be autoplastically adaptive (Main 1977), these behaviors, when used elsewhere, are relatively maladaptive. Outside the home, the same less-than-optimal responses to others are ordinarily quite ineffective, or, even worse, provocative of reciprocal suboptimal responses. Nevertheless, these children can be understood as attempting to relate, in their inadequate way, according to their internal model of relationship, including assaults. Thus, A and C children were much more likely than B children to present behavior problems in school. In kindergarten, although A and C children were more negative than Bs, there was no significant difference in the number of attempts to be near the teacher. The nature of these attempts, however, did differentiate the children. The A children approached the teacher in oblique or disguised ways that were less effective in drawing positive attention unless the teacher was alerted to them (Sroufe 1983).

The point is not that the status of insecure attachment at 12 months *causes* maladaptive behavior in the preschool years but that it strongly *predicts* it. The inconsistent or rejecting care that brought about the early assignment to the insecure group tends to continue and in the absence of meliorating factors, seems to produce the less-than-optimal ways of relating to others later. Had the quality of care changed for the better for a significant time after one year, then a more favorable result could be expected in preschool (Sroufe et al. 1984). These findings are generally supportive of Bowlby's second hypothesis, that internal working models of attachment, once formed, tend to be stable and to determine how the child construes subsequent relationships. Cassidy (1988) found children's patterns of self perception at age 6 were related to SS status at age 1. Sroufe's group has recently followed up a portion of its sample, 28 children by then in the third grade. Again they found an association between security in the SS at age 1 and competence with peers at age 8. (Erickson et al.1985, Sroufe 1988). Thus, among many other findings, children assessed at 12 months as insecure–avoidant later got along poorly with others in school, tended to isolate themselves, and yet drew attention by negative action. Insecure–resistant children were seen later as being sad, fearful, and alternatingly amiable and hostile, seemingly to attract positive attention and then spoiling it (Main and Cassidy 1988).

The above findings were all on cohorts of normal children but they point the way to diagnostic possibilities. One recent report compared clinic-referred children with disruptive behavior and nonproblem controls. It was found that the children with behavior disorders in nursery school, ages 3–6, were much more likely to have insecure relationships with their mothers, assessed by separation/reunion behavior at the time of referral, than were matched normals (Speltz et al. 1990).

*Security Classification and Psychopathology.* Some have been tempted to regard anxious attachment, especially avoidant and disorganized attachment in the SS, as a reliable indication of significant future personality problems. This is unwarranted. Security in the SS at age 1, although a good beginning, cannot be expected to protect the child from all future difficulties, nor is a child assessed as avoidant condemned to a life of psychopathology. These patterns can and do change, in lawful ways now being discovered and described. The possible relationship of insecure attachment to the phenotypic expression of temperament and biologically influenced mental illnesses such as schizophrenia, manic–depressive disorder, and childhood psychosis remains to be defined. It is unlikely that more than a small percentage of anxiously attached children assessed at age 1 will come to psychiatric diagnosis, and there is little evidence that insecurity in the SS affects intelligence, cognition, or learning *in the absence of stress*. This does not mean, however, that the early relationship paradigm is not important. The Sroufe Minnesota study described earlier showed dramatic differences in self-esteem and relationships with peers and teachers for children who had been secure, as against those who had anxious attachments, with almost no overlap between groups (Sroufe 1983). In addition, and of singular importance to child therapists, there were significant differences in the elaborateness, flexibility, and quality of the fantasy play. For those children who had been assessed as avoidant, there was almost a total absence of fantasy themes concerning people. The avoidant children produced more conflict-laden play situations without bringing them to satisfactory conclusions (Sroufe 1988). This is a common observation in child therapy but requires more stringent examination.

It would be too tidy to expect to find that adult psychopathology neatly issues from the three insecure groups in the SS, the more neurotic from the resistant group and the more severe and infantile types from the avoidant and disorganized groups. Nevertheless, it would be surprising if the serious emotional disorders of later life were not drawn from the last named groups grown up, especially if the insecurity lasted a long period of time, since maldevelopment in the oral phase is so often identified as the substrate from which later, more serious behavioral pathology emerges. Because the

traits under consideration here require substantial object relationships in order to occur at all, very early attachment deficiencies of
the third variety seem unlikely to play a prominent part in the
development of hysterical personality. It is possible, however, to
correlate some of the striking characteristics of hysterical style with
behaviors that are frequently seen in those infants in the insecure–
resistant group. The insatiable attention-seeking of the hysteric
may have some of its origin in the partially frustrated attachment
behavior of signaling to the mother. The intermittent frustration
has the paradoxical effect of increasing the behavior rather than
extinguishing it. A close study of analogous behaviors in the
resistant group might reveal a number of hysterical antecedents
inaugurated by these partial frustrations by the mother coupled
with encouragement to continue the attention-seeking.

Utilizing the findings of these developmental psychologists,
Bowlby continued to enlarge what has been called "attachment
theory" (despite his objections to that term) until his death in 1990.
In characterizing the importance of attachment in personality, he
emphasized the primary position of these personal bonds between
the child and the (emotional) caregiver and held that within these
relationships there are formed internal working models (IWMs) of
the world and people (1988a). In his concept of attachment, the
IWMs are synonymous with the internal libidinal objects of
psychoanalytic theory. "As a child grows older, the patterns [the
IWMs] become increasingly a property of the child himself, which
means that he tends to impose it . . . upon new relationships
such as with a teacher, foster mother or a therapist" (p. 127). Seen
in this light, the period we are concerned with in understanding
hysterical personality would be age 4 or 5, when the child's
behavioral repertoire reflects the beginning solidification of the
IWMs on the one hand, and the continuance of parental relationships on the other.

The window on the first life relationship offered by the development of the SS instrument has led to a major concentration of
research on the infant–mother attachment and its effect on development. The quality of attachment, however, does not encompass
all aspects of the child–parent relationship, nor presage every type
of future adaptation. In addition to the security of attachment,
Emde (1989) sees affect, the achievement of emotional balance, as

a core psychological experience having a principal role in the development of the self. He holds both are strongly prompted by biology, but their effectiveness is a function of early relationships. He describes multiple interdependent axes of development in terms of the child's part and the parents' part: attachment in the child, bonding in the parent, affect regulation in the child, empathic responsiveness in the parent. To these he adds a number of other lines such as vigilance/protection, self control/discipline, learning/teaching, and so forth. As with Greenspan's system (1989), perturbations can arise in any one of these axes, at any time in the early life of the child, and if not met with mutual adaptation may solidify into disturbance and eventually disorder; the perturbation is in the relationship, the eventual disorder can come to reside in the child.

Arnold Sameroff (1989) has evolved a developmental scheme based on general systems theory that is congenial with the findings discussed here. He describes the social environment, the patterns of expectation of family and culture, as the *environtype*, by analogy to the biological *genotype*. The individual child, as the specific expression of the genotype, is the *phenotype*, and transactions occur between the child and the environtype. The child is affected by the environment, which in turn triggers gene activity on the one hand and environmental response on the other. This system evolves a dynamic balance within which learning and development occur. Because after birth the environmental regulation is mediated primarily through relationships, these become the major source of variation in all personality and pathology. He feels, therefore, a clear understanding of the normal and abnormal dynamic transformations in children's behavior can be the only basis for the study of personality and development.

Many workers since Ainsworth have focused on the increasingly sophisticated systems the young develop from birth to relate to the caregivers: seeking stimulation, exploring, and mastering. The infant becomes a child who attempts to control and be effective within the constraints of a personal relationship to the attachment figures. By about the end of the second year, symbolic representations are advanced to a point where language increasingly joins affect as the medium of relationship exchanges in normal families. The progress of this type of research, and its pertinence for psychoanalytic theory and psychotherapy, are well summarized in Zeanah and colleagues (1989).

> The continuing mutual reciprocal relationship between infant and environment requires an understanding of continuity as a product of this increasingly complex process [the attachment relationships] and underscores the importance of considering infant development within its environmental context. [p. 656]

These authors propose a *continious construction* model that substitutes evolving relationship patterns as the central process of development, normal and abnormal, rather than the linear traumatic event/fixation/regression model. The debate about such a shift is very current (Shapiro/Zeanah et al. 1990). Research with normal infants, showing continuities and correlations of affect attunement, joint referencing, mastery, reciprocity, and internal representations, as spoken of by Zeanah's group, by Stern, and many others, seems to indicate that much personality disorder (that is, a psychiatric condition or diagnosis) has its origin in pervasive abnormalities in social relationships. Sameroff, Emde, and colleagues (1989) have put forward a cogent system for ordering the psychopathology of relationships, which promises to correlate a synthetic developmental theory with what is now being learned about the function of play and fantasy in the oedipal period by analytic methods such as Cohen's.

## THE ORIGINS OF PERSONALITY

The sources of personality may be organized under two broad categories: the constitutional and the environmental. The constitutional sources produce their influence through the gene chemistry, which finds its expression in the configuration of the body and the structure of the nervous system, including the sexual hormones, which influence appearance and behavior. The environmental sources are those effects and experiences that meet the organism where it is in its development and shape it through all manner of learning, thereby contributing to the epigenetic ontogeny for good or ill. We have spoken some here about the biological substrates of behavior and personality, and these will be considered specifically, if briefly, when dealing with the sources of hysterical personality. But before entering into a discussion of the learned factors in hysterical personality in children it would be well to outline three categories of learning that emerge successively in infancy and that apply to the formation of every personality type: (1) the intrinsic direction taken by the biological drives, (2) the overt parental example, and (3) the shaping effect on the child's behavior of interpersonal affects and signals of the caregivers, conscious and unconscious.

*The drives*. Although spoken of somewhat differently by the variety of theorists concerned with development, the constitution of the child is thought to be innate and responsible for the direction and character of the behavioral systems present at birth. These drives, already discussed above under the mother–infant bond, seem to contain the earliest and most biologically linked of all learning processes.

The newborn begins by preferring certain general visual configurations over other configurations and seems more attuned to a female voice than to a male voice. Later, the infant will attend more to the human face—any face presented straight on—and still later it will prefer its mother's face. These behaviors assume at this point a distinct social cast. After attachment to the primary objects (emotional caregivers) is complete, somewhere between the 6th and the 12th month in home-raised infants, it is difficult to interrupt this attachment and reestablish it with another primary object. This progressive narrowing of attachment to a few specific figures has the quality of imprinting (the behavior described originally by Lorenz in ducklings), and has had its most thorough exposition for humans by John Bowlby (1969/1982, 1973, 1980).

*Overt parental example*. The second type of learning is not present at birth, but it shortly begins to be obvious and gradually becomes the most important source of all personality traits: the example of behavior that the child observes in those around him. This learning begins in simple mirroring of fragments of adult and sibling behavior before any attachment or true object relationship is apparent. Certain body movements, especially those to do with the mouth, face, and head, have a tendency to reflect similar movements in the caregivers. Head bobbing and mouth opening, lip smacking and tongue play are a few of the early mimicry behaviors that anyone familiar with infants will recognize. Later, more complete series of actions will be mimicked as the child willfully imitates and identifies with the behavior and thought processes of one or both parents. The peekaboo, pattycake, and verbal babytalk games of the first six months of life are familiar examples. Further on, the toddler will begin to show whole blocks of rather complex imitations derived from close observation of his parents without grasping the purpose of these behaviors. "Shifting gears" while in the child's car seat is such a behavior.

Social learning theorists have now recognized that learning of adult behaviors by mimicking what he or she sees plays an important part in an infant's grasp of what is appropriate and rewarded in the family. There seems to be a primary impetus in children to learn social rules and to become competent (Bandura 1977, Mischel and Mischel 1983). This incorporation illustrates not only the increasing mastery of the physical body but also the progress of the internalization of the child's idea of the meaning of the parents' behavior, their motivations, and their thought processes. The cat will be petted or its tail pulled, teddies will be punished or rewarded, and all manner of adult everyday activity will appear in miniature, especially while the adult is actually doing that activity.

It is important to remember that these imitative behaviors are not indiscriminate but skewed in favor of the social and personal context within which they are experienced. The more intimate and affect-laden these relationships are, the more the emulation. This is perhaps why children who are already given to violence, or experience it personally in their everyday lives, are harmed the most by viewing television violence.

*Shaping effects of parental intervention.* The third type of learning situation relevant here is one that becomes progressively more important as the object relationships mature. Although it may begin as early as the 3rd month, it reaches its greatest intensity after the age of 2, when the child begins to grasp its mother's intentions, her plans, and especially her affects in relation to its own impulses and feelings. These perceptions of parental overt and covert inhibitions and reinforcements will cause the child to shape its behavior, to some extent, to conform to these parental interventions, including the acting out of parental unconscious impulses by the child (Szurek et al. 1942, Massie et al. 1988).

One common example could be the 18-month-old whose mother subtly encourages him to hit her, trample on her feet, and pull her hair, reflecting her attitude about herself and/or her wish to do that to others. A little later, when cognitive functioning is more mature, the child's impulses and his attitude toward these impulses will be revealed in his play dialogue, which will be a reflection of how he perceives his mother's feelings. For a 3-year-old runabout, the making and serving of imaginary tea will show this imitation: who gets served first, what is said, the distribution of praise and correction, and so forth. At first, one may see clearly the youngster's thoughts played out, as yet still externalized and not yet imbued with qualities of goodness or badness. A little later the bad will be firmly suppressed from play and then from consciousness altogether. The tea party of the 4-year-old will more often be quite proper and correct, as the avenues for behavior and for admission of impulses to consciousness are increasingly controlled by the child himself, especially if all the while these attitudes are supported by consistent parental behavior. This internal conflict and control will be seen again as normal children in analytic research playroom sessions negotiate between protective/loving and attacking impulses (Cohen et al. 1987).

The communication between the mother and the child can thus be viewed as the template for the communication within the child's mind between instinctual derivatives emerging into awareness and what is permitted in mental representation. Any necessity imposed on the child—or assumed by him or her to be expected—to distort or ward off certain tabooed impulses will provide the child with the cognitive signposts indicating what must be repressed, denied, or projected.

As with attachment, which will come about for good or ill regardless of how an infant is treated, identification occurs even with the negative or ineffectual behaviors of immature or abusive parents. A split of such identification can have an important sparing effect on a child who has at least one figure with whom the identifications are good. The worst results obtain when all attachments to caregivers are insecure.

Of course, the three categories of learning spoken of here do not exhaust the list of possibilities, but they do cover those that have to do with interpersonal relationships and attachments, without which, certainly, no appropriate psychological development will occur.

## ANALOGY WITH RADIATION OF SPECIES

After the initial attachments are secure and the child enters the active, runabout phase, between 18 and 36 months, new behaviors seem to stream out and diversify much like radiations of variety in a species that has come to occupy a favorable ecological niche. Like the favorable environment, which tolerates these radiations, some parents allow much experimentation, guiding and shaping behavior only when appropriate to the child's best interests and those demands of society that the parents feel are justified. In healthy families, these guidelines change with the stages of development so that both behavioral and emotional growth keep pace with the chronological age of the child. For example, father might stay close to his daughter at play when she is 18 months old in order to see to it that she doesn't attempt activities that her coordination could not handle. The same protection at age 3 would tend to give the child the idea that she is fragile or uncoordinated, in need of protection.

The analogy to the radiation of species can be carried one step further in that parents who provide the milieu within which hysterical traits occur in their children are like those stringent, negative-feedback environments wherein the alternative radiations are severely restricted. As long as these conditions apply, the species remains static in its physical structure and behavioral adaptation to its limiting environment. The capacity for radiation remains, however, latently waiting for more favorable conditions. With a child, the latent capacity to develop is present also, but it is inversely proportional to the length of time that the restriction is in effect. If the environment provided by the parents is static and thus increasingly inappropriate as the child reaches the oedipal period and beyond, then the capacity to learn and originate new and more adequate behavioral systems decreases. If this continues through the usual personality thaw and reorganization of the period of adolescent conflicts, an internal structure of personality is formed and operates with little regard for external feedback and may be relatively impervious to outside obstruction or encouragement to change. In short, a personality disorder results.

This analogy may be illustrated, in an oversimplified way, by seeing the environment as a template, superimposed on the radiating forms of the organism. As long as the negative feedback operates, the animal species rapidly conforms and thereafter remains the same—adapted to that environment. When the restriction is lifted, the organism radiates new forms again (see Figure 3–1).

This is, of course, only one dimension of the situation. Reciprocal interaction between the child and its caregiver affects them both. The infant's constitutional givens play an important role, potentiated by the adult's preexisting attitudes about these givens. The child helps shape its own environment (Scarr and McCartney 1983). An upset, irritable infant may invoke feelings of guilt and helplessness in its mother, and her behavior then may contribute to the tension rather than relieve it. Some rigid parents, if they once conceive of their child as difficult, see the child's subsequent behavior as difficult no matter what the child does (Zeanah et al. 1986).

In the evolution of the behavior of any child, the parents (society, the physical world, and so on) provide the template. If this template is static and restrictive, it will resemble the ethological analogy, except that if the restriction goes on too long in any given child, the capacity to generate change is reduced. In the hypothetical ideal situation, the templates laid down by the parental and societal environments would have wide apertures and would shift with the necessities of the successive developmental stages so that by the time evolving personality becomes a structure after adolescence, there would be considerable adaptedness as well as adaptability already present (see Figure 3–2).

Clinical experience testifies to the potential for growth in children when pathological templates are lifted, whether through psychotherapeutic intervention with the child and/or his parents, favorable shifts in his environment, or the naturally healthy impetus of the developmental thrust, especially in adolescence.

It is important to bear in mind that the analogy to species radiation discussed here relates only to the behavior that one can

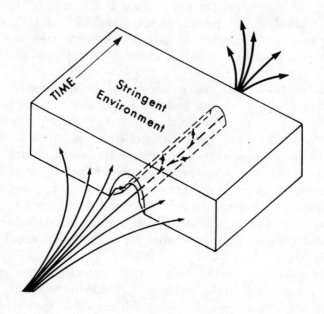

## FIGURE 3–1

Species with radiations

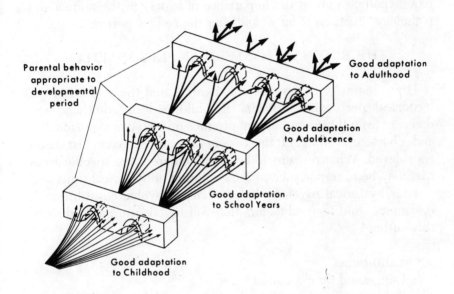

Parental behavior
appropriate to
developmental
period

Good adaptation
to Adulthood

Good adaptation
to Adoléscence

Good adaptation
to School Years

Good adaptation
to Childhood

FIGURE 3–2

Effect of environmental templates on psychological development

observe. What the child's intrapsychic constellations are can be inferred from the child's play, through psychological testing, through psychotherapy or analysis in childhood, and to some extent through all these modalities in adult life. The relative importance of the intrapsychic aspects in childhood is very much a matter of debate. It is here that further research is necessary to validate the psychoanalytic hypotheses about the importance of fantasy in the normal and pathology situations of life at and after the oedipal period.

## THE ROOTS OF HYSTERICAL PERSONALITY

There seems to be no reason to assume that the sources of the hysterical personality disorder in childhood or adulthood are different from those sources that produce other types of personality and character. Some of these general sources have just been considered. What remains to be discussed are some specific areas that may be of importance in the evolution of hysterical traits and of later hysterical psychopathology. These involve constitutional, epigenetic, and learned factors that will be taken up according to this outline:

Constitutional
  Congenital temperament
  Behaviors fixed or strongly determined by gender or hormonal influence

Learned factors
  Constitutional givens that affect environmental response
    Gender of child
    Physical characteristics of the child
    Early behavioral characteristics of the child
    Physical illnesses of the child in early life

  Effects of parental conflicts and anxiety on child's behavior
    Encouragement of dependency
    Suppression of anger and aggression

  Inappropriate sexualization of the parent/child relationship

*Constitutional or inherited factors.* We still know almost as little as ever about the possible predispositional factors in *any* character trait, to say nothing of interpersonal styles as epigenetically evolved and complicated as those under examination here.

Since Charcot, few have doubted hereditary–constitutional factors are important in the disposition of people to develop hysterical personality, but their expression, the timing and method of their appearance, are hidden from view and contaminated with the epigenetic constitution–environment interaction that operates all along the line to complicate the definition of endowment at birth. Genetic markers and defects of biochemistry are being discovered that contribute to some of the serious disorders of childhood and adult life, but nothing of the kind has been linked to personality disorder. Pollak (1981), in reviewing the literature bearing on the inherited factors in the genetics of hysterical personality, was constrained to say it was virtually nonexistent. Since that time, behavioral genetics, through twin and adoption studies, has provided for the separation of genetic and environmental effects in research on the heritability of some behavior. This has led to advances in the molecular biology of such severe conditions as schizophrenia and manic depressive psychosis and demonstrated the importance of general environmental conditions such as poverty, parental strife, and social deterioration on the development of children. But in addition to these overall factors which impinge on each family member equally, very recent findings point to the importance of individual and personal factors that are different for each child in the family. These are called "nonshared environmental effects" (Reiss et al. 1991). The isolation of these nonshared differences promises to help identify specific social and environmental experiences that correlate with the development of specific personality traits and psychopathology such as we are concern with here. As yet, little data is available (see Plomin et al. 1990).

*Temperament.* Today the congenital temperament of the child is often cited as one determinant of the attachment process as well as a significant element in later personality and personality disorder (Rutter 1987). The topic of temperament, practically invented by Thomas and Chess (Thomas et al. 1968, Thomas and Chess 1977), has become, along with the topic of attachment itself, a veritable industry within developmental psychology. Certain inborn tendencies of behavior are demonstrable early but do not stabilize until older childhood, after a great deal of life experience. But even then, what raters see, and especially what parents see, tends to be biased by the beholders' preconceptions (Belsky and Isabella 1987). Correlations of temperamental ratings are low among people with different relationships to the child (Achenbach et al. 1987). Most students of the subject agree with Buss and Plomin (1984) that there is some heritability of activity type, emotionality and sociability but that temperament seems to relate to the activity level of the contact-seeking (Belsky and Pensky 1988), and not to security of attachment. What may be inherited is a general tendency, an inclination, to develop certain types of behavior rather than others that influence the direction and quality of the initial interaction between mother and child. For example, a child who was especially alert and responsive might draw an early overstimulation in certain families and for this reason become unduly attuned to outside stimuli, an often noted characteristic of hysterical personality. Such correlations of apparent constitutional diathesis and hysterical traits depend on the solidity of the hypothesis of congenital temperament, a proposition by no means firmly established (Goldsmith et al. 1987).

The greater frequency of hysterical traits in women than in men continues to be provocative but thus far seems most satisfactorily explained by reference to cultural influences, since dependency, egocentrism, and the like are more often tolerated or even encouraged in girls than in boys. Blacker and Tupin consider this issue in detail in Chapter 2. The part played in the evolution of typical "feminine" or "masculine" behaviors by the influence of sex-linked substrates in the genes or the effects of sexual hormones before birth or at pubescence has been confirmed in several species of mammals and is now being explored in humans. For example, one group of girls, androgenized in utero, showed more tomboyism and low-parenting play or interest, both in childhood and adulthood, than matched controls. Yet their behavior was well within what is acceptable for females in our society. Some even became mothers (Meyer-Bahlburg et al. 1986). For another group of such girls the hypothesis was not confirmed (Lish et al. 1991). Whether these factors further influence the presence or absence of more pathological "hysterical" traits is entirely unknown.

*Constitutional givens and environmental response.* There are important factors in the constitution of the infant that are givens at birth but that stimulate parental responses that then affect what the child learns. The most striking of these is the gender of the child. Whether it is a girl or a boy, has blue eyes or brown, is assertive or passive—all these variables will tend to elicit different responses from the parents in line with their hopes, fears, identifications, and preconceptions. These responses feed back into the child's developing behavioral systems in a way that shapes the direction taken by his own responses, and later his attitude about himself. Those who deal with newborns and infants often hear parents attribute qualities to their children that are not at all obvious to others. Boys are commonly seen as tough, aggressive, and destined for success in sports; girls are often described as sweet, shy, and in need of their father's protection, even though the children in question may be of identical size and behavior to an objective observer.

*Physical illness.* The child who develops hysterical traits starts life, as all others do, with the basics described above, but may experience early in life special events that predispose to these traits. Beginning with Schilder (1939), many authors call attention to the occasion of physical illness in infancy or childhood, with its focus on the body, as fundamental for later hysterical symptomatology. Abse (1974) points out that often the parents are neglectful when the child is healthy and then remorsefully attentive when the child is sick *or distressed* (Abse's emphasis). Such a primary focus on the body might be another impetus toward seeking attention through the physical modalities.

The issue of parental misemphasis on real bodily illness or special attention to only transient or insignificant infirmities needs statistical confirmation but appears to be central, at least to those hysterics who somatize. This point recollects Freud's description of Schreber's paranoid delusions, which seemed to take their origins from actual bizarre behavior toward him in his childhood by his father.

Just how much the somatic disabilities of infancy—colic, eczema, and (later) asthma—are intrinsic failures of physiological balance and how much they are the individual infant's unique somatic response to a poor object relationship is not well understood. Spitz

(1965), in his consideration of the psychotoxic factors in these illnesses in the first year of life, attempted to delineate the special conditions that exist between the mother and the child which produce the various symptoms. Although this correlation was not confirmed by later studies, it is well known in both adult and child psychiatry that specific illnesses or physical traits in a child affect parents, and that parents may dwell on or develop phobias of these attributes of their child. Again, whether such a focus predisposes the child to hysterical preoccupations with the body later in life can only be settled by anterospective studies.

*Parental conflicts and anxiety.* A second important source of pathological learning in children showing hysterical traits is the inhibiting effect of the anxiety provoked in the child when he becomes aware he is acting in a way that causes anxiety in the parent. If the child is insecurely attached and seeking the reassurance of parental attention and approval, the recognition of parental anxiety will be a stimulus for the child to retreat to commonly successful maneuvers to attain this reassurance. These behaviors will mark one pole of the unconscious conflict of the parent. The child remains relatively fixed at certain immature behavioral levels due to this reciprocity between his behavior and what the parent wishes unconsciously. This direction may even be opposite to what the parent says and believes he or she wants.

For an example we can return to the 18-month-old who ends up stepping all over his or her mother and pulling her hair while she is trying to talk to her friend. The child sees mother's attention fixed on someone else and attempts to elicit reassuring signals that mother is attending to him or her also. Mother may be anxious that her child make a good impression, but she also may have pressing needs of her own to relate to the friend. This anxiety and competition is communicated to the child by ambivalent attachment signals from mother, which are unsatisfying. Mother continues to look at her friend, her flow of speech gets faster and more tense, and she mechanically handles the child in a way that excludes the youngster from the main channel of exchange between the two adults. The mother is fearful that her own needs will not be met if the child intervenes. At this point, the child becomes aggressive in its attempts to get on mother's lap and in that effort steps on mother's feet and shoves its way in. Mother responds by giving her full attention then to the child, rewarding the regressive behavior and consolidating the cycle.

Millon (1969) suggests that the hysterically inclined child, whom he refers to as the "active-dependent" personality type, may have had many different caretakers in infancy who supplied intense, short-lived stimulus gratifications that came at irregular intervals. He notes that irregular schedules of reinforcement establish deeply ingrained habits that are highly resistant to extinction. He feels that the persistent yet erratic dependency behaviors of this type of personality may reflect a pathological form of intense stimulus-seeking traceable to highly charged, varied, and irregular stimulus reinforcements associated with early attachment learning.

*Encouragement to look to others for fulfillment and help.* A predominant constellation in the early life of a child with hysterical traits (or such an adult, on recollection of childhood) is the overt encouragement to expect and demand help, guidance, and the good things of life while covertly signaling that these are beyond the child's competence and can only be supplied by the parent. It is important here to differentiate between a normal and necessary *instrumental dependency* (Sears et al. 1957), where children need and use adults to help when the problems to solve are beyond their ability. The negative connotation of the word "dependency" does not apply here. This is a proper and healthy attachment function. *Emotional dependency*, the need for continuing attention, direction, and support in order to function, and not just when upset, seems to have its origin in the quality of the early relationship between the child and the caregivers (Sroufe et al. 1984). In this regard, the parents treat the child as they would have liked to have been treated themselves, that is, indulged. When the child responds by inhibiting its own alternatives of action and conforming to the behavior indicated, the parent is flattered by the attention and gives it in return; but the parent is consciously disappointed and disapproving, as was the mother in the last example: she says no, but takes it.

The child's healthy emotional development is inhibited by innumerable repetitions of these double instructions by parents whose fixed and inappropriate expectations neither adapt to the child's immature level of understanding nor shift with the advance of the child's capacities. The parents are *narcissistic* in this regard. Even if the developmental thrust carries the child further in specific age-appropriate behaviors, as it often does, these islands of reciprocal social expectation remain as points toward which the child and the parents orient, and to which they habitually regress. These points will be among the main features when a child is finally brought for psychiatric evaluation, usually for symptoms other than the hysterical behavior.

It is common, for example, for the child to be seen as physically delicate. While overtly emphasizing the importance of physical conditioning or sports, the parents, who themselves may be active, give the child the message that he or she must not become proficient or competitive, but rather remain weak and in need of help. This is again a projection of the parents' own yearnings. It seems clear that, in such circumstances, part of the hysterical propensity to repression is brought about by the necessity to square the inconsistency of the two parental messages by acting on the covert one without being aware there was such a message. The use of repression in the child seems a reflection of the importance to the parents that these yearnings of their own for attention and help remain firmly repressed. With such families it is not so much rejection that causes a feeling of insecurity in the child as the capricious alternation of approval and disgust that keeps the child hoping to please but never sure of what will please, and thus more dependent on outside direction.

*The suppression of anger and assertiveness.* Sperling (1973), describing in detail an adult patient, reminds us of the importance of the mother in the evolution of hysterical personality and conversion. Indeed, she sees the basic conflicts of the hysterical diathesis as originating in the mother–child relationship. She emphasizes how certain mothers, caught in unconscious conflict, do not permit expressions of anger and assertiveness, or even anxiety, in the child but encourage dependency and passivity instead. At the same time, the mother does not expect the child to be able to cope with anxiety-provoking situations without her help. The child becomes aware that anger and assertiveness threaten the already insecure relationship with mother and thus learns that these responses must be early and firmly repressed from consciousness. The submissive behavior, in addition to its attention-getting value, wards off the awareness of anger and frustration. There is quite a difference between a mother who says don't express it so strongly or don't do it that way and the mother who says, in effect, don't express it at all, or, don't even think it. It is the displaced and "immature" acting up, the reactive self-isolation and the autoerotic activity that finally brings such a youngster to the attention of a child psychiatrist, as is the case with the first clinical example to be described presently.

*Inappropriate sexualization of the parent/child relationship.* Children whose parents have been physically overstimulating—especially when the parents infantilize the child as a projection of themselves—will elicit the early and intense development of sensuality in the child, which may divert him or her from other exploratory interests if it continues at high levels beyond the first year or so. Since this inappropriate sensuality is connected with the social interactions that are the vehicle for its transmission, this may lead in later life to the need to maintain a similarly high level of egocentric and sexually oriented interactions typical of the hysterical personality. Since such interactions serve a stereotyped function for the parents that is referable only to their own unconscious preoccupations, these interactions are not fitted to the child's changing need for social reciprocity. Stimulation of this kind may not even be what the child actually wishes and reaches out for, but may have a teasing, incomplete quality that keeps him coming back for more but not often getting the truly satisfying response at the appropriate level that he seeks.

When the sensual stimulation is specifically sexual or contains pronounced sexual features, and especially if the adult involved is conflicted about such behavior and represses the awareness of the sexual elements, the situation predisposes to a hysterical outcome. The closer the physical interaction approaches actual sexual stimulation, the more likely it is that the child will respond by a strong surge of participation, accompanied by complete repression of the awareness of his own interest: again, the typical hysterical result.

The younger the child, the more he or she will experience the interaction as part of an attachment pattern. The paradigm is the focus of the infant on its attachment figure. The seduced child is schooled to respond to the intensely stimulating sexualized attention but to forget the adults' invitation to gain pleasure by these means (Bowlby 1988b). What is left is an overinvestment of the bodily functions at the expense of other learning.

It is as yet unknown how often seduced and sexually misused children become hysterics. It seems most likely that the earlier the abuse occurs the more the child will show serious character malformation reminiscent of oral-stage pathology, not only because of the premature stimulation of sexual behaviors, but because of the grosser nature of the adults' misuse of the child for their own purposes and the likelihood that such caregivers will be significantly abusive and deficient in other ways as well. As far as seductions of older children are concerned, we know that Freud had to retreat on his conviction that his patients had fallen ill of neuroses because of actual parental seduction. Nevertheless, it seems likely that children and adults with sexualized, hysterical traits have actually experienced unconsciously sexualized behavior at the hands of their caregivers, if not actual physical seduction.

If there is little interest in the question of whether a hysterical diathesis exists in childhood and is a precursor of such a personality in adults there is a good deal of energy being expended at present on a related topic: multiple personality disorder (Putnam 1989). Here the impressive symptoms and behavior that characterize the syndrome in child and adult sufferers (and overlapping considerably those native to hysterical conditions) are being linked with known pathogenic events in childhood, such as physical and sexual abuse, to suggest that a new diagnostic category, "Dissociating Identity Disorder" be added to the child section of *DSM-IV* (Peterson 1990). The implication is that there is a developmental syndrome, or even a diagnosis, that is the origin and necessary precursor of the adult condition, Multiple Personality Disorder. Research on this, when it has winnowed out the bias introduced by the current enthusiasm for this new category, may illuminate the developmental history of all personality, but should be especially pertinent for hysterical phenomena.

## THE DIAGNOSIS OF HYSTERICAL DISORDER
## IN CHILDHOOD

*Hysteria.* The relationship between manifest symptoms of hysteria, paralyses, blindness, paresthesias, and the like, and the preexisting personality type is even more unclear in childhood than it is in adult life. Children of all ages and personalities seem more amenable to suggestion and hypnosis than are adults, and this is likely to hold for conversion reactions as well, but statistical evidence is lacking. They seem independent but interrelated (Pollak 1981).

There are as yet few studies of personality formation in children that have included samples of youngsters who have shown overt hysteria in one form or another, although there is no dearth of reports on striking symptoms of this kind in children (Sheffield 1898). Robins (1966) showed that girls diagnosed as having hysteria during their childhood were only slightly more susceptible to falling ill with hysteria (not hysterical personality) in adult life than were others. None of the boys with hysteria in childhood had such symptoms when they grew up. What concerns us here is not the overt hysteria, which apparently can occur in children and adults of all personality types, but whether something like adult hysterical personality can be identified in childhood.

*Hysterical personality.* Very little has been written about the matrix out of which hysterical diathesis in childhood grows. Indeed, a sharp differentiation of hysterical psychoneurosis from hysterical personality in childhood is nowhere in evidence. The Group for the Advancement of Psychiatry report (1966) on classification of childhood disorders did not list hysterical psychoneurosis at all. Recognizing the transience of the child's intercurrent development the report rightly kept clear of character classifications. It provided "hysterical personality disorder" as a diagnostic category instead, and so preserved the class. *DSM-III-R* made no provision for histrionic personality disorder in childhood, nor does *DSM-IV* augur to do so, but they permit an Axis II diagnosis of the adult type, should the criteria be fulfilled. A Medline search through 3400 citations under the headings "childhood hysterical/histeroid-personality/character" covering the period 1967 to 1990 produced one, in Dutch.

In one sense it might be said that there can be no such thing in childhood as a mild hysterical personality, since the cardinal features of the adult disorder, egocentrism and urgent attention-seeking behavior, are not as inappropriate in the school-age child as they are in the adult. As for the more disturbed children, the context of their family and the continuity of distorted care they receive there seem to be the key to the understanding of the severity of the disorder and the direction of treatment.

Rosner (1975) has briefly reported the successful analysis of a 6-year-old girl whose sexual symptoms were so intense that he felt she already had a serious character deformity of the hysterical type. Treatment had been precipitated when she developed acute regressive symptoms subsequent to being denied access to her 3½-year-old brother when he went to the toilet. Her mother reported that *for about 2 years* (emphasis added) this child had accompanied her younger brother into the bathroom and was overheard telling him: "I'll rub it and then you will be able to make." Unfortunately, beyond this piece of provocative data, Rosner mentions little information about the parents, who seem to have been aware of this girl's habits over those 2 years.

*Three representative types.* Of the spectrum of children between ages 6 and 13 who appear to have hysterical traits, three representative types can be isolated to serve as descriptive of the whole group.

The first and most mature of these types is a youngster who would almost never be seen as disordered, since he or she rarely presents any disturbance or distress within the family during latency. Such children are like early editions of the "good" or "healthy" hysteric as described by Lazare (1971) and Zisook and DeVaul (1978). There is a predominance of oedipal over oral conflicts and, if the youngster in question is a girl, she will be focused on her relationship with her father, which will be colorfully romanticized. She might have some difficulties in mastering the cognitive part of schoolwork because of her tendency to overgeneralize, her lack of acute attention to detail, and her deficiency in analytical ability, but she would more than make up for this socially by animation and attentiveness to others. Her social skills, which are apt to be precocious, equip her to make her way well with peers and teachers alike. She may be quite artistic. In her background, we would expect to find a relatively intact family group, good attachment as an infant, intense and emotional relationships with her father and brothers, and a depreciated relationship with her mother, whom she would see as drab and uninteresting compared with herself. Such a well-developed and extroverted child and family are diagnosable, in theory at least, if she and her parents become sufficiently well known to the psychiatric observer. This is unlikely to happen in childhood but may come to pass when such a child seeks psychotherapy or analysis in her adult life. Just what percentage of children of this type actually become ill with hysterical character disorder as adults is not known, but the hypothesis presented here holds they would not. Rather they would show neurotic traits unless serious stress overwhelmed their adaptive ability.

The other two types of children with hysterical traits comprise those who are most commonly brought to pediatricians and child psychiatrists for evaluation and treatment. They have occasioned some disequilibrium within the family, or have provoked such negative response outside the family that help is sought. These children and their parents are quickly seen to be more disordered than the first type of child described above and cluster in either a second, less seriously disturbed group, or a third, more seriously disturbed group. The less seriously disturbed group resembles the more disturbed in *reported* behavior, but they can be told apart at some point in the diagnostic process. The prognosis for the two poles of the pathological continuum they represent are significantly different. Often, differentiation can reliably be made only through assessment of the relative impoverishment of the child's ego development and the relative level and rigidity of the parents' personality by means of a course of psychotherapeutic evaluation of the family, individually and as a system.

*Common complaints in both pathological types.* General complaints about children in these two disturbed categories are the following: Although they tend to be outgoing, engaging, and charming initially, they are often soon seen as irritating and intrusive, impulsive, and more "selfish" than even the norm for their age. They are more than usually emotional, but in a superficial way, yielding quickly to indications that others have different feelings by abruptly changing their tack. This trait gives them a fickle and capricious quality that loses comrades as fast as their gregarious and shallow friendliness gains them. Above all, such youngsters seek approval and attention, as if they were trying to fill themselves up. This has a pronounced intaking quality that accounts for the striking pregenital impression these children make on the observer, despite whatever overt sexual behaviors they may be mimicking. They have learned that their satisfactions are dependent on others, and that this satisfaction is variable and may be withdrawn at any time. Therefore they press for more now. They crave stimulation and excitement and seek it through inter-personal contacts, often with much younger children who are liable to give them respectful attention but who may not yet be able to demand reciprocation. Genital exposure and confused sexual play that is mixed with aggressive components are frequently among the presenting complaints. Such children are uneasy in the give and take with peers; they are labile in their emotions and either erupt in inappropriate and sometimes bizarre piques or retreat from the field.

One of the most impressive traits of these children is that they have an uncanny sensitivity to the moods and unexpressed thoughts of the adults with whom they have a relationship. They search the adult's face for clues and act on what they imagine is there. With those they know well, they are often accurate, especially in the recognition of unconscious motivations. With others, they are quite often inaccurate, since their conclusions spring from their confused and misleading ideas strongly colored by their excitable interest in all bodily orifices and functions. If the unconscious attention of the adult is focused on the same eroticized topics, such a youngster will not fail to become excited. They give the impression of being used to receiving some sort of positive response from adults in this regard and become confused or frightened when it is not forthcoming, as in the first playroom sessions. Their pseudosexual provocations, both with adults and peers, seem to result not in satisfactions but in a heightening of diffuse tension and excitement that is then discharged in tantrums and aggressive motor behavior, often self hurtful. This brings on further guilt and feelings of worthlessness, another round of ingratiating obsequiousness and an attempt to obey the rules. These attempts are fragile and fail, often because of a breakthrough of negativism, resulting in further punishment.

*Sexual behavior.* The sexuality of the hysterical personality in childhood is deceptive. The overly "feminine" or seductive traits are only superficially sexual; they really express the identifications with the orally seductive parent as a means of retrieving or maintaining love or the acting out of hostile manipulations. The hysterical child is seldom seeking a sexual partner but is absorbing the eroticized positive or negative attention of the parent. If the mother is hysterical or infantilizing in her encouragement or competition with her pretty child, any fixation of the child in this style is easy to understand. If the mother, herself neurotically restricted and repressed, identifies with the child's eroticized behavior, the youngster will express these impulses for her if not spared by the influence of a firm, mature father.

Alternatively, a little girl who is deprived of adequate mothering may turn to an abnormally close tie with her father. If this relationship becomes sexualized because of father's conflicts, the child learns this technique and uses it to earn dependent gratifications from future father figures at the cost of submission and passivity to those who respond to this and quick rejection of those who don't. The relationship remains superficial because at the point it is elicited it is based on the young child's inability to love in a mature way, that is, to seek the other person's best interests as well as her own. Hysterical personality can have its beginning when the little girl manages to turn her father into a seductive substitute mother (Hollender 1971). Slipp (1977) describes fathers of children with hysterical disorders as often narcissistic and exploitative men who devalue their wives and gratify their need for dependency and nurturance through their daughters; they are seductive but simultaneously condemn any overt sexuality.

If it's the father who inaugurates the overmothering, he sees his daughter (or, as is sometimes the case, his son) as weak and young. These are essentially projections of his own oral neediness. In his solicitous attitude toward the child, including his special interest in his or her body, he is almost literally taking care of himself as a small child. If he leads into petting games, thinking of the child as a less threatening sexual partner than her mother, the child's flirtatiousness will reflect this skin erotization. Perhaps the strongest, most persuasive setting for the development of hysterical personality in childhood is the combination of both such parents, as shown by the first family presented below.

*Learning skills*. The ego abilities of these patients vary. Some youngsters operate well in school, where the reciprocal distorting interpersonal cues may be absent. Most suffer truncation of their cognitive development, with the inevitable limiting of learning skills and learning. Their tense, sexualized play testifies to the anxiety attached to seeing and hearing, an anxiety which contributes to their impressionistic style. They are so busy acting on their sexual and aggressive theories and then forgetting the actions that they have little time or interest in the mastery of learning. If this occurs early in life, during the 3rd and 4th year especially, instrumental skills can be so poorly acquired that the child may develop special learning disabilities that add to and complicate the youngster's emotional problems (Anthony 1961).

*The mechanisms of defense*. In differentiating between the less and the more seriously disturbed youngsters with hysterical traits, an assessment of their current and habitual defense systems is in order. The hysterical style is born not only in the need, for example, to ward off libidinal impulses from awareness (which might be accomplished by any number of defensive styles), but in the use of particular mechanisms and not others. How are these likely to arise?

The earliest defensive systems evolve to preserve homeostasis in the biological drives, to master reality, and to handle object anxiety. They become more elaborate and specific as they develop in concert with appropriate shifts in parental expectations. The level of defense increases in complexity as maturation proceeds, the more sophisticated systems evolving in an epigenetic way from the less mature previous stages. The child elaborates its defensive structure in collaboration with the mother, incorporating and identifying with gross segments of the mother's overt behavior and unconscious conflicts. Through thousands of interactions, overt and covert, blatant and subtle, the mother's cognitive style and habitual ways of cognitive processing shape and determine to a major degree the child's selection of certain defenses over others. Later, in the context of the playroom session, or in psychotherapy as an adult, the child's defenses will again be displayed in characteristic types of resistance to the treatment and avoidance or distortion of topics introduced by the therapist as well as those that emerge from within the patient. When these observations of the child can be put together with an assessment of the level of parental defensive functioning, a clearer understanding of the cause and likely prognosis of the child's pathology is possible.

Although it may be that the first type of child described in this section—the healthiest—generates his or her style for the most part as an array of adaptive techniques to the demanding interpersonal world of the 4–6-year-old, it is certainly obvious from clinical work that the two categories of children with more serious pathology are heavily influenced in their maldevelopment by their interaction with their mother and also sometimes with their father. In the first family to be described, the mother, abetted strongly by the father, acted out her libidinal wishes through encouragement of her daughter's sexualized behavior while suppressing expressions of anger and assertiveness in her. This appeared to lead toward the elaboration of relatively mature defenses in the child, such as repression of the awareness of the sexual elements in her behavior and reaction formation and intellectualization to handle the self assertive impulses and her anger at frustration. In the second case described, we will see that the child acted out the mother's eroticized aggressive impulses and continued to use more primitive and immature defenses such as schizoid fantasy, in which she retreated to mental images and playroom scenes of great violence and sadism.

The descriptions here are not of the mechanisms of defense per se, which are evanescent, waxing and waning in complex interaction with each other as glimpsed during a psychoanalytic hour or playroom session. They are, rather, what the observer can see that can be recorded: the defensive behavior, the characteristic style of the child, from which the various mechanisms of defense can be inferred. Vaillant (1971) identifies four progressive levels of defense structure: (1) the narcissistic defenses, (2) the immature defenses, (3) the neurotic defenses, and (4) the mature defenses. The two categories of latency children showing hysterical traits tend to cluster their defensive systems in either of the middle two of these four levels.

Although the healthier children of the two pathological types show immature defenses some of the time, or when under severe stress, they mostly have recourse to the neurotic types, especially "forgetting," that is repression and dissociation (neurotic denial). "I don't know" is likely to be the first answer that comes to their lips on being questioned on practically any topic. This is not simply a ploy to avoid self-incrimination but often a fact, for memories are frequently not accessible to them, and when they are, they are vague and impressionistic. The earlier this defense forms, the more impoverished the actual fund of information retained in memory will be, again increasing the child's dependence on the outside world for signs of self-worth. Identification, taking on as one's own the behaviors of the parents, provides a global method of coping without integrating. This results in a poor sense of self and a tendency to variable response and a cognitive style unequal to intellectual pursuits despite excellent endowment (Shapiro 1965). Reaction formation and displacement are also characteristic of the more developed hysterical types in childhood and serve to assist repression in the conflicts over unacceptable instinctual impulses, especially those having to do with getting and giving, as in oral and phallic periods.

In contrast, conflicts around rage and issues of power and dominance, so much more pressing for the less developed of the children, are not always well handled by repression. Some combination under the general category of intellectualization may be required: isolation, rationalization, ritual, undoing, and magical thinking. For the more disordered child whose parents are unable to present appropriate models or responses and expectations, more immature defenses such as projection, hypochondriasis, passive aggression, and especially schizoid fantasy are much more usual. Such a child is not defending because of conflicts over sexual thoughts and impulses but in response to the parental expectations that the child be a protagonist in scenes from the parents' unconscious fantasies—fantasies that are almost always a sadistic distortion of narcissistic struggles for survival with figures from the parents' past. In these situations, neurotic repression, usually developed later to handle oedipal impulses, is prematurely and malignantly evoked to furnish out the child's inadequate repertoire of defenses, and this causes a tendency to repress all intrapsychic life rather than just the forbidden libidinal impulses, as in other types of pathology.

*Prognosis*. Briefly, children falling into the less disturbed portion of this group have had adequate attachments in early life (often the girl is attached more prominently to her father than to her mother), but for their own reasons mother or father or both continue to treat the child as if she were much younger than she is. This may continue even though she shows more mature behavior elsewhere than in their presence. The parental expectations are communicated in the behavior they encourage or inhibit, and they usually demonstrate in their own personality style the basics of the traits the child has picked up, by osmosis as it were, from the earliest years. Close acquaintance with these children reveals that they have achieved some or even many developmental landmarks but are treated by their parents as if they were much less capable than they are.

If such a situation were recognized early enough in the life of the child, treatment of one or both parents alone would likely be sufficient to prevent fixation in the child. Once the cluster of traits develops fully, the youngster's future development will depend on the natural course of his or her parents' disorder and the opportunity for the influence of other significant adults including psychotherapists. A certain portion of such children probably recover with positive experiences during adolescence. Starr (1953) holds that in many cases of hysteria and anxiety neuroses in childhood, the impact of pathological parental attitudes and traits not only acted as determining factors in the genesis of the problem but were *current* elements that kept the child's illness active at the point of diagnosis. Those who maintain that the psychoanalytic treatment of a child with hysterical personality is as long and arduous as an adult's with the same disorder should remember that without significant shift in the parents, the small patient has to contend with a caregiving system that supports the disorder.

The prognostically less hopeful portion of this group will have had poorer relationships with their mothers and a more blatant hysterical style. They are less amenable to treatment. The disorder in their parents is more severe and resistant to therapy also, even if the parents were willing patients, which they are not. At times, only a trial of treatment will differentiate between the more seriously ill child, with immature defenses and intense parental stimulation, and the less disordered child, with defenses dominated by repression but with greater development concealed behind symptoms. Although it may be that the more developed child can be successfully treated alone, therapy for the parents is a great adjunct to accurate diagnosis and good outcome and may be virtually the only chance, short of residential placement, for the sicker child (Szurek 1954).

The hypothesis advanced here is that the more mature child with hysterical traits who does not get treatment or otherwise escape the limiting environment will form the major portion of that group from which the hysterical personality disorders emerge in later life. Further, the sicker, less-developed children who do not get treatment will not achieve even that level of function but will instead comprise the group from which the more disabling personality forms emerge, the grossly immature and impulsive personalities, the infantile personalities, and perhaps the addictive and sociopathic characters as well. Thus, in later life these more disturbed children with hysterical traits would not ordinarily be identified as hysterical personalities, or even necessarily, hysteroid disorders of pregenital type, but show one of a wide variety of personality disorders.

## TWO FAMILIES

These theoretical considerations can now be cast into more palpable form by two clinical illustrations derived from the evaluation and long-term treatment of two families, each with a child who manifested hysterical traits. One family had a child with a milder disturbance; the other had a child with more severe developmental impairment. Of course, what we know about the etiology of the hysterical personality, or any personality, is considerably less than the sum of the conclusions catalogued here. If these assertions are too firm for the evidence, it is hoped that the complexity of the examples to follow will temper this tone and indicate that even though explanations cannot be reduced to simple cause and effect, some useful differentiations can be made.

## CASE HISTORY

### Therapy with a Family in the Favorable Group

Ann C. was 9 years old when brought to psychiatric evaluation for what her mother described as "something wrong from the beginning." She had a problem minding, was consistently immature, oppositional, and "forever doing things she's too old to be doing." This included being forgetful, impulsive, emotional, and having special interest in "bathroom" topics. The request for help came at that time because Ann was getting worse in her behavior and performance despite one year of a special school for remediation of "auditory dyslexia." The parents disagreed over whether Ann's behavior was her problem or whether it was due to their faulty discipline. They accused themselves and each other alternatingly. They were alarmed at the apparently sexual way Ann and her 5-year-old brother would continually hold wrestling matches with each other, rolling on the floor together clutching each other's genital areas and getting more and more excited until they had to be sent to their separate rooms.

Ann was a consciously wanted first child whose gestation and delivery were unremarkable. Her mother never considered nursing, so Ann was bottle fed. She had colic and was quite irritable from the first, "never went to sleep without crying," and "cried every night from twelve to four," which didn't stop until she was a year old. The home was so tense that the pediatrician prescribed a tranquilizer for both mother and child and recommended a vacation away from her. The parents did take a nine-day holiday away from Ann when she was 9 months old, leaving her in the care of a nanny. This prolonged separation at a crucial phase of attachment may have played a part in Ann's vulnerability to a hysterical diathesis.

Ann was a picky eater, but her developmental landmarks were achieved early and she was large for her age. Her parents showed many snapshots of her in infancy which indicated Ann had no problems with social smiling or positive response to her family. During her 2nd and 3rd year she had trouble moving her bowels and required suppositories and laxatives. This culminated in the formation of a fissure that was not diagnosed for some time. Ann was always afraid of defecation and used to run around excitedly before a movement. Otherwise her health was good.

By Ann's 3rd birthday, she was dressing herself and tying her shoes. During this year her brother was born. Her father mentioned that he felt she always considered her brother an interloper. When she entered nursery school at age 3, she was a watcher, not a joiner. The school kept her with younger children even though she was the largest of them. Her teachers didn't feel she was ready when it was time for kindergarten. She loved to color and draw for fun, but it was not until the end of kindergarten that she was able to draw representationally.

During the first and second grade she had a very hard time handling herself with the other children and was pushed about despite her size. She was tutored at home during one summer, but she never did her homework and couldn't learn the flash cards. Her mother thought of her as helter-skelter, running, laughing, and acting in a very immature way but did not think much of this, since "all her friends are also that way—immature and giddy." These friends tended to be a year or more younger than she.

Ann's father, Mr. C., a highly paid partner in a successful firm, originally called to ask for help in protecting his children from his wife's bad influence, claiming they differed greatly on how to handle the children. He said his wife wouldn't come in, but she appeared with him on the first visit, during which he described their differences in a very accusatory manner.

In the course of conjoint and individual psychotherapy with the parents, it became evident that there was a great deal of sensual contact between Ann and her father, which Ann had experienced as very exciting (she spontaneously told of this herself in the playroom). He frequently bathed both the children and carefully dried them after the bath. It seemed clear from the context within which this was reported that neither parent was conscious of the frustration and tension engendered in the sexually stimulating play between Ann and her father and between her and her brother. In an early playroom session she told of how exciting it was for her to be caught in the trap of her grandfather's legs and how much fun it was for her to ride horsey on his foot. She was eager to know whether the therapist tickled his children and described how much she enjoyed it when her father tickled her until she "couldn't stand it." Her capacity for immature attention-getting and the physical nature of this behavior was well illustrated by an episode that occurred early in treatment. Her brother messed his pants in a slight bout of diarrhea. When Ann saw her father was affectionately bathing him and telling him it was all right, she pushed out some formed stool into her own pants as she stood watching them. Her mother was furious, feeling that the child was old enough to know better.

In subsequent individual sessions with the father, the topic of his children seldom came up. He was aware that this concern about the children and his wife's behavior was, in part, a rationalization for his own return to treatment. He had been in psychotherapy twice before in the last ten years and was in psychoanalysis for more than a year until nine months before the beginning of the present treatment. This information emerged well after treatment had begun. He said he had quit the analysis because he wasn't getting anywhere.

Mr. C. quickly showed himself an obsessive person, riddled with guilt about his strong sexual and aggressive impulses (not actions), and filled with resentment at what he felt amounted to his being deprived of what he deserved from those around him. The theme of his competition with his brother was prominent. Behind his repetitive thoughts and fantasies was a great deal of hostility covered by a smile. He was afraid of destroying others with his brightness and success and therefore dissembled the brightness and undercut the success by an excessively deferential manner, which he immediately applied in his treatment. He hoped to enlist the sympathy and help of the therapist in diagnosing his wife as the cause of all the family's problems. This attitude yielded intermittently to an awareness, to his chagrin, that his own behavior with her and the children played a prominent part in the situation.

Mrs. C. was a strikingly intense, very slim woman who, without being aware of it, communicated great physical tension in the way she moved and held her body and flexed the muscles of her neck as she talked. In her individual sessions she indicated her concern about her awareness that she did not love Ann in the same way she loved her son, David. She described Ann as a very great responsibility who yielded little gratification in return. She was obviously trying to do her best to care for her daughter and had been doing so for years, but within her very rigid and organized program she recognized that her child was not flourishing.

Mrs. C. liked to iron and did a good deal of it. She was passionately insistent on arranging her schedule so that she could swim two miles twice a week "to work off my aggressions," she said. She often could not fall asleep after a full day of activities and regularly took a mild tranquilizer for this just after her ritual shower at night. Much of her early sessions was taken up with descriptions of how Ann failed to change her school clothes into play clothes or jumped on the bed or put toys in the wrong place. She was irritated that Ann needed so much attention, and she feared she might be too "analytical" and "organized" for the child's good. In sexual matters she gave the initial impression of being a prude. She was willing to come for psychotherapy, her first such experience, if the therapist thought it might help her daughter.

The psychologist who examined Ann early in the child's treatment concluded that her intellectual functioning was clearly limited and on an overall basis fell to a below-average level. In some areas, particularly but not exclusively those affected by school achievement, her functioning was even poorer, although on three of the ten Wechsler Intelligence Scale for Children subtests her score did reach the average level. Ann's perceptual–motor problems were varied and substantial. It was felt that there was an approximate two-year lag in the development of perceptual–motor skills, which seemed great enough to produce the obvious impairment in Ann's academic skills. Ann was seen to have a substantial emotional disturbance and to be highly immature. She was quite anxious, almost openly so in affective interaction with others in the projective testing. She indicated strong interest in others but found interaction threatening and tended to turn away toward fantasy to escape the threat. The psychologist's findings suggested that her relationships with both adults and peers had the quality of an open wish to be loved and accepted, but she sustained feelings of being inadequate and undeserving and was preoccupied with sensual impulses. Action on these impulses failed to bring satisfaction, causing instead frustration and anger and a turning toward confused fantasy. The fantasies were not satisfying enough to prevent her continued attempts to achieve more satisfying relationships; but instead of achieving these, she seemed to be in the process of developing hysterical personality patterns. Psychotherapy was strongly recommended.

Treatment began with twice-weekly playroom sessions for Ann and one weekly conjoint and one weekly individual session for each of her parents, all conducted by the same therapist in private practice. In the first several months of playroom treatment, Ann displayed the phenomena of an immature childhood hysterical style in a striking way. She was always cheerful and smiling and usually brought a number of things from home, dolls and cuddly bears. She searched the therapist's face and appearance for signs of change and continually tried to guess his thoughts and reactions to her—how many children does he have, does he ever get angry with them, could she see his angry face, and the like. Later, a good many comments about his breath, his hair, and his moustache made it clear she was acutely aware of his physical nearness. This attention did not have a seductive or even an endearing quality but was delivered inappropriately and with a heightening of tension that was deflected but not relieved by attempts at interpretive comment.

The playroom hours were almost always active and physical, scattered and labile; and for this reason it was often difficult to see associations between the conjoined activities. Inquiry along this line produced the child's ever ready "I don't know." Often the main theme of a session would be either some sexualized activity between the Barbie dolls, usually two preteen girl dolls and a rather busty woman doll, or formless aggressive fights between the wolf and the alligator handpuppets, alternately held by each participant. The impoverishment of her fantasy was impressive. Handpuppet play always had a very elementary story line, without plot, elaboration, or variation; just straight biting, to the tune of the therapist's growling. With the dolls she would say, for example, "You want to see something?" and then pull up the mature doll's blouse to expose her breasts, after which there was usually a good deal of aggressive spanking and reproaching by the older doll of the two child dolls and also some (very French) kissing and making up by the dolls. With the pingpong-ball guns she added no embellishment, no sallies or retreats; just peppering away at point-blank range, followed perhaps by, "Do you ever get angry at a child in here?"

Ann's performance of physical activities such as throwing and catching, darts, and other endeavors was grossly poor, although her fine motor movements were normal. Suggestions on how she might do the activity better resulted usually in deterioration in her performance. Nevertheless, she would, perhaps the next hour, ask for the instructions again and then be able to follow through on them, as if she was freer to use and learn when she herself requested the help. Later in the first year of treatment she wanted very much to learn how to use a yo-yo and practiced until she mastered the rudiments of that skill.

Ann's worst behavioral deteriorations would come at points where she found herself behind in a game or unable to solve an addition problem in keeping score or unable to understand a move in checkers. She would impulsively condemn herself, become agitated and want to quit the game. She several times reached the point of saying, "I don't want to come here any more" as an expression of her frustration. She had difficulty waiting for her turn in board games or card games and often just took one turn after another, oblivious of the therapist.

Ann maintained an interest in the physical bodies of her dolls but was flustered and confused when specifics were involved, as if the details were cloudy in her mind. In trying to tell a story about a sick cousin in the hospital she couldn't clarify what she wanted to ask about the tubes going into his body. She retreated into violent sexual play with the dolls when she was uneasy about the therapist's questions after a bout of stealing candy bars from the school's treat box. There were many repetitions of the bad mother theme, with the mother punishing the children and the children retaliating. These sequences were frightening to her, and if the therapist said something like "Sometimes a girl can get pretty angry at her mother," she would ask when the hour would be up. Once when she was ordering the therapist around, she said, "Pretend you never will be mad at me."

The early conjoint sessions with the parents concentrated mostly on ways of dealing with Ann, and there were frequent discussions of the handling of the sexualized physical play between the two children and between the children and their father. This led to effective techniques for separating the children at those times and for diminishing the father's sexualized bodily care. Both parents acknowledged in the course of time that they recognized in themselves an element of inappropriate sensual enjoyment in the physical handling of the children. As soon as this came to open discussion in the treatment, the problems of Ann's sexualized behavior at home greatly diminished, and her preoccupation with the Barbie dolls and fighting handpuppets in the playroom gave way to activities more characteristic of latency.

After this, the conjoint sessions turned to the parents' relationship with each other. When the couple began to address themselves to their own problems in their treatment and found more effective methods of handling their children, it had the effect of lifting their static and distorted constrictions, and this released their daughter from the reciprocal stimuli that had kept her from adequate development. She then rapidly moved toward a more normal pattern for her age. She began to be more interested in games of skill and in improving her technique in the various physical activities of the playroom. She watched the therapist's face less and persevered when failing. More form and content entered her fantasy play at the same time that the aggressively sexualized and assaultive elements diminished. She began to cast the therapist in more elaborate oedipal roles appropriate to her age: having him, as her father, rescue her with an ambulance, cooking for him, caring for him while mother was away, and speculations, such as, "Maybe I'll marry you." There were glowing reports from the school that her comprehension and performance there had improved greatly as had her social relationships with peers.

After eight months of twice-weekly treatment, Ann was so improved that her sessions were reduced to one per week and the conjoint treatment to one per month so that the parents, by that time both deeply engaged in their own treatment, could go to two individual sessions per week each. Both were working in the same way they would, had they sought individual treatment for themselves, and both were making significant progress. This was especially true of Mrs. C., whose rituals had decreased to the extent that she had time to begin preparation for entry into a postgraduate professional school. She said, "For the first time in my life I feel like a real mother."

After a year of treatment, a repetition of psychological testing showed six subtests of the WISC in the average range, and there was no longer any question that Ann's potential intelligence was average. Her skill deficiencies in learning had clarified themselves to difficulty with maintenance of directionality, with sequencing, with rotational errors, and with integration of parts into a whole. With this specificity, an improved special program was mounted at her school to focus on these deficiencies. She was still emotionally disturbed and immature but seemed to be integrating her inner experience more adequately and was not so overwhelmed by her anxieties. She was expected to do well in further psychotherapy.

From material developed in the treatment of her parents over sixteen months' time, it was possible to identify some of the factors that played a part in the development of Ann's hysterical style. Ann's father identified with her against her mother, whose strict ways of doing things annoyed him as his own father's rules had in the past. In his attempt to defend her and oppose his wife, he interfered with her adaptation, communicating to her his feeling that she was weak and incapable. He also identified with her in this weakness and incapacity, for he felt that way about himself in his competition with his brother. This led him to indulge her in those ways he himself wished to be indulged, that is, to be attended to physically in every possible way. These attentions excited Ann but also elicited anxiety and repression in her, since she was dimly aware of his own conflicted feelings. It seemed possible that this stimulating–repression cycle started early in life, affecting her curiosity and her retention of the details that she was learning at the time, thus contributing to her failure to learn the instrumental perceptual–motor skills during the nursery school years.

For her part, Mrs. C. recognized in Ann the pretty, father's favorite child that she herself had been in the preschool years. She saw her as a rival for her husband's affection and was angry at her for the load of responsibility she represented. At the same time, she felt sorry for her as Ann fell behind in maturation, and she felt guilty for whatever part she might have played in that, just as she was guilty about her behavior toward her own brother, to whom she felt superior and who was a failure in her father's eyes. Her mother's evaluation of her was clear to Ann and undermined her self-respect. Mrs. C.'s guilt motivated part of her toleration of Ann's immaturity, but this indulgence alternated with repressive rules in all areas and a sharp, almost fanatical, stickling on details of dress and demeanor. Although at the point of beginning treatment Mrs. C. presented almost a classic obsessional personality, she had quite obviously retreated to this position from a well-developed hysterical style in latency. A good many of Ann's outbursts at home had elements in them that her mother could recognize as her own. She held herself responsible for Ann's deficiencies, as she had blamed herself for her brother's problems. When she clarified some of these things and began to handle better situations with the children at home, she felt less guilty and more competent as a mother.

Ann is an example of a child whose development was held back substantially by the static interaction dictated by her parents' unconscious conflicts and projections, which prevented them from providing for her needs. When these constrictive templates were lifted in psychotherapy, the child quickly began catching up to what would be expected from a girl her age.

## CASE HISTORY

### Therapy with a Family in the Less Favorable Group

Cathy B. was 6 years old when she was brought to the child psychiatric clinic for evaluation for her excitable, argumentative, and manipulative behavior for which her mother found difficulty setting limits. Also, she had developed a tendency to be flirtatious and coquettish with her mother's boyfriends in the past and was now approaching her stepfather by stroking and whispering profanity in his ear and by touching his genitals through his clothing. Her mother felt competed-with but helpless.

An extended clinical evaluation through work with all family members indicated that Cathy had grown up in a disturbed and disrupted environment and that her symptoms appeared to be reactions to problems within and between the adults with whom she lived. She did not appear markedly disturbed, but there was concern that the direction of her development augured for future personality disorder of the hysterical type. The family accepted the offer of individual therapy. This treatment went on for three years with a succession of psychiatric residents on six-month rotation in children's psychiatry. Each family member saw the same therapist for once-weekly individual sessions.

Cathy's stepfather, Mr. R., was 26 when the treatment began. He spent his time as a potter and volunteer "art therapist." He had been unable to find a suitable direction for himself after graduating in philosophy from a small college and was contemplating attending theology school. He did begin this training during the period of his therapy but dropped out after a short time. He contributed to the family's income, but his wife's business provided the largest share.

Initially, Mr. R. was concerned that the evaluation might have a negative effect on his own mental stability, and reluctance to be in treatment characterized much of his contact with the clinic. Twice he temporarily discontinued before finally saying he would come only once a month to talk about Cathy. In the last year of treatment, he and his wife had become interested in self-improvement through the Gurdjieff system, and when the episode occurred that precipitated the family's withdrawal from treatment, he expected to help Cathy through involvement in that method.

During his therapy hours, Mr. R. was concerned about both his anger at and his sexual feelings for Cathy, and his inadequate handling of these by detachment and immobility. He was conflicted about his role as a limit-setter and disciplinarian and worried about his wife's demanding dependency and his own passivity. Although he made some changes, especially after the birth of his own daughter, he responded poorly to changes in therapists, a common result with patients with his degree of disorder, and it was felt he was of little help to Cathy or her mother in their interpersonal struggles. Of the three, he made the least progress in treatment. Intellectualization was his primary defense, and he appeared to be intermittently psychotic in his thinking.

Mrs. R., also 26 at the time of the evaluation, was much more voluble and dramatic than her husband. Her personality was scarcely more stable than his, but she supported the family, and later her second daughter (the patient's half-sister), and an unwelcome friend of her husband's through an increasingly successful photography studio. Mrs. R. was the only child of her parents' marriage, which ended in divorce when she was 3 years old and after much physical and verbal abuse between her parents. She recalled that during this marriage, her father, an alcoholic, would take her with him when visiting his girlfriends. Her mother was a vain, self-absorbed person whom she could remember sitting before a mirror for long periods admiring her breasts, combing her hair, and trying on clothes. Mrs. R. felt her own most successful portraits and model posings were of a type that would have complimented her mother's appearance. Their relationship was that of "bickering sisters," and Mrs. R. recalled feeling lonely and unloved, often being left at home after school and in the evenings by both parents. After her mother remarried, Mrs. R. remembers hearing her mother and stepfather's loud and rough sexual play through the bedroom wall.

After one year of junior college Mrs. R. married her first husband, John B., and Cathy was born eleven months later, when her mother and father were 20. Mrs. R. reported that the marriage went downhill from the beginning, but the couple stayed together, nursed Mrs. R.'s mother in her last illness, and moved to California, where they both occupied themselves with work and Mrs. R. quickly became quite successful. There was another pregnancy, not very much wanted even in the beginning, and it ended in a stillbirth. After this, when Cathy was about 4 years old, the parents separated for good, and she and her mother moved to a nearby metropolis where Mrs. R. began a frantic dating spree ("fifty men in six months"). She said she enjoyed controlling these relationships by her teasing and coquettish behavior. Cathy watched her mother with these dates, including embraces, and would herself seek attention by being boisterous, putting herself between her mother and the dates, and by imitating her mother's flirtatious and sexual approaches to men. About a year before seeking help for Cathy, Mrs. R. met and began to live with Mr. R., who became her second husband as soon as her divorce was final.

Mrs. R. participated actively in the evaluation and subsequent treatment but in a flighty and disorganized way so that she managed to avoid talking about specific incidents or emotions most of the time. Her initial diagnosis was hysterical personality, but further acquaintance prompted a more ominous formulation. Her investment in the treatment was more intense than that of her husband,

and her work was more useful to her, but it also fell short of major success. During the therapy, she gave birth to another daughter, in the hope that by having a child of his own her husband would feel more real involvement in their marriage; yet at the same time she began to have an affair with one of her work associates and described him as the first person with whom she felt sexually fulfilled.

Major issues in Mrs. R.'s therapy were a yearning to be cared for, fear of being neglected, and anger at men. She was quite fearful of expressing these angry feelings lest they end relationships, but she was aware she often acted bossy and guileful. As a mother she was self-critical for neglecting her children, but at the same time she envied them their child status and saw her own needs as theirs. It was clear her inability to set limits on Cathy's misbehavior was due to her own vicarious pleasure in observing the acts. She behaved toward Cathy as if Cathy were a peer with whom she could bicker, as she had done with her mother. She was teasingly provocative with two of her male therapists, and both of them observed that her coy approaches at times were a vehicle for anger rather than positive feelings. Her attitude toward her treatment was consistently that of questioning and challenging the therapists on their personal life, tastes and styles, habits and beliefs. There were constant doubts of the therapists' competency, implicit criticisms and dissatisfaction, advice-seeking and postures of helplessness. She brought in a wealth of material, dreams and associations, but veered away from affect-laden issues, seeming to lose the details when asked for particulars. She had rapid fluctuations in emotion, but usually she was not consciously experiencing the emotion even as she expressed it. A thorough working transference was present intermittently but with only one therapist. Her husband had stopped coming in regularly during the last six months of treatment and she herself began to find reasons for not attending her sessions. When the fee was reassessed upward because of the increasing success of her business, she felt great anger, betrayal, and a sense of being punished. The cumulative resistances could not be resolved, and the family dropped out of treatment.

Despite the fact that very little progress was made in the therapy of her mother and stepfather, both of whom had been described by several therapists as borderline (the stepfather at one point being called "psychotic-like"), Cathy's intellectual and learning abilities and her immediate emotional relationship to the therapist seemed to indicate that, whatever the chaos at that point in her life, her early attachment and development had been adequate. Her parents were not yet estranged in the first year of her life, both were attending junior college, and there was apparently some support from the grandparents. It may be that Cathy was attended to during that time much as she herself later attended to the dolls in the playroom—adequately. Her mother must have identified with the parental role sufficiently because Cathy's first 2 years of development seem to have been relatively normal.

Difficulties arose when Cathy was 2 and the family returned to the Midwest to nurse Mrs. R.'s mother through to her death from cancer. It was known from Mrs. R.'s treatment that she felt her mother didn't give her the "right kind of attention," and it may be that whatever support she derived from their relationship evaporated during her mother's last illness.

In spite of these difficulties, Cathy seemed capable and normal at age 3 in nursery school when the parents moved to California. There was then another pregnancy and a deterioration in the parents' relationship, which was hastened by the unwanted child, born dead. This was followed by the separation and divorce during Cathy's 4th year of life. From what was subsequently revealed in the playroom, it appears that it was during this 4th and 5th year that Cathy began the behavior that revealed conflicts to which she so easily returned later during times of stress and disappointment. Certainly, after age 2 she was picking up on her mother's cognitive style, and it seems likely that this took on the trappings of the hostile erotization of her mother's relationships with men and of arguments and competition with women. There was evidence that Mrs. R. used her daughter as a peer with whom to argue and act up, and whom she could manipulate. At that point, Mrs. R. appears to have regressed and become promiscuous, and Cathy and she began to be rivals for the attention of the men callers. Just at the time that Cathy's cognitive structure was being shaped, and her own sexual-sensual feelings were able to focus on a father-image in the dates, her mother's own conflicts here were being expressed as hostile behavior in the guise of seductions. Cathy had to share her mother's attention with the men, for which she was angry, while at the same time competing with her mother for the attention she craved from the same men.

It became clear in Mrs. R.'s treatment that she felt very inadequate, neglected by her own mother, inferior to men, incomplete as compared to them, and angry at them, expressing the anger in hostile seductiveness, which accomplished three purposes at once: to control, punish, and attract attention. The "many dates" stopped with her remarriage when Cathy was 5½, but the competitiveness between mother and daughter for the new husband continued. He was essentially paralyzed by Cathy's seductiveness, attracted by it and uneasy. Her mother felt "envy" but couldn't intervene.

When evaluated at age 6, Cathy was active, voluble like her mother, and expressed immediately in the playroom a rich fantasy life concerned with the interpersonal relationships that character- ized her chaotic family life. It was not difficult to correlate the playroom scenes with the happenings in her family life as reported by her parents. At the point of initial evaluation, she was preoccu- pied with the idea of brothers, and that children must intervene to regulate the violent life of the adults. (Her mother had asked during the evaluation, "Is the child forced to be an adult if the adults in the family act like children?") Psychological testing found her of bright normal intelligence, with castration fears, but not very disturbed as yet in her development.

In the playroom treatment, there were early aggressive attacks on the dolls, biting and stabbing predominating. Much of this was directed toward the genitals of the human dolls. She was consis- tently destructive toward the genitals of the male figures. If the dolls were made to have intercourse, they bit each other's heads off afterward. It appeared here that she was resonating with her mother's hostile use of seduction. Over time, these playroom themes were reenacted with a different outcome. She did not repeat a feint at the therapist's genitals in that early period after he had responded firmly and calmly. Not long after this, tender and caring themes emerged that were intermixed with destructivity.

During this period, it seemed her oedipal inclinations were being contaminated by the underlying acting out of her mother's hostility toward men, and her own frustrated needs for fatherly attention without sexuality, both pregenital strivings. Her own father was distant and unavailable; her stepfather was aroused and paralyzed. Only the therapist remained for any adequate working through of these mixtures of needs and impulses. The success of the therapist's efforts was measurable in the caring themes and psychiatrist ideal- izations that appeared later in treatment. Cathy seemed to be sorting out two major inclinations in her relationship to the male therapists: tenderness and aggression. When the therapist calmly turned away first her attack on his genitals and a later, more seductive, invitation, she began to take care of him with proper tea parties and the loving care of babies, in which he was involved in a fatherly way. But before this type of play emerged, there was

messiness in the playroom, disorderly fingerpainting and water
play, and an attempt to forcibly feed the therapist. Normal oedipal
themes could not emerge before the pathological preoedipal strivings, so abetted by her home environment, could be worked
through.

With this disturbed family there were, of course, many intersect-
ing and conflicting themes to be winnowed in assessing how this
particular youngster developed her hysterical style. There is, for
example, the event of the stillborn brother, whom Cathy reportedly
accused her mother of killing, and the birth of a sister subsequent to
the beginning of treatment. When she was 7, a weird boarder
stayed with the family for some months and caused a great many
problems, the father ambivalently admiring him and the mother
hating him but not able to evict him. Cathy regressed during this
time to playing out fantasies of mayhem and murder culminating in
a scheme to cut off the boarder's penis. Such ideas were apparently
provoked or encouraged by Cathy's finding a wooden dildo around
the house.

Despite the lack of progress in her parents, the themes across the
three years of psychotherapy reflected substantial advance in
Cathy's cognitive and psychological development: clearly the direct
result of playroom work. It was inferred that the concomitant
therapy with the parents had a sparing effect that intermittently
lifted the static and inappropriate interactions between them and
the child. Nevertheless, Cathy remained vulnerable to rapid disorganization under stress (such as her sister's birth or the boarder) to
those sadistically "sexual" and hostile behaviors that typified her
behavior when she first came to the clinic. In this regard, Cathy's
relationships were not characteristic of regression or fixation to any
normal preoedipal state but, rather, distorted and inadequate as a
function of her parents' inability to support normal interpersonal
development several years earlier and continuingly. When met with
consistent responses in therapy she developed, if slowly, age-
appropriate behaviors with the therapist, resulting in more maturity
in her play. However, at the breaking-off of treatment it was feared
that these advances could not be sustained, given the ongoing
interrelationships at home.

This family showed an impressive interweaving of the sexual
behaviors with aggressive and hateful impulses in both mother and
child and suggests one avenue through which hysterical styles with
less favorable prognoses arise. It seemed that in her therapy Cathy
moved through her oedipal phase into latency, but retained her

vulnerability to regression. Had she not had this help, it appears she would have been in great danger of developing a very inadequate personality. Taking her parents' immature personalities into account, Cathy's psychological future, despite her progress, must still be considered problematic.

## CONCLUSIONS

It remains to summarize these theoretical abstractions and clinical implications and their meaning for the concept of hysterical personality in childhood.

The last two decades have yielded little new information to the understanding of hysterical conditions, but they have validated earlier impressions that the enduring qualities of personality, especially those underlying interpersonal relationships, are more important to the diagnosis and treatment of the adult patient than the overt symptomatology.

What *is* new is the ethological approach to the study of normal children from birth, focusing on what appear to be the two main systems that determine the internal representation of the self and the environment: a sense of connection to others, and competence. These two lines have precursors present at birth and accrue characteristic forms vertically as the child experiences the caregivers and the world. They change, not from one discontinuous developmental stage to the next, but ongoingly, diverging from normal at any point that inappropriate social responses have continued long enough, and reapproaching normal when appropriate responses are reintroduced. The presence of psychopathology in childhood, or later in life, called fixation or regression, does not refer to any behavior of the patient at some prior *normal* developmental level, but implies divergent behavior and distorted context at that prior level. The findings of new research bearing on this will eventually require change in our concepts of normal and abnormal development and bring the theory derived from treatment of adult patients more into line with what we are now learning about normal infants and children.

As far as hysterical personality is concerned if one were to use only the *DSM-III* or *IV* to assess the presence or absence of a hysterical personality in a child between the ages of 3 and 7 or 8, only some would escape that diagnosis. Clearly, such classifications are too inclusive for use with most children who show hysterical traits. The state of development of the child, his or her age, and the relative balance of ego structure as compared to psychosexual and psychosocial maturity are of crucial importance. The quality and quantity of interpersonal relationships, especially with parents, play a part in the manifest behavior that is characteristic of the child. How long that influence has been present, how rigid or flexible, static or progressive it is, will figure in the result and must be taken into account in diagnosis.

In adult personality disorder, the traits described appear relatively fixed, as if they are characteristic emissions of an internal cognitive structure. In children, however, character is determined by the appropriateness of their interpersonal environment in relation to their age and social milieu and is in constant flux toward maturity due to the impetus of biological givens. The degree to which this impetus realizes its aim will be determined by the quality of the interaction of the growing child with the parenting persons and especially by the length of time inappropriate interactions persist. In general, the earlier a deficiency appears in the reciprocity of the first attachments, the more serious the subsequent maladjustment.

The labels appended to patients are abstractions designed to facilitate our thinking and understanding and therefore our treatment. They do not fully describe any disease state, nor do they indicate the balance between strengths and weaknesses even in adulthood, to say nothing of childhood. Thus, to identify a child as having a hysterical character disorder would be such an oversimplification as to operate more as a hindrance than a help. Fuller understanding of the parent–child interactions and a psychotherapeutic acquaintance with the inner life of all three will often reveal the framework from which pathological and protopathological traits in the child emerge. These are shaped (and sometimes elicited) by parental attitudes, conscious and unconscious, which are a reflection of the parents' own immature intrapsychic life and are more than the child can tolerate without distortion and constriction.

With the art and science of diagnosis as it is, it might be too much to expect to discover and treat incipient hysterical personality in the nascent state in school-aged children with any frequency. The most that can be said is that a large group of children with commonly recognized hysterical traits can be identified. It is proposed here that if we exempt those who are showing such traits because they are normal for their age, and if sufficient data can be obtained through evaluation and treatment of the remaining children and their parents, two subgroups can be differentiated. The children in the more mature group are in danger of remaining at the level of symptomatology, which if unchanged by therapy or other environmental factors may later be diagnosed as hysterical personality disorder. With treatment of these children, or their parents, or both, the prognosis is good. The other subgroup, those children who are less developed, have more disturbed parents, and are at risk for a variety of disabling personality disorders of later life, only one of which is the so-called good or oral hysterical personality. For them the future is more ominous. They do not often reach effective treatment and the prognosis must be guarded.

What holds here must also hold for the formation of all personality and pathology. The scientific validation of this proposal, and its likely effects on psychoanalytic theory will have to wait for long-term observation of many children and their parents in their own environments, and in psychotherapy or analysis, but it is a prospect now being actively pursued.

## REFERENCES

Abse, W. (1974). Hysteria within the context of the family. *Journal of Operational Psychiatry* 6:31–42.

Achenbach, T., McConaugh, S., and Howell, C. (1987). Child/adolescent behavioral and emotional problems. *Psychological Bulletin* 101:213–232.

Ainsworth, M., Blehar, M., Waters E., and Wall, S. (1978). *Patterns of Attachment*. Hillsdale, NJ: Lawrence Erlbaum Associates.

Anthony, E. (1961). Learning difficulties in childhood: report of a panel. *Journal of the American Psychoanalytic Association* 9:124–134.

———(1982). Hysteria in childhood. In *Hysteria*, ed. A. Roy. New York: Wiley.

Bandura, A. (1977). *Social Learning Theory*. Englewood Cliffs, NJ: Prentice-Hall.

Baumbacher, G., and Amini, F. (1981). The hysterical personality disorder: a proposed clarification of a diagnostic dilemma. *International Journal of Psychoanalytic Psychotherapy* 8:501–532.

Belsky, J., and Isabella, R. (1987). Maternal, infant and social-contextual determinants of attachment security: a process analysis. In *Clinical Implications of Attachment*, ed. J. Belsky and T. Nezworski. Hillsdale, NJ: Lawrence Erlbaum Associates.

Belsky, J., and Pensky, E. (1988). Developmental history, personality, and family relationships: toward an emergent family system. In *Relationships within Families: Mutual Influences*, ed. R. Hinde and J. Stevenson-Hinde. London: Clarendon Press.

Bleiberg, E. (1987). Stages in the treatment of narcissistic children and adolescents. *Bulletin of the Menninger Clinic* 51:296–313.

Bowlby, J. (1969/1982). *Attachment*. New York: Basic Books.

——(1973). *Separation*. New York: Basic Books.

——(1980). *Loss*. New York: Basic Books.

——(1988a). The role of attachment in personality development. In *A Secure Base*, pp. 119–136. New York: Basic Books.

——(1988b). On knowing what you are not supposed to know and feeling what you are not supposed to feel. In *A Secure Base*, pp. 99–118. New York: Basic Books.

Buss, A., and Plomin, R. (1984). *Temperament: Early Developing Personality Traits*. Hillsdale, NJ: Lawrence Erlbaum Associates.

Caspi, A., Elder, G., Jr., and Herbener, E. (1990). Childhood personality and the prediction of life course problems. In *Straight and Devious Pathways from Childhood to Adulthood*, ed. R. Robbins and M. Rutter, pp. 14–32. Cambridge, England: Cambridge University Press.

Cass, L., and Thomas, C. (1979). *Childhood Pathology and Later Adjustment: The Question of Prediction*. New York: Wiley.

Cassidy, J. (1988). Child–mother attachment and the self in six-year-olds. *Child Development* 59:121–134.

Cohen, D., Marans, S., Dahl, E., et al. (1987). Analytic discussions with oedipal children. In *Psychoanalytic Study of the Child* 42:59–83. New Haven, CT: Yale University Press.

Cramer, B. (1975). Outstanding developmental progress in three boys: a longitudinal study. In *Psychoanalytic Study of the Child* 30:15–48. New Haven, CT: Yale University Press.

Emde, R. (1989). The infant's relationship experience: developmental and affective aspects. In *Relationship Disturbances in Early Childhood*, ed. A. Sameroff and R. Emde. New York: Basic Books.

Erickson, M., Sroufe, L.A., and Egeland, B. (1985). The relationship between quality of attachment and behavior problems in pre-school in a high risk sample. In *Growing Points in Attachment Theory and*

*Research*, ed. I. Bretherton and E. Waters. Monographs: Society for Research in Child Development, No. 209, Vol. 50, Nos. 1–2:147–166.

Erikson, E. (1963). *Childhood and Society*, 2nd ed. New York: Norton.

Freud, A. (1963). The concept of developmental lines. In *Psychoanalytic Study of the Child* 18:245–265. New York: International Universities Press.

———— (1965). *Normality and Pathology in Childhood*. New York: International Universities Press.

Freud, S. (1920). The psychogenesis of a case of homosexuality in a woman. *Standard Edition* 18:147–172.

Garmezy, N. (1974). Children at risk: the search for the antecedents of schizophrenia, part I. *Schizophrenia Bulletin*, No. 8, pp. 14–90. National Institute of Mental Health.

Goldsmith, H., Buss, A., Plomin, R. et al. (1987). Roundtable: what is temperament? Four approaches. *Child Development* 58:505–529.

Greenspan, S. (1989). *The Development of the Ego*. Madison, CT: International Universities Press.

Group for the Advancement of Psychiatry (1966). Report of the committee on child psychiatry. In *The Psychopathological Disorders of Childhood*. New York: Scribner.

Hollender, M. (1971). The hysterical personality. In *Comments on Contemporary Psychiatry* 1:17–24.

Horowitz, M. (1987). *States of Mind*. 2nd ed. New York: Plenum.

Kernberg, P. versus Shapiro, T. (1990). Resolved: borderline personality exists in children under 12. In: Debate Forum, *Journal of the American Academy of Child and Adolescent Psychiatry* 29:478–483.

Krohn, A. (1978). *Hysteria: The Elusive Neurosis*. New York: International Universities Press.

La Barre, M., and La Barre, W. (1965). The worm in the honeysuckle. *Social Casework* 46:399–413.

Lazare, A. (1971). The hysterical character in psychoanalytic theory: evolution and confusion. *Archives of General Psychiatry* 25:131–137.

Lish, J., Erhardt, A., and Meyer-Bahlburg, H., et al. (1991). Gender-related behavior development in females exposed to diethylstilbestrol in utero. *Journal of the American Academy of Child and Adolescent Psychiatry* 30:29–37.

Ludwig, A. (1972). Hysteria: a neurobiological theory. *Archives of General Psychiatry* 27:771–777.

Main, M. (1977). Analyses of a peculiar form of reunion behavior seen in some day care children: its history and sequelae in children who are home reared. In *Social Development in Childhood: Day Care Programs and Research*, ed. R. Webb, pp. 33–78. Baltimore: Johns Hopkins University Press.

Main, M., and Cassidy, J. (1988). The stability of reunion behavior with parents from infancy to six years of age. *Developmental Psychology* 24:415–426.

Main, M., and Solomon, J. (1986). Discovery of a new insecure-disorganized/disoriented attachment pattern. In *Affective Development in Infancy*, ed. T. Brazelton and M. Yogman, pp. 95–124. Norwood, NJ: Ablex.

Marmor, J. (1953). Orality in the hysterical personality. *Journal of the American Psychiatric Association* 1:656–671.

Massie, H., Bronstein, A., Afterman, J., et al. (1988). Inner themes and outer behavior in early childhood development: a longitudinal study. In *Psychoanalytic Study of the Child* 43:213–242. New Haven, CT: Yale University Press.

Meyer-Bahlburg, H., Ehrhardt, A., and Feldman, J. (1986). Long-term implications of the prenatal endocrine milieu for sex-dimorphic behavior. In *Lifespan Research on the Prediction of Psychopathology*, ed. L. Erlenmeyer-Rimling and N. Miller, pp. 17–30. Hillsdale, NJ: Lawrence Erlbaum Associates.

Millon, T. (1969). *Modern Psychopathology*. Philadelphia: Saunders.

Mischel, H., and Mischel, W. (1983). The development of children's knowledge of self-control strategies. *Child Development* 54:603–619.

Mitchell, S. (1988). *Relational Concepts in Psychoanalysis: An Integration*. Cambridge, MA: Harvard University Press.

Mueller, W., and Aniskiewicz, A. (1986). *Psychotherapeutic Intervention in Hysterical Disorder*. Northvale, NJ: Jason Aronson.

Opler, M. (1969). Culture and child rearing. In *Modern Perspective in International Child Psychiatry*, ed. J. Howells, pp. 309–320. Edinburgh: Oliver and Boyd.

Peterson, G. (1990). Diagnosis of childhood multiple personality disorder. *Dissociation* 3:3–9.

Petti, T., and Vela, R. (1990). Borderline disorders of childhood: an overview. *Journal of the American Academy of Child and Adolescent Psychiatry* 29:227–337.

Pierloot R., and Ngoma, M. (1988). Hysterical manifestations in Africa and Europe: a comparative study. *British Journal of Psychiatry* 152:112–115.

Plomin, R., DeFries, J., and McClearn, G. (1990). *Behavioral Genetics: a Primer*, 2d ed. San Francisco: W.H. Freeman.

Pollak, J. (1981). Hysterical personality: an appraisal in light of empirical research. *Genetic Psychology Monographs* 104:71–105.

Putnam, F. (1989). *Diagnosis and Treatment of Multiple Personality Disorder*. New York: Guilford Press.

Rangell, L. (1959). The nature of conversion. *Journal of the American Psychoanalytic Association* 17:632–662.

Reiss, D., Plomin, R., and Hetherington, E.M. (1991). Genetics and psychiatry: an unheralded window on the environment. *American Journal of Psychiatry* 148:283–291.

Robins, L. (1966). Childhood behavior predicting later diagnosis. In *Deviant Children Grown Up*, pp. 135–158. Baltimore: Williams & Wilkins.

Robins, L., and Rutter, M., eds. (1990). *Straight and Devious Pathways from Childhood to Adulthood*. Cambridge, England: Cambridge University Press.

Rosner, H. (1975). Clinical and diagnostic considerations in the analysis of a five-year-old hysteric. *Journal of the American Psychiatric Association* 23:507–534.

Rutter, M. (1987). Temperament, personality and personality disorder. *British Journal of Psychiatry* 150:443–458.

Sameroff, A. (1989). General systems and the regulation of development. In *Systems and Development*, ed. M. Gunnar and E. Thelen, Hillsdale, NJ: Lawrence Erlbaum Associates.

Sameroff, A., and Emde, R., eds. (1989). *Relationship Disturbances in Early Childhood*. NY: Basic Books.

Scarr, S., and McCartney, K. (1983). How people make their own environment: a theory of genotype-environment effects. *Child Development* 54:425–435.

Schilder, P. (1939). The concept of hysteria. *American Journal of Psychoanalysis* 95:1389–1413.

Sears, R., Maccoby, E., and Levin, H. (1957). *Patterns of Child Rearing*. Evanston, IL: Row, Peterson.

Shapiro, D. (1965). *Neurotic Styles*. New York: Basic Books.

Shapiro, T., Zeanah, C., et al. (1990). Exchange on psychoanalytic theory. In Letters to the Editor, *Journal of the American Academy of Child and Adolescent Psychiatry* 29:667.

Sheffield, H. (1898). Childhood as it occurs in the United States of America. *New York Medical Journal* 68:412–416, 433–436.

Silverman, M., Ries, K., and Neubauer, B. (1975). On a central psychic constellation. In *Psychoanalytic Study of the Child* 30:127–157. New Haven, CT: Yale University Press.

Slipp, S. (1977). Interpersonal factors in hysteria: Freud's reduction theory and the case of Dora. *Journal of the American Academy of Psychoanalysis* 5:359–376.

Speltz, M., Greenberg, M., and Deklyen, M. (1990). Attachment in preschoolers with disruptive behavior: a comparison of clinic-referred and nonproblem children. *Development and Psychopathology* 2:31–46.

Sperling, M. (1973). Conversion hysteria and conversion symptoms: a revision of classification and concepts. *Journal of the American Psychoanalytic Association* 21:745–771.

Spitz, R. (1965). *The First Year of Life*. New York: International Universities Press.

Sroufe, L. A. (1983). Infant-caregiver attachment and patterns of adaptation in preschool: the roots of maladaptation and competence. In *Minnesota Symposiums in Child Psychology*, vol. 16, ed. M. Perlmutter, pp. 41–81. Hillsdale, NJ: Lawrence Erlbaum Associates.

———. (1988). The role of infant-caregiver attachment in development. In *Clinical Implications of Attachment*, ed. J. Belsky and T. Nezworski, pp. 18–38. Hillsdale, NJ: Lawrence Erlbaum Associates.

Sroufe, L. A., Fox, N., and Pancake, V. (1984). Attachment and dependency in developmental perspective. *Child Development* 54:1615–1627.

Starr, P. H. (1953). Some observations on the diagnostic aspects of childhood hysteria. *The Nervous Child* 10:231.

Stern, D. (1985). *The Interpersonal World of the Infant*. New York: Basic Books.

Szurek, S. (1954). Concerning sexual disorders of parents and children. *Journal of Nervous and Mental Diseases* 120:369–378.

Szurek, S., Johnson, A., and Falstein, E. (1942). Collaborative psychiatric therapy of parent–child problems. *American Journal of Orthopsychiatry* 12:511–516.

Thomas, A., and Chess, S. (1977). *Temperament and Development*. New York: Brunner/Mazel.

Thomas, A., Chess, S., and Birch, H. (1968). *Temperament and Behavior Disorders in Children*. New York: Brunner/Mazel.

Vaillant, G. (1971). Theoretical hierarchy of adaptive ego mechanisms. *Archives of General Psychiatry* 24:107–118.

Walker, J., and Szurek, S. (1973). Early childhood development of psychotic children: a study of anamnestic methods. In *Clincial Studies in Childhood Psychoses*, ed. S. Szurek and I. Berlin, pp. 390–413. New York: Brunner/Mazel.

Widiger, T., and Frances, A. (1985). The *DSM-III* personality disorders. *Archives of General Psychiatry* 42:615–623.

Zeanah, C., Anders, T., Seifer, R., and Stern, D. (1989). Implications of research on infant development for psychodynamic theory and practice. *Journal of the American Academy of Child and Adolescent Psychiatry* 28:657–668.

Zeanah C., Keener, M., and Anders, T. (1986). Adolescent mothers' prenatal fantasies and working models of their infants. *Psychiatry* 49:193–203.

Zeitlin, H. (1986). *The Natural History of Psychiatric Disorders in Childhood.* Maudsley, England: Institute of Psychiatry, Monograph 29.

Zetzel, E. (1968). The so-called good hysteric. *International Journal of Psycho-Analysis* 49:256–260.

Zisook, S., and DeVaul, R. (1978). The hysterical personality—I. The healthy hysteric. *British Journal of Medical Psychology* 51:363–368.

# CHAPTER 4

# Basic Treatment Issues

**DAVID W. ALLEN,** M.D.

The initial phase of treatment in an average treatable case of hysterical personality is often one that is an urgent appeal for attention. This phase is followed quickly, once a therapeutic attachment is established, by a period of regression in which unresolved conflicts and childhood fixations of the patient are manifested within the therapeutic relationship itself. Ideally, this second phase overlaps with a period of working through, the therapeutic antidote to the multiply determined nature of the patient's state at onset of treatment. Finally, termination of treatment encompasses the difficult task of separation, itself a phase of important work on self development for the hysterical personality.

This chapter focuses on major themes during these phases, especially on initial problems. Since the extended and complete treatment of a single case is described in thorough detail elsewhere in this volume, a broad view will be given here through the use of case vignettes. As described in a prior chapter, hysterical symptoms are not synonymous with hysterical personality. Nonetheless, persons who do fall within this typology often present for treatment with a conversion or dissociative symptom, and so treatment of such complaints will be included.

The techniques of psychotherapy cover such a wide gamut that any discussion must be circumscribed by boundaries. The approach here is that of brief or extended treatment guided by

This chapter was prepared originally with the assistance of Sarah Peelle and the editorial help of JoAnn diLorenzo. The quotation from Allen and Houston, *Psychiatry* 22:41–49, 1959, is reprinted by permission of the William Alanson White Psychiatric Foundation.

psychoanalytic theory, using the basic ground rules of psychody-namic psychotherapy (Abse 1974). The main patient type under consideration is the hysterical or histrionic personality who has developed a separated, although conflicted, self-representation and who has advanced, in capacity for relationship, to at least the beginning of genital aims and conflict configurations. For the more severely impaired hysterical personality, who has not advanced developmentally from pregenital levels of character formation, the addition of techniques for treatment of narcissistic and borderline character disorders would be appropriate (Giovacchini 1975, Kernberg 1970, 1974, Kohut 1971).

## MOST COMMON TREATMENT THEMES

Running through the chronicle of hysteria treatment are several colorful themes. One is that the nature of symptom onset, and even the cure, may be quite dramatic. The course is often variable and associated with difficulties in differential diagnosis. Another important theme, although often expressed only vaguely or intuitively, is that sexual and aggressive impulses were repressed and yet returned in a distorted expression through somatic or behavioral symptoms. Finally, there is the theme of the conflicting emotions aroused by hysterics in those who treat them. These themes are illustrated in the following case example.

### Case History of an Athetoid Teenager

A young psychiatric resident was called in consultation to see a pretty 16-year-old farm girl who had been referred to the university hospital with the diagnosis of a possible rheumatic fever athetosis. About two weeks prior to admission, she had developed a rhythmic, slow, writhing movement of her right shoulder that continued in spasms almost unabated day and night. Since the onset the patient had hardly slept and had had very little to eat or drink. When the resident first saw her, she was lying in bed, and every few seconds her right shoulder made a twitching shrug. In spite of this symptom and the fact that she looked rather dehydrated and pale, her demeanor was bland and calm. The history was of a sudden onset without apparent cause. There was no history of fever or cardiac symptoms other than somewhat elevated pulse rate, and no history of joint pain.

The past medical history was not remarkable and neither was the initial family history except for the fact that her family belonged to a strict fundamentalist Protestant sect. Mental status examination indicated no loss of contact with reality or other evidence of psychosis. Except for the symptom as described, neither her physical examination and a careful neurologic examination nor routine lab work and a sedimentation rate test revealed any abnormalities. The resident, proud of his neurologic and medical acumen, was troubled that, despite repeated questioning, the patient, although apparently cooperative, was totally unable to recall any possible traumatic emotional situation connected with the onset.

The resident presented the case to his superior, a psychoanalyst, who insisted that in addition to the motor symptoms without evidence of physical lesion, and despite the patient's calm mental attitude, the resident should be able to demonstrate other positive psychological findings before diagnosing a conversion reaction. The psychoanalyst also said that there should be a stress of onset, with efforts to ward off some unacceptable impulse and a fantasy that had partially escaped repression and returned to the consciousness in the form of the symptom. The psychoanalyst insisted that the writhing and twitching of the patient's shoulder in some way symbolized the conflict, and that the patient's inability to relate the symptom to any emotional stress was evidence of the resistance in her own mind—the manifestation of a defense against anxiety.

When plagued by the resident for more tangible help, the analyst said that undoubtedly through hypnosis or Amytal interviews not only could the patient's symptom be relieved temporarily but relevant history obtained. However, he suggested that it would be more therapeutic to enlist the patient's conscious cooperation in recovering the memory and fantasy, and that this could be done from available clues. Her shrugging might represent, for example, he said, a warding off of a wished-for and feared incestuous impulse such as a caress from her father. She might have been sleeping in the same bed with him with her shoulder up, imagining his hand on her shoulder.

The resident thought his consultant's hypothesis almost bizarre. But he returned to the patient and asked her to describe the sleeping arrangements in her home. Without hesitation she said that her grandparents had come to visit shortly before the onset of her symptoms and that she had had to move into the bedroom with her parents. Further questioning quickly elicited the fact that she had slept next to her father, facing the wall, on her left side, with her right shoulder up. During the night she had had to crawl over her father to get out of bed in order to visit the outhouse. And it was upon her return to bed, just as she was starting to fall asleep, that the uncontrollable twitching of her right should had begun.

I shall not go into further detail on this case except to say that I was the resident, not the psychoanalyst. And the very day the patient talked about being in bed with her parents and next to her father, her shoulder twitching began to diminish, and in another day or two she was completely free of it.

## INITIAL PHASE

### Approaching the Presenting Symptoms
The hysterical symptom should not be assaulted by direct interpretation. One of Freud's early cases (1913) is instructive on this point.

> In one particular case the mother of a hysterical girl had confided to me the homosexual experience which had greatly contributed to the fixation of the girl's attacks. The mother had herself surprised the scene; but the patient had completely forgotten it though it had occurred when she was already approaching puberty. [p. 141]

Freud learned then that "every time I repeated her mother's story to the girl she reacted with a hysterical attack, and after this she forgot the story once more" (p. 141). Clearly the patient's resistance stiffened against knowledge being forced upon her. The patient finally simulated feeblemindedness and developed a complete loss of memory in order to protect herself against the conscious knowledge of the incident (pp. 141–142).

While perhaps extreme in demonstrating the forcefulness of resistances, this case of Freud's is certainly not atypical of the ineffectiveness of an attempted direct attack on a firmly placed symptom, especially when the symptom has a strong function in the patient's psychic economy. Any attempt to remove a patient's hysterical symptom by direct reasoning tends to produce a negative result. It is just as futile to attempt to rid the hysteric of a symptom by explaining the functional nature of the reaction as it is to attempt to reason away the paranoid's delusions. To approach treatment along the expected lines of layman logic only strengthens the patient's symptoms and intensifies the patient's negative feelings toward therapy and the therapist. The patient's defensive system is a reaction to inner anxiety, and anxiety is heightened and defenses further excited by threats of external attack. Resistances are stiffened even if the patient is able to agree with the therapist's evidence and reasoning. The patient's symptom is impregnable from the front, as it were, and only a well-prepared and well-timed flank attack or encirclement will relieve it.

The usefulness and effectiveness of the oblique approach is more apparent in long-term therapy, but to a degree it applies in even the briefest psychotherapy, as the following case illustrates. In even an hour's time, information was collected and rapport developed; interpretation did not directly assault the symptom but dealt with it gently through the roots of the underlying dilemma. This is not to say that there need be any concealment of the therapist's intent to try to understand the patient, nor concealment of the therapist's wish to have the patient's active cooperation in the process—quite the contrary. Nor is it to say that the therapist may not ask appropriate questions, request clarifications, or juxtapose meaningful information.

## Case History of a Premedical Student

A premedical student appeared in the emergency room with a history of acute onset of feelings of a mass in his throat, sensations of gagging, and uncontrolled vomiting for 48 hours. He was given parenteral thorazine, and the retching stopped, but he continued to complain of the feeling of the mass in his throat, and he experienced distressing gagging sensations.

In consultation I discovered that the onset of symptoms began a few hours after he had been to the dental clinic, where a male friend of his, a few years older, had done the dental work on him, his hands and instruments in the patient's mouth. A brief review of the patient's background revealed that since childhood he had been highly industrious, helping a competent mother run a family business. The father was affectionate but passive and ineffectual. The patient felt that he himself carried the family aspirations. I asked the patient to describe the mass in his throat. He said that it was a greasy mass and indicated with his hand that its dimensions were about 6 inches long and 1 ½ inches in diameter. My tentative formulation to myself was that the young man defended against passive tendencies and oral-dependent longings by his characteristic independence and industriousness. Further, I felt that the patient had probably had difficulty in attaining a comfortable masculine identification. In childhood he might have wished for a closer relationship with a strong and capable father. All of these factors probably conspired to produce a latent homosexual conflict that became acute at the time of his oral-physical contact with his friend the dentist.

What should the psychiatrist's intervention be? Should he reassure the patient? Prescribe more thorazine? Tell him that he needs long-term psychiatric treatment? Offer him a genetic-dynamic formulation of his case? Or interpret the phallic symbolism of the mass in his throat by suddenly thrusting a large hot dog in his face, as Lionel Blitzsten is once alleged to have done with a woman opera singer with aphonia? Blitzsten caused the singer to scream and thereby relieved her loss of voice (Orr 1961, p. 46). She developed this hysterical symptom shortly after her first experience with fellatio, and Blitzsten's rather dramatic action interpretation was an attempt to relieve her acute aphonia a few hours before she was scheduled to sing an important role. Blitzsten's dramatic action interpretation had the advantage of surprise in connection with an acute symptom in which the symbolic meaning seemed almost flagrantly preconscious and easily relatable to the recent memory of fellatio. While Blitzsten's action interpretation might seem to run counter to the rule that a hysterical symptom should not be frontally assaulted, it should be remembered that this symptom was a fresh one that had not become fixed or chronic. But it was a gimmicky treatment, and while it may have a place in the technique of certain peculiarly gifted therapists such as Blitzsten presumably was, it was risky and is generally to be avoided.

The problem with the premedical student was to do neither too little nor too much within the context of the rapport the psychiatrist had built up in the hour of the interview. I said to the patient, "It sounds as if you've always been a pretty independent guy, and it's difficult for you to accept help even from a friend and colleague." In my opinion, this statement touched on the essential issues, and at any rate it was acceptable to the patient, who smiled and agreed and, in a short while, announced that the lump in his throat was beginning to go away. If at some subsequent time he required further psychotherapy, he had at least had a helpful, nonthreatening introduction to it.

Since direct assault on symptoms is often contraindicated, it follows that one must work on underlying causes. In such an approach, the relationship established between patient and therapist becomes a key concern for alteration of the pathological situation. For in the transference phenomena that usually emerge, the core problems that underlie symptom formation and characteristic maladaptations can be gradually explored.

## Transference

Hysterical patients make contact immediately, and it is a reparative contact they seek. Their anxiety and acting out against deeper involvements derive from fears and fixations going back to earliest object relations. The narcissism of the hysterical personality bespeaks an impairment in the earliest experiences of loving and being loved and in the conditioned expectations arising out of these body experiences with self and others. These early impairments interfere with normal gender-identity development and result in the compensatory, intensified pseudosexuality described in the previous chapters.

For the beginning therapist, hysterical patients give the clearest and most accessible evidence of transference. The dynamics are less obscure than in most other kinds of patients. The crux of the treatment of the hysterical personality *is* the transference. If we give wrong interpretations, we can correct them in the light of later information. If we miss opportunities to interpret, they will occur again and again. But if we mishandle the transference, the treatment is in trouble. *Mishandling the transference or failing to establish a therapeutic alliance is almost the only vital mistake*, and it is exceedingly difficult to repair. The history of handling the transference is virtually the history of the evolvement of the treatment of hysteria, which became systematically understandable only with the advent of psychoanalysis.

Transference was a stumbling block for Freud's colleague Breuer and a stepping-stone for Freud (Jones 1953). When Breuer treated

Anna O., she had developed a museum of symptoms—paralyses, contractures, anesthesias—after much physical contact in nursing her dying father. A highly intelligent and attractive young woman, she first pointed out the value of cathartic talking, but she became very attached to Breuer, and his consuming interest in her began to make Mrs. Breuer jealous. When the patient developed a phantom pregnancy, Breuer was profoundly shocked, but managed to calm her and then fled in a cold sweat. The patient's accusation that he was the father of the child was too much for Breuer. He broke off treatment and left the next morning with his wife for Venice. Ten years later, when he called on Freud in consultation on a case of hysteria, and Freud pointed out evidence of a developing pregnancy fantasy by the patient, Breuer, without saying a word, picked up his hat and cane and left the house (pp. 224–226).

In reviewing the history of the treatment of hysteria, certain principles—approaching the symptom through its underlying causes, and attending to the proper management of the transference— become clear. An adequate theoretical basis for consistent, understandable, repeatable, and teachable application of the therapeutic principles became possible with Freud. Prior to that, treatment results were more a matter of chance and the personality of the therapist.

## Countertransference

Now, with nearly a century of psychoanalytic treatment of hysteria behind us, we have little excuse for not knowing the principles of treating hysteria and for not knowing the limitations of the method. Practical experiences of many analysts and therapists are available to supplement the personal practical experience of the individual therapist.

In the treatment of hysterical personality, the therapist should not avoid the eroticized transference. He or she should allow it to develop, and in time, like the hostile transference, the therapist should analyze it. But the therapist must guard against possible eroticized and hostile countertransferences. A brief review of such countertransferences may help alert the beginning therapist to this issue and provide an interesting reminder to the experienced clinician.

Before Freud was born, a young English physician in the early 1800s, Robert Brudenell Carter, described by Veith (1970), developed a method of treating hysterics that was essentially free-associative and cathartic in that he encouraged the patient to "fill the outline" (p. 207). Carter cautioned against suggesting motives to the patient. He clearly understood much about overdetermination and sexual and narcissistic factors. What he apparently did not understand—even intuitively—was the transference. And he had countertransference problems. As Veith notes, "Underlying his perceptiveness one senses an antipathy towards his hysterical patients, perhaps the expression of his youthful impatience with the whims and foibles of women and their 'moral obliquity'" (p. 209). Perhaps it was his antipathy to hysterics as much as the lack of recognition of his work by the Victorian generation that led Carter to discontinue treating hysterics and become an eye surgeon (pp. 199–209).

Both Breuer and Carter had countertransference reactions to patients, which made it difficult for them to work with the patient's transference. And when the inquisitors of the Middle Ages and Puritan New England imputed secret sensuous pleasures and practices to the hysterics of their times, they were probably having countertransference reactions as well. The harsh treatment rendered by those judges says almost as much for their own suffering as for that of their victim.

In the past, however, nonexploitive, intuitive psychotherapists whose personal maturity immunized them against countertransference entanglements have often been able to be helpful to hysterical patients. William Osler (Schneck 1963) wrote of S. Weir Mitchell's ability to be helpful to hysterics. Emaciated, nervous, full of whims and fancies, the patient was unable to digest any food unless she lay upon her back with her eyes shut. Standing at the foot of her bed, Mitchell felt that every suggestion he made as to treatment had been forestalled. Every physician had urged her to exercise, to keep on her feet, to get about.

M. [Mitchell] on the inspiration of the moment told her to remain in bed. She took food better but found that on attempting to get up she was so weak that she could scarcely stand from lack of exercise. M. says he felt that he had run up against a stone wall. About this

time he had seen on several occasions a quack named Lyons, who
professed to cure, by passes and rubbings, a confirmed ataxic in
such a way that he could get about for an hour or more at a time. The
idea occurred to him to substitute for exercise the movements of the
muscles caused by rubbings and friction and . . . [after giving
several lessons to an aide] he instructed her to rub Mrs. S. for a
certain time each day. The improvement began to be noticed and to
the rubbing was added the electrical stimulation of the muscle also
substituted for the active movement. The food was taken more
freely, she gained in flesh and gradually recovered and was sent to
her home. . . . The improvement persisted; she has since borne
several more children and has been the soul of many enterprises in
her native town. An incident, postpartum so to speak, was a letter
from Mrs. S.'s mother, a wealthy New England woman, a speaker at
temperance meetings, full of 'isms, *etc.* She wrote to Dr. M. to say
that bodily comfort and ease, health and enjoyment might be dearly
bought if at the price of eternal peace. For he had recommended
her daughter to take champagne and to have a maid to assist her in
her toilette. The former she considered not only unnecessary but
hurtful, the latter quite superfluous, as any well-instructed New
England husband was quite capable of helping his wife in her
toilette. [p. 895]

It will be obvious here that Mitchell's encouragement of libidinal
gratification, his permission of regression, and his countering of an
overly severe superego influence are understandable in the psychoanalytic view. He is not put off by any feelings of "moral
obliquity"; he does not dislike his patient. He is her ally against her
inner enemy.

Often negative to psychoanalysis, Mitchell is like Freud in his
empathy for his patient's humanity and in his intuitive understanding of the depth of her needs. And how interesting that he notes
and reports on the reproach of the patient's mother to him in a way
that connects the patient's difficulties with the mother's attitudes.
But he does not reproach the mother either.

### Beginning Treatment and the Emergence of the Transference

The general principles of psychotherapy apply in the treatment
of the patient with a hysterical personality, but clinical experience
teaches us that there are a number of rather predictable kinds of

therapeutic difficulty and opportunity that are likely to be encountered in various phases of treatment. It is important during the initial phase that the therapist not act in ways that will make the resolution of the later phases of treatment more difficult or impossible. Freud's (1912) advice on this is still most pertinent:

> Young and eager psycho-analysts will no doubt be tempted to bring their own individuality freely into the discussion, in order to carry the patient along with them and lift him over the barriers of his own narrow personality. . . . The doctor should be opaque to his patients and, like a mirror, should show them nothing but what is shown to him. [pp. 117–118]

This advice has too often been misinterpreted to mean coldness and passivity. Its meaning is more simple and direct: it is not useful in overcoming patient resistance to give glimpses of one's own problems or intimate information about one's life, for it is the patient with a hysterical personality who is most likely to demand and provoke a therapist to reveal her or his own problems. The patient may feel alone in exposing her or his thoughts in treatment, find it unfair, and feel that trust in the intimacy calls for similar revelations by the therapist. This feeling of unfairness is further evidence of the working of the unconscious resistances to understanding by the patient and of anxiety about regression into conflictual areas of childhood thought and feeling. The patient feels vulnerable, but exactly to what the patient does not know.

If the therapist adopts a familiar attitude with the patient, it may induce earlier revelations of certain consciously suppressed information, but the initial gain is lost later a thousandfold in the impediments the familiarity places in the way of the development of a clearly delineated transference that can be seen and felt by the therapist and interpreted and made conscious to the patient. If the therapist is to find the role the patient tends to project on to the therapist and use it to clarify the patient's reaction, then the therapist must not interfere with the process of the patient's attributions by bringing the therapist's own life into the patient's treatment.

The therapist stands at the interface of the patient's unconscious fantasy world and the real world. The therapist needs to be able to demonstrate that what the patient attaches to the therapist is the last part of a long thread winding back through the patient's life to childhood.

Sometimes, out of anxiety about self revelation, the patient seeks to reverse the roles of patient and therapist. The patient wants to know all about the therapist's thoughts and life as a prerequisite to revealing herself or himself, or because the patient thinks the therapist more interesting, or because the patient thinks of the therapist as a model to pattern after. Often, indeed, such patients feel they had a defective parent model in childhood. That attitude, then, is already a forcible manifestation of the transference as the patient seeks to reexperience and remake her or his childhood and past. The patient is already searching for the defects in the therapist, which *the patient knows* must be there as the patient seeks to recreate the relationship with the parent imago.

In analysis and in extensive uncovering psychoanalytic psychotherapy, an attitude by the therapist that is too intimate and self-revealing is incorrect technique. In psychotherapy, however, the therapist has more leeway for self-revelation when the goal is for limited and immediate symptom relief, and the therapist does not contemplate more extensive working through of character defenses and cognitive style. More than ever in such instances, the therapist must know what he or she is doing and what is being sacrificed for an immediate gain.

### The Therapeutic Alliance

Establishing a relationship with the patient, collecting information about the patient, organizing the information, and using it to communicate what may be useful to the patient are appropriate tasks for the therapist. The establishment of the therapeutic role within the relationship is a matter of utmost priority. The therapist asks herself or himself—and in various ways the therapist asks the patient—what's wrong, why now, and how did it come about? The therapist attempts to understand those critical areas of human life having to do with stress reactions and character development: the patient's object relations, past and present; the patient's relationship to the patient's body and self-image and identity; and the patient's concepts and values and how they are experienced.

As clinical data begins to accumulate, answers will reveal that the hysterical (histrionic) personality has strong narcissistic needs and seeks constant reassurance of worth, admiration, and love. And the hysteric is exquisitely sensitive to even the faintest sign of rejection. In part, the hysterical personality seems to need constant narcissistic gratification in order to maintain ego integrity and to reduce the anxiety constantly generated by a gender-identity confusion underlying the compensatory pseudosexuality.

Lacking constant narcissistic supplies and a sense of connectedness with the therapist, hysterics or patients with hysterical personality experience anxiety, frustration, and anger. They become demanding, ashamed, and guilty. In turn, confidence in their own integrity and worth diminishes. They then seek reassurance that by destructive impulses and global rage they have not harmed the therapist as a potential supplier for their narcissistic needs. Patients may then increase demands for favors and special recognition. They require extra time at the end of the session or on the telephone, or they may ask for prescriptions for sedatives or tranquilizers.

Reacting sexually or aggressively in an attempt to define gender identity, hysterics try to force the therapist to have more "real" contact with them. They thereby hope to gratify and counteract unconscious fantasies of omnipotence and helplessness. These inward dilemmas of omnipotence and helplessness and longings for merging and separateness manifest themselves in the relationship with the therapist, often in the form of demanding total gratification or nothing. It is as if the patient is saying, "Either you give me everything or I break off treatment; and if you give me everything it will destroy us." And now there is a dilemma and an opportunity for the therapist. In fact, the therapist knows the dilemma is coming and waits for it to develop so that the therapist can make an emotionally meaningful interpretation.

If therapists attempt to gratify patients' demands, the demands become endless. Then patients' feelings of omnipotence increase, they manipulate the therapist at will and feel guilty and frightened of loss of control. Any effective therapy ends. Many a beginning therapist has been usefully if painfully instructed by the experience of going this destructive route with a patient. On the other hand, if the therapist takes a harsh stand or a punitive or critical attitude and refuses any concession, the patient may not be able to tolerate the deprivation or rejection and the resulting engulfing anxiety and rage. The patient may be unable to continue in treatment and will break off or react with stubborn uncooperativeness or an ultimatum. And the same new therapist who was painfully instructed about permissiveness often fills out her or his experience in this opposite direction.

The splitting tendency of the patient—manifesting and externalizing itself in the relationship with the therapist—is the therapist's opportunity. The therapist's only way out is also the way out for the patient. The therapist must maintain a neutral, steady therapeutic attitude without either indulgent gratification or retaliation. The therapist reminds the patient of the therapeutic task and focuses on the patient's feelings of frustration, anxiety, and anger. As the patient is able to express these feelings verbally, it becomes possible to examine and interpret the patient's underlying fantasies of power and impotence, belief in the power to destroy and rescue, feelings of worthlessness, and need to be rescued. Often the female hysteric, whom we do see more commonly in treatment than the male hysteric, seems to be demanding rescue by a magic, powerful parent figure.

The therapist must avoid being drawn into the patient's cycle of acting out, gratification, shame or guilt, self-punishment, suffering, guilt relief, and more acting out to obtain gratification. The therapist must avoid participating in the cycle while helping the patient examine and understand it. In so doing, the therapist helps the patient to have a learning experience of delaying action and of tolerating some deprivation and frustration, and thus finding better forms of gratification.

A word is in order here about how the patient comes to treatment or the manner in which the patient is referred, since these events make the beginning and the continuation of treatment more or less difficult. Sometimes a patient has been evaluated by a good psychiatrist or psychoanalyst, has been thought to be analyzable, and has been prepared for analysis or intensive psychotherapy through consultation with the referring doctor. In such a case, the patient has a general knowledge of what to expect in terms of time, frequency, continuity, cost, and the nature of the treatment. I usually take this patient, at least on a trial basis, right into analysis or psychoanalytic psychotherapy. I do this even if the patient has a history of repeated and intense but rather superficial personal relationships outside of therapy and even if the patient has seen a number of previous therapists and at some point has broken off treatment with them.

If the patient does not come to me referred in the most appropriate manner, however, or is self-referred but has a history of brief and broken-off relationships, including disrupted therapy with previous therapists, I generally undertake a kind of transitional therapy. I do this either for the purpose of making an adequate referral to another therapist for more definitive work or with the idea of possibly preparing the patient for more extensive therapy with me. Either way, I probably tell the patient something like the following: "Well, this pattern of your breaking off relationships at some point seems to be pretty clear, and I suppose the same thing will, in time, threaten to happen to us if we are going to be working together. You understand, of course, that either of us will be free to discontinue treatment at any time. But I want to call to your attention that it might be important to understand, if we can, what it is that drives you to that pattern of repeatedly breaking off your relationships, why it's necessary for you to do that. Anyway, I just want you to know that in time, the pattern is almost certain to come into the treatment here. And when it does, do you think you might wish to consider taking the opportunity to see what the breaking off could be guarding against, rather than just automatically or reflexively reenacting the same pattern?" Some such statement, made initially, may help later to gain the patient's conscious cooperation when the dilemma of the transference develops.

## MIDDLE PHASE

### Work on Gender Identification

In time, it can become possible to examine the patient's sense of gender-identity confusion, the absence of inner certainty and integrity, and the core fantasies of merging and destruction, of being destroyed or made whole or perfect by some sort of unification and splitting or rebirth experience. The manifestations of all these fantasies in the treatment relationship and other relationships need to be examined and related to their beginnings in early object experiences. Then the patient can be helped to see what kinds and degrees of gratification are realistically possible and what is realistically possible in therapy.

During this phase a romantic or erotic transference may develop. The patient believes he or she is in love with the therapist and as a resistance to working this through may insist on a "real" relationship with the therapist. If the patient resists interpretations and tests the therapist with threats to quit, it may be necessary to confront the threats quite directly. For example, the therapist may say: "Here we are again at the breaking-off point. We can see that we are on the horns of a dilemma. You say that you love me and that it is real. But if we were to have a romantic relationship, however gratifying it might be, it would certainly go the way of previous relationships in your life and you would be no better off than before. On the other hand, if I don't go along with you on such a 'real relationship,' and if I insist that we need to analyze what's happening, you can always feel hurt or angry and use that to break off treatment. That, too, will defeat us. We can see that it's a damned-either-way thing unless we manage to understand it and work it through."

These situations occur in both gender-matched and gender-opposite parings of patients to therapists. For example, a male patient with an essentially hysterical character makeup, including hypermasculinity or pseudomasculinity, will also have a pattern of moving on in personal and occupational relationships when intimacy-stirred tensions build up. In some ways male hysterics are more difficult to treat when the therapist is a man. The patient may not only be frightened off by the welling up of homosexual undertones in the relationship with a male therapist but by the intensely threatening dependency aspect of the relationship. He feels a strength in making demands but a weakness in asking for help or even in accepting it. The male stereotype calls for independence, assertiveness, and concealment of tenderness with other males—hence the urge to flee treatment if these threatening feelings begin to arise with a therapist. Dependency and sentiment are more acceptable in the female stereotype and do not so sharply threaten the early treatment relationship.

Society, incidentally, tends to treat men who have a hysterical personality differently from the way it treats women with this style of behavior, particularly if the acting out tends to infringe on legal constraints. Society is more punitive to the male hysteric. An attractive young woman hysteric who runs up charge accounts or bounces checks is never held as accountable nor is her social reputation as damaged as the male hysteric who may rather rapidly become embroiled in legal entanglements that further impair his social adaptation and that may even result in his being labeled sociopathic. As Blacker and Tupin have pointed out in their earlier chapter, however, it is more accurately a pseudosociopathy.

## Working Through Interpersonal Dilemmas

Attractive, provocative, manipulative, young hysterical women are often difficult for young male psychiatric residents to treat. Houston and I (Allen and Houston 1959) wrote of our experience in a training clinic working with some of these patients and young male therapists. We described typical clinical situations and countertransference problems and demonstrated how, by setting limits and sometimes by working with spouses or families, hysterical personalities can be effectively treated.

The following case, taken from that study, illustrates the development of the relationship and adequate data gathering before attempting significant interpretations of the patient's interpersonal dilemmas as these dilemmas begin to be double binds for the therapist. The reader will note that the interpretive approach with this hysterical character is through the defense against feeling, although the patient acts as though she is free to feel and consciously believes that she is. The interpretations are within the cognitive style of the patient and enable the patient to reestablish thought connections which in turn make her acting out understandable, less automatic, and more under voluntary control.

## Case History of a Dismissed Student

A young woman had repeatedly been involved in various kinds of activities that in effect harmed both herself and her family. Both of her parents had already been in treatment for reasons of their own but had in the course of their therapy come to recognize their daughter's need for help. She had been sexually promiscuous, had had an illegal abortion, had been dismissed from a well-known women's college because of drunkenness, and had been involved in a number of serious automobile accidents with a group of young hot-rod enthusiasts.

Often she came into the office dressed in a very provocative manner, and several times she came directly from the beach in her bathing suit or from the tennis court in shorts.

After a time the therapist was able to point out to the patient that her acting out occurred at times when she felt tense, and always after a period of external pressure had passed—for instance, following school examinations. The patient acknowledged this and said that at these times she had the feeling of wanting "to rebel, do something different, kick over the traces." At this point she was not aware that this wish concealed an underlying fear of losing control of herself, which, in turn, covered a guilty wish for abandoned behavior. The acting out thus served as a counterphobic defense against the fear and at the same time provided a displaced discharge for the original warded-off impulse. The patient emphasized that she believed in individual freedom, was against stereotyped thinking, and admired the expression of natural feelings.

In connection with a bit of the patient's acting-out behavior, the therapist suggested that the patient actually was not free to choose her course of action, that she had to act out in a rebellious way. The patient at first insisted that she did not *have* to, that she *wanted* to. But the therapist said, "It may seem that way to you, but I think you might agree that you are at least unable to control what you will want to do—that is, you are unable to want to put off action at these times of tension." The patient demurred, saying that the therapist was simply trying to lay a semantic trap for her. The therapist said, "If you feel that I am trying to trap you, it seems that you imagine that the problems we are trying to understand are between us rather than within you. You are aware that you distrust me, but apparently you are not aware that you distrust yourself."

At a later session she gleefully confronted the therapist with the fact that she had not acted out in a period of tension according to the pattern the therapist had anticipated. The therapist agreed that the patient had indeed been able to refrain from action, but pointed out that she was able to do so not for the sake of understanding the tension, but in order to rebel against the therapist—to prove him wrong. The patient grudgingly admitted that such was indeed the motive. Later, both the therapist and the patient came to see how the patient was engaged in a complicated sequence of mental gymnastics, trying to anticipate the therapist's unspoken predictions about her acting out, and then doing the opposite. The therapist remarked that her behavior in these respects was not free but was in fact controlled by what she imagined he expected of her. The patient again grudgingly agreed. Later, the therapist pointed out that the patient used her mental image of his approval or disapproval as reason to do what she herself wanted to do to discharge tension. She used either the therapist's imagined approval to support what she wanted to do, or his imagined disapproval as justification to rebel and do what she wanted to do. Her use of the imagined support or prohibition alleviated the guilt associated with hitherto unconscious fantasies. After this interpretation was examined repeatedly by the patient, her acting out diminished, but she expressed much anger verbally against the therapist and against her parents.

The result of all this psychological maneuvering was that the patient got into a position where she could explore her relationship to her parents—particularly her reactions to what she felt were their repeated violations of her trust in them. Ultimately, it became clear that the patient had a great deal of conflict about closeness to anyone—fear of it and desire for it—because of her early disappointing experiences with her parents. She was able to work this conflict through in her relationship with the therapist. As the therapy proceeded, her acting out gradually stopped; she became more successful in her university work; and her relationship improved at home and with her peers. [p. 47]

### Recurrent Danger of Countertransference

In clinical fact, all of us are driven irresistibly to repeat our childhood, and it is helpful to know this and to know in what ways our childhood drives us. One of the great recurring difficulties in doing psychotherapy happens when there is a blind overlap of the transferences that both patient and therapist bring to treatment. Then overidentification occurs, and the therapist is unable to interpret correctly. And then he or she is in serious jeopardy of acting out with or against the patient. In either event, the reaction is utterly destructive to therapy. It is not just certain therapists who have a tendency toward nontherapeutic involvement with hysterics. People other than therapists sometimes also have an affinity for distressing relationships with hysterics, as in the following case.

## Case History of a Creative Businessman

An intelligent, intuitive, and creative businessman whose work was on the fringes of the entertainment industry came to treatment. He was quite consciously manipulative, and to some extent his skillful manipulativeness and his own acting-out tendencies had contributed to the success of his work. He was pragmatically honest in his business dealings and very effective in maintaining harmony in his business organization, largely because of his sensitivity to the feelings of others. This man, however, was driven irresistibly to relationships with beautiful, intelligent women with hysterical personalities. And he had been married to a succession of them. Each time tensions built up, there was a lack of mutual reciprocal nurturing; he became wildly distressed and angry with his wife; he broke off the relationship to go with another woman who was already, literally, in the offing.

It may come as no surprise that this patient's mother—beautiful, intelligent, histrionic—ran away with another man when the patient was at the end of his oedipal period, leaving him with his father and grandparents. Incidentally, this man was not postmaritally vindictive with these women and often found a place for them in his business organization, where he maintained a friendship and in a sense took care of them as he did his mother, who lived some distance away.

One can imagine the difficulties in treatment if this man were the psychiatrist, psychologist, or social worker treating a histrionic or hysterical woman if he had not been well trained and well analyzed. Probably the best that could happen would be that out of ethical considerations he would refer her to another therapist—while he prepared to marry her.

## Review of Treatment Guidelines

Let us pause to reconsider four treatment guidelines. First, don't make an initial interpretative attack directly on the patient's symptom. Second, cultivate a good working alliance with the patient, a positive relationship, before making interpretations. Third, allow clinical data to accumulate until conclusions seem almost obvious, before even tentatively pointing them out. It would follow that usually no attempt should be made to deprive the patient of secondary gain attending a symptom or behavior pattern until there is enough understanding of the primary gain, that is, the forces that initially converged to produce the symptom or character trait. When this is understood, it is sometimes possible in the context of psychotherapy to suggest better and more direct gratification of conflicting needs. And finally, the fourth rule, a rule that is simpler to state than to apply, is to establish and maintain the relationship with the patient and the manner of working so as to maximize analyzing throughout the whole treatment and to minimize any reality basis for the patient's conscious expectations of any other form of gratification, such as acting out together with the therapist.

## Tailoring Treatment to the Hysteric's Thinking Style

The bland affect of the hysteric in the acute conversion reaction is one indication of the effectiveness with which the mental mechanism of repression can work: repression blanks out anxiety and the anxiety-producing ideas. In the hysterical or histrionic personality, there seems to be an excess of affect; but it is also pseudoaffect, an as-if feeling, which in part functions to screen out the intensity of the threatening feeling. This pseudoaffect may counterphobically permit partial gratification.

With the obsessional, in contrast, small amounts of anxiety are permitted into consciousness but are kept within manageable limits by the mechanisms of isolation of affect—doing and undoing, reversal, reaction formation, and regression. In contrast with the narcissism, sensitivity, and emotionality of the hysterical personality, the obsessive–compulsive seems emotionally blunted. In the obsessive, the forgetting or repressing is mostly limited to dissolving the feeling connections between memories and ideas, leaving the ideas isolated but conscious. Conclusions with appropriate feeling tone, however, may not be drawn even though anxiety and other distressing affects are avoided. The obsessive–compulsive consciousness focuses on, dwells on, certain thoughts and lines of thinking, and in so doing excludes certain feelings and other thoughts leading to threatening or unbearable feelings.

In short, the hysteric has repressed or dissolved the ideational connections between *feelings* to defend against certain affects; the obsessive–compulsive has repressed or dissolved the feeling connections between *ideas* to defend against certain threatening affects.

Curiously, these two styles of thinking, though in a sense opposites, are not mutually exclusive and to some extent can coexist in the same person. And there is a sense in which the obsessive–compulsive and hysteric are similar in that the obsessive–compulsive dwells on the *thought* content without appropriate conclusion of thought and feelings; and the hysterical or histrionic personality dwells on *feeling* without appropriate conclusions of feeling and thought.

In the anxiety-hysteric or phobic person, anxiety may be intense but it is limited to the phobic situation or stimulus. The phobic is to an extent intermediate between the hysteric and the obsessive–compulsive and shows some elements of the thinking styles of both the hysteric and the obsessive.

Shapiro (1965) wrote of the factual memories of obsessive–compulsives. He believed the obsessive's thinking provides material on which the recollection must be drawn. He contrasted the obsessive's thinking style to the hysteric's thinking style in terms of apperception, apprehension, data gathering, and recall:

[The hysteric's thinking is] global, relatively diffuse, and lacking in sharpness, particularly in sharp detail. In a word, it is *impressionistic*. In contrast to the active, intense, and sharply focused attention of the obsessive–compulsive, hysterical cognition seems relatively lacking in sharp focus of attention; in contrast to the compulsive's active and prolonged searching for detail, the hysterical person tends cognitively to respond quickly and is highly susceptible to what is immediately impressive, striking, or merely obvious. [pp. 111–112]

Shapiro believed that the lack of detail and definition in hysterical cognition is neither the result of the mental mechanism of repression nor of the exclusion of specific ideational or emotional contents from consciousness; rather, he thought that it is a form of cognition in itself, a form that results in vagueness or diffuseness rather than explicit exclusion (p. 113). Some of both the hysteric's and the obsessive–compulsive's symptomatologies suggest a physiological substrate in the central nervous system's ability to focus attention—as in sight, hearing, and feeling—that goes awry in excess.

We can look at the hysteric's lack of sharp definition and thought content in another way, one that has implications for therapy. To the extent that the hysteric still unconsciously seeks to reestablish the nurturant child–mother relationship, there is an expectation, an unconscious demand, for an intuitive, primarily nonverbal, global understanding from others. Hysterics seem forever surprised at not being understood; they seem to feel that, of course, others know what they are feeling, and they seem to feel that if their needs are misinterpreted or not met, it is out of some sort of lack of love, rejection, or even hostile perversity by the others. When, for instance, a female hysteric and male obsessive–compulsive are in a close relationship like marriage, the hysteric often seems amazed and offended at the failure of her husband to apprehend her feeling state. And the obsessive–compulsive in that marriage just as often seems astonished at the wife's failure to comprehend what seems to him logically obvious in his linear style of thinking.

One of the frequently experienced misunderstandings with hysterics is that manifestations of need for elements of preverbal closeness, such as the wish to be held or cuddled, are reacted to by the other person as an overture for genital sexuality. "I just want to be held and kissed, but my husband always gets turned on and wants to have sex," a female hysteric may complain.

I have described some of the similar ties and differences in the way hysterics and obsessive–compulsives react that affect the strategy and tactics of therapy with them. Every experienced therapist knows that narcissism, libido, mental mechanisms of defense, phase-specific learning, object loss, and many other perspectives can all be used to scrutinize the healthy and unhealthy elements of mental life. One such perspective I have found useful in understanding the hysteric's thinking style is that of scopophilic-exhibitionistic conflict.

Much of the hypercathexes of these looking–showing factors can occur in the phallic-oedipal period that is critical and familiar in contributing to the hysterical constellation. But how does a therapist use a perspective such as the scopophilic–exhibitionistic to understand the hysteric's cognitive style in a clinically useful way? Let us examine a case of late-onset hysteria in which the patient's rather typical emotionality and the vagueness of thought content were gradually understandable as defenses against fears of intimate seeing and being seen. The treatment in fact pivoted in this case on scopophilic-exhibitionistic genetic-dynamic factors. How these factors were conditioned in the patient's early life, how they were constantly being played out again and again in the patient's daily life and in the transference, and how they affected the treatment technique can be seen in the following account. Clarification of these problems was to be an essential ingredient in the treatment process.

In this case, as in all cases, the principles of overdetermination and multiple functioning are operative. The relevant factors, as in all cases, need not immediately dance right up and introduce themselves to the therapist, although they are in there dancing. It is their interconnections that are elusive. We must be open to seeing these elusive interconnections in order to fit the treatment to the hysteric's thinking style.

### Case History of a Matron and Her Trembling Hand

An intelligent, attractive, gentle-looking, 50-year-old woman with a high school education came to treatment with a complaint that her right hand trembled when she attempted to sign her name in public. She had a fear of signing her name in any sort of public situation—filling out a questionnaire, signing a check, and so on. She also had a fear of going to see doctors and was afraid of hospitals, although she had done volunteer work in them. She had complained of anxiety and depression for many years, but especially in the last two, and more recently after a visit to see her son, daughter-in-law, and grandchild on the East Coast. On that visit, her mother who suffered from parkinsonism with considerable trembling of her hands, had returned West with her.

The patient was afraid that her own symptoms had something to do with menopause because her menstrual flow had been scanty and irregular during the previous year. She reported feeling more tense and irritable for several days before menstruation.

When she came to treatment the patient wondered whether anyone had ever had a similar symptom or fear of hand trembling. She thought that maybe it could not be understood and that maybe she could not be helped. Her internist had attempted to reassure her about her nervousness. He had told her she did not need to see a psychiatrist. Her gynecologist, however, had encouraged her to seek psychiatric treatment.

Family and past history revealed that the patient had grown up in the southeastern United States, as had her husband. She was the middle of five children. The oldest brother had been killed during World War II, and the next oldest brother was somewhat alcoholic. A younger brother was married and apparently had a stable life. The patient's sister, four years younger than the patient, had committed suicide after giving birth to a second child, a girl.

The patient said her mother had had a hard life. Her mother's father had been an alcoholic and the mother's early life was very insecure. Her mother had had parkinsonism for a good many years, and she, too, was afraid of going out in public. At the time the patient initially came to see me, she was attempting to do everything for her mother's visit that was possible, but she was finding that she felt nervous being with her mother so much.

The patient's father was described as distant but hardworking. He had become a heavy drinker after his oldest son was killed. The patient's paternal grandfather had died when the patient's father was a young man, leaving him without much education but with a crippled brother, a dominating mother, and a farm. The patient's father worked mostly as a construction worker and carpenter and was considered very "good with his hands" in various kinds of skilled labor. The patient said that she had never been able to talk to her father, that he was a very silent man, seldom speaking except when he was drinking, and that she was troubled by the estrangement between her parents. Her mother said there was nothing good about the patient's father at all. And yet the patient loved both of them.

The paternal grandfather had been the head of a school, and he left a large library that remained in the family, although the patient was never allowed to read the books. Early in treatment the patient hesitantly scanned the bookshelves in my office and asked if I could recommend something for her to read that would help her. I replied that, offhand, I did not know of anything that would necessarily be of much help to her. "The main thing that I think you'll find helpful is just to talk to me about whatever is on your mind while you're here," I said. "It's not necessary to do any homework."

"If I read something I feel like it might help me understand better," she said, "but I've heard that sometimes it's not a good idea, that it can interfere with treatment. Do you think I shouldn't read about psychiatric things?"

"Well, there are pros and cons on that," I replied. "I guess reading *can* be used in ways to avoid understanding oneself, but it does seem to help people sometimes, too. Why can't you just feel free to read whatever you'd like, and we'll see how it goes?"

The patient's paternal grandmother lived with the family while the patient was growing up. The grandmother tended to give a great deal of unasked-for advice. The patient, however, spoke of her grandmother as having had "kind hands." The grandmother was a midwife and knew about sexual matters but the patient did not feel she could discuss such things with her. The grandmother had had an illegitimate child, although it was never clear as to when this had happened.

Another of the grandmother's children, the patient's crippled uncle, about five years older than the patient, also lived with the family while she was growing up. The uncle apparently had a Pott's disease kyphosis from tuberculosis of the spine. He was never sent to school, and he may have been somewhat mentally retarded. When he approached puberty, he began sleeping with the grandmother, displacing the patient from that comforting position.

The patient knew her husband in high school, where she had been elected a beauty queen. He grew up in a tenant farmer's family. The patient was fond of her husband's parents, especially of her husband's father, who had died about a year and a half before the patient came into treatment. After World War II, her husband had worked his way through the state university and had done well. The patient believed that the frequent moves she and her husband had had to make in the course of his career had done much to cause her to feel insecure. Her husband was a vice-president of an industrial firm with interests all over the country, and he had been something of a troubleshooter for them.

The patient looked younger than her stated years. She had a kind of little-girl manner about her, often smiling in a "cute" way. And she dressed somewhat like a young girl, often wearing little white boots, rather frilly clothes—all a bit out of keeping with her years. Often, too, she wore a dark outer garment, such as a dark dress or dark slacks and sweater, while underneath she wore a white blouse. With the white boots she suggested a total whiteness underneath the dark outer layer of clothing.

There was also a feeling of gentleness and kindliness about this patient. By all accounts, she was, in fact, a gentle and kind mother to her son, who was getting along well with his wife and two children. He lived in the area where the patient had grown up; he worked the family farm, although he had a master's degree and had done work in educational counseling. The patient and her husband had raised her sister's daughter after the sister's suicide. Both the patient and the patient's husband were fond of this niece who had been almost like a daughter. And they were distressed that she had married a man who had a drinking problem and was abusive to her. The niece lived in the Midwest and occasionally came to visit the patient.

In addition to the hand-trembling that brought the patient to treatment, she had a fear of being looked at. She was something of an artist but was afraid to show her work. The past history indicated that she had always been somewhat fearful in public situations, was afraid in school of being called on to read aloud or recite in class, and was often afraid to go to school for fear of being put on the spot in the classroom. In the second grade, after her family had moved from the farm in connection with her father's construction work, the patient did not know the way home from school; she remembered vividly one incident when she cried, being ashamed to tell the teacher she did not know her way home. She often pretended to be sick in order to avoid having to go to school.

The patient also had anxiety about looking at people closely or looking at things. In the office with me it was apparent that she was even fearful of looking very directly at me or of looking around the office. For a long time she did not realize the office had a second exit door.

While it did not come out in the first interview, it evolved ultimately that the patient was fearful of having her husband of more than thirty years see her nude. She had refused to have sexual relations with him except in the dark. She wore underclothing under her nightgown or pajamas when she went to bed, and in fact wore heavy underclothing at all times for protection against being seen. Her mother, incidentally, was not afraid of wearing sheer nightgowns. The patient had never examined her own genitals with the aid of a mirror. In foreplay she permitted her husband to touch only her breasts, never her clitoris or genitals. On one occasion, after several months of treatment, she asked me whether I thought her husband's buying magazines like *Playboy, Oui,* and *Penthouse,* which showed nude women, had anything to do with her refusal to let him see her undressed.

The patient's husband, incidentally, was supportive of her continuing treatment. Several times he came and talked with me, both with the patient and separately, because he was concerned that the patient seemed to be increasing her consumption of alcohol in the evening. Because of the history of alcoholism both in her family and in his, he was afraid she might be becoming an alcoholic.

The patient's husband was totally unaware of her having any sexual difficulties except for the fact that she had not been willing to have intercourse with him in the light. In the past, she had not been able to achieve orgasm, although she had regularly feigned it. The husband felt the patient was satisfied with their sexual life together. She did not feel, however, that this was the case.

In describing how to fit treatment to a hysteric's thinking style, it is relevant to know that this patient made a point of keeping scrapbooks for persons she cared about—her son, her niece, and others. Periodically she presented these scrapbooks of photographs and memorabilia to them. In the course of her work with me she developed a kind of scrapbook for me in the sense of bringing me clippings, sending me scores of pages of notes, and bringing in written notes. It was through showing me these scrapbook pieces that the patient was able to reveal some things that had been difficult for her to speak about in more direct ways.

For some time after beginning treatment and the taking of the initial history, the patient found it difficult to talk with me. She became increasingly apprehensive about keeping her appointments and felt she did not know what to talk about. She often wanted me to direct her as to what she should say. I pointed out that in the nature of treatment I needed to be relatively quiet and that, although this was part of what bothered her, as had her father's silence, she was also made anxious by feeling on the spot to reveal herself. The patient often brought in the notes I have mentioned and referred to them or read them aloud to be able to have something to talk about. And sometimes the notes she sent between times were about being sorry that she had not been able to talk more freely.

At first, I saw this patient only once or twice a week for several months. Because of her difficulty in looking at me or in having me look at her, the patient *wanted* to use the couch. We talked about it for a while, and then I saw her four times a week in more or less full analytic treatment with the patient using the couch and attempting to report her associations freely.

After the patient had been in treatment for about a year, she learned I had written *The Fear of Looking* (1974), and she wanted to read it. I did not discourage her but asked, "Why can't you read whatever you wish, including my book? Is there some connection with not being allowed to read your father's books?"

"Maybe so," she replied. "I never thought of that." She was clearly pleased at the idea of reading the book. She was much relieved in reading it to discover that other people shared her anxieties about looking and being looked at; and as a result of having read the book, she seemed more confident that there were possibilities of working out her difficulties in treatment. Also as a result of having read the book, she decided that one of the ways of helping herself overcome her difficulties was to abandon the use of the couch and to resume sitting in the chair opposite me and to force herself to look at me.

To show herself and me that she was looking at me acutely, she would often make reference to some article of my clothing, usually my tie—describing the color of it or alluding to the fact that I was wearing a bright yellow striped tie—or the like. The patient, incidentally, made her husband's ties for him, and they were usually of bright colors. She began to paint more. According to her husband her paintings were quite good, but she refused to allow her handiwork to be exhibited or to allow her husband to show them to any except close friends. Most of them she kept hidden at home.

Early in treatment this patient tended to gloss over specifics and to talk in generalities. Sometimes she would dismiss my request for detailed information with, "Oh, you know what I mean; we don't need to go into that." Partly this wish to gloss and evade grew from feelings of shame and guilt. As treatment progressed, however, her interest in understanding and the value she saw for understanding by going into details helped override her sense of shame. Her style of talking, if not of cognition, was observably altered.

Over the years there were many reasons why the patient felt ashamed of her family and background in spite of her love for the various members of the family. She was ashamed of her father's drinking, of her grandmother's illegitimate child, of her crippled uncle. As an adult she was ashamed of sexual acting out on the part of her sister and of her sister's suicide. She was also ashamed of her brother's alcoholism. And she was ashamed of having sexual impulses of her own toward men other than her husband.

As the patient gradually worked over various aspects of her shame about herself and her family, new information came to light. One of the significant things that evolved was an early childhood memory that the patient dated as occurring shortly after the birth of her sister—when the patient was 4 years old. At that time, the new baby was sleeping in the bed with the patient's mother, and the patient was sleeping in the father's bed in the same bedroom. The father apparently had been drinking, and during the night the patient recalled that she awoke to find her father fondling her genitals. The patient made a moaning sound and pushed his hand away. She was sure he was awake and conscious of what he was doing, but neither she nor her father ever acknowledged what had occurred. The patient never disclosed the incident to her mother, but after that she was always fearful of sleeping with her father.

The patient remembered another sexually traumatic incident that occurred when she was about 8 or 9. The crippled uncle attempted to have intercourse with her in the presence of her brothers, who were encouraging the uncle to make the attempt. The uncle got on top of her but made no genital penetration. The patient was terribly ashamed of this incident and again remembered being unable to tell her parents about it, although apparently her mother had some inkling of what had happened, since she spoke to the patient of having to keep an eye on the uncle because of his tendency to exhibit himself sexually and to molest small girls.

Slowly it became possible to link the patient's fear of signing her name in public and a fear of being good with her hands to her frequent previous statements about her father being good with his hands—meaning in a manually skilled way—and the childhood traumatic masturbatory incident with him. These disclosures, however, did not altogether alleviate the patient's anxieties. In fact, when I first linked them up, the patient was made so anxious she felt extremely faint in getting up from the couch and felt it necessary to sit for several minutes in the waiting room before she could recover enough sense of strength and equilibrium to walk the several blocks to her home.

While the patient went through a period of some erotic transference attachment to me, she got over that. She was finally able to have a true orgasm in intercourse with her husband. The first time orgasm occurred she was frightened enough to exclaim, "Oh, I'm going to have a heart attack!" But she began to feel more comfortable about that, too, and she was pleased at the results of treatment, although for a long time she was still quite anxious about some elements of showing herself more freely to me through her talking.

While this patient is primarily classifiable as hysteric, I believe the scopophilic-exhibitionistic factors were active determinants in the course of treatment. Crucial as determinants of her psychopathology and cognitive style, these looking-showing conflicts were also determinants in the development and handling of the transference. The case illustrates a therapeutic tailoring of the treatment to fit the thinking style of the hysteric.

## Comment on the Right and Left Cerebral Hemispheres

Of theoretical interest, and tending to support contrasting thinking styles for the hysteric and the obsessive–compulsive, are the studies of the right and left cerebral hemisphere functions (Galin 1974). It would seem that the thinking styles described for the hysteric and for the obsessive–compulsive in many ways correspond, respectively, to the thinking functions of the right and left cerebral hemispheres of the brain that have been reported by investigators. When the corpus callosum, the great tract connecting the two cerebral hemispheres, is transected, it becomes possible to demonstrate the separate functions of each hemisphere: the right is global, holistic, impressionistic, and aesthetic in its apperception; the left deals in details, verbal memory, logic, discrete recall, linearity, and time sequence (Callaway 1975). Both these left–right hemisphere modes of functioning have obvious adaptive value, and each complements the other. One is tempted to speculate that when a clearly defined hysteric or obsessive–compulsive style of thinking exists, it may have resulted from a suppression or repression of the functions of the complementary cerebral hemisphere or that the functions of the complementing hemisphere were not fully activated at some critical time in a specific maturational period.

Among hysterics and obsessive–compulsives of comparable levels of intelligence, it seems to me more common to find the hysteric lacking in mathematical ability and the obsessive–compulsive more able in mathematics (at least in arithmetic calculations). Obsessive–compulsives may be good at bridge and routine money matters; the hysteric, rarely. But the hysteric is often better at such activities as acting, art, and interior decorating.

## Thinking Style—Continued

The so-called vagueness or emptiness of the hysteric's thinking is apparent but is not the whole story by any means. For example, I treated a very creative woman artist who had a hysterical style in talking, dressing, and behavior. And she clearly had a degree of gender-identity confusion. For this patient, making art forms equaled remaking her body image. She had even had a plastic surgeon remodel her breasts, making them smaller to fulfill an unconscious wish to be more like her brother. In her usual talk, this artist reacted in global terms, often impressionistically, or with seeming vagueness. But in fact she had much specific information and ability to deal with detail both visual and otherwise.

As repressions are lifted in the course of therapy with hysterics, it is often even more apparent that details of events do indeed register with the patient but are immediately pushed from consciousness with only a kind of blurred afterimage available in symbolic outline.

Consider the following familiar example. A therapist is a couple of minutes late in starting an appointment. The patient shows a definite negative response. She is uncharacteristically silent or slow to start talking. She reports feeling "down," but she does not consciously relate her reaction to the narcissistic hurt of the therapist's lateness. Asked if she were possibly reacting to the therapist's lateness, she says that she did not notice he was late. Almost always she gives a large real-life reason for her depressed mood or asserts she doesn't know why she feels down. But in any event, she implies that the therapist is not as important a part of her life as might be inferred from his question about her reaction to his lateness. While her denial or lack of awareness can be either a narcissistic protection or a counterstrike at the therapist or both, it is clear that the detail registers and the patient reacts, albeit in a rather totalistic way, as though the therapist's lateness constituted a major rejection.

To better to understand how you treat the hysteric, it may be helpful to recognize both the contrast and the similarity between the hysteric and the obsessive–compulsive.

I oversimplify to assert that we teach the hysteric to think and the obsessive to feel. To put it another way, the obsessive–compulsive has to rediscover the feeling links between thoughts, and the hysteric needs to relearn the thought connections between feelings. In treatment, the obsessive–compulsive tends to intellectualize without feeling and the hysteric seems to emotionalize without thinking clearly. The hysteric is in a sense phobic about thinking and the compulsive phobic about feeling. But I wish to emphasize that with the hysteric and the obsessive–compulsive what is ultimately being defended against—by their mental mechanisms and by their styles—is feeling. The therapist must treat the feeling part, must help the patients work through the defenses and reexperience the warded-off ideas. In treating hysterics, however, you first have to point out that they really do not feel as much as they seem to be feeling. The woman hysteric may be frigid and not feel sexually, but in other areas she also does not feel as much as she seems to be feeling, or she has by quick and premature expression of feeling aborted the intensity of its full development. Just as her sexuality is a kind of acted sexuality, a role-played sexuality, her anger is often a kind of acted anger. The problem with this patient is to help her learn how to think better about certain situations. To do this, the therapist might first point out that her anger is a kind of as-if feeling. It is a pseudofeeling, an acted feeling, and that is one of the reasons this patient is called histrionic or theatrical—because she is acting and not fully feeling what seems to be felt. In the acting there is a defense against the very feeling that is portrayed, and that defense is what the therapist must first point out. The therapist directs attention toward what the hysteric is having trouble feeling.

The obsessive–compulsive—for example, a male obsessive–compulsive—who seems to think so logically and linearly, up to a point, and has such a good factual and technical memory, is also having trouble with feelings and is defending against feeling. He has trouble making decisions and yet may be dogmatic in defense against his uncertainties. He constantly reverses and undoes things he says. He will, for example, compliment the therapist and then immediately have to take it back or revise it. Or he attacks the therapist and says something derogatory and then must take it back: "Sometimes I think you're full of crap. But most of the time what you say makes sense." You see the immediate reversal and taking back. The reason for this reversal is that the obsessive–compulsive defends against certain feelings that he senses would evolve if he continued that line of thinking. This reversing mechanism serves to let through only a little anxiety, a little feeling, and maintains a control with which he is constantly struggling. He is both afraid of losing control and yet wishes to let go.

With the obsessive–compulsive you bring the patient's attention to this mental mechanism of defense, of doing and undoing; you invite the patient to continue the line of thinking he or she is prone to shut off. You direct attention first to what the patient is having trouble thinking. If the patient is attacking and you have called this mechanism to the patient's attention, you may be able to say, "Now, at any moment, you are automatically going to feel like taking all that back." To some extent this nudges the patient to go a bit further than usual. The patient begins to loosen up the constricted switching back and forth and goes further in each direction. As he goes back and forth further and further, the patient *feels* a bit more of what he or she has been guarding against.

So en route to teaching the hysteric to think and the obsessive–compulsive to feel, the therapist first teaches the hysteric to *feel more* and the obsessive–compulsive to *think further.*

To summarize, both the hysteric and the obsessive–compulsive defend against feeling by the use of their characteristic mental mechanisms of defense and thinking styles. The therapist must help the patients work through the defenses and reexperience the warded-off feelings before their styles of perceiving and thinking can change.

The hysteric and the obsessive–compulsive deal with words differently. If the hysteric says something about being "irritated" and you reply with the word "anger" it will not bother her or him. An obsessive–compulsive, on the other hand, often makes excessively sharp distinctions between related words and is sometimes pedantic about it. For example, I have a patient who says, "I didn't say *angry.* I said I was *irritated.*"

I say, "Aren't these things pretty closely connected?"

"No," he says, "they're very different. I certainly was not angry. I was irritated, not angry," he emphasizes.

"Well, granted there's a difference between irritated and angry, and you've emphasized the difference, isn't it mainly a difference of degree? Aren't they related—at least second cousins maybe?"

If the patient's resistances are so strong that he or she treats all this with grim seriousness, further irritation, or intellectualizing, you generally let it go and press no further on the connection at this time. And here the therapist must bear in mind that it is in communicating with the patient through the patient's cognitive style that the therapist can be most effective. It is of little use to ask the hysteric at the outset to think in a manner almost utterly foreign to her or him. And it's just as useless to ask the obsessive–compulsive to feel feelings he or she cannot sense.

Therefore, the first therapeutic step, as I've mentioned before, is for the hysteric to feel more fully and for the obsessive–compulsive to think more logically. The initial interpretations are in these directions. To the hysteric, for example, you may say, "Perhaps you are really not feeling that so intensely." To the obsessive–compulsive, you may say, "If you extend that line of thinking without taking it back or counterbalancing it, where might it lead?" Patients are usually unconscious of their thinking styles without an outside observer to help them be aware of it. It works the same way with characteristics of culture—members of the culture are unconscious of their lifestyles when a basis for comparison is lacking.

## TERMINATION PHASE

By the termination phase, patients will have worked through many of their core neurotic conflicts and reduced their anxieties in the context of the transference, in the examination and alteration of their current interpersonal relationships, and in the review of their life stories. Because of their need for attention, they will have tested the therapeutic situation in many different ways and will have experienced turbulent emotional episodes: unconscious aims to recapitulate the past and obtain "this time" a more satisfactory outcome will have been frustrated and analyzed. But they will have found some gratification in the treatment situation itself, in the undivided attention and concern of the therapist, in finding that they have not been misused by the therapist, and in the pleasure of insight.

As separation from the therapist and the therapy situation is contemplated, there will be repetition of many of the earlier themes in the context of giving up the gratification of being in treatment. At this point, the hysterical personality will often reveal aspects of fantasies of rescue and nurture that have remained previously veiled. Especially prominent may be fantasies of relationships beyond the treatment conclusion. Only during this phase may residual symptoms be relinquished, especially symptoms that were maintained because of the fantasy of a particular kind of secondary gain. The patient may have a covert wish for indefinite continuation of treatment, for example, and only in the termination phase is it possible to examine and resolve the desperate need for an enduring sustaining relationship.

All the dilemmas of how to relate to other persons, to gain attention, to fulfill an authentic sexual role will be reviewed in the termination phase in connection with the important issues of separation and the transience of all human relationships. The patient may wish to continue a transference as a defense against the risks of a real relationship outside of the therapeutic situation, as illustrated in the following case example of a course of treatment (for further details of this case see Allen 1974, pp. 93–97).

### Case History of a Student Nurse

An intelligent, attractive, foreign-born student nurse sought psychiatric treatment near the end of her training. She complained of feeling mixed-up, depressed, anxious, and a compulsion to overeat and then to gag herself to vomit. These symptoms had begun several months before when she was kissed by a young doctor, at which time instead of feeling pleasurably aroused sexually, she felt as if she were going to be smothered. She felt gagging and nausea. These symptoms had occurred repeatedly after that when kissed by other men. She was a virgin and felt herself unable to work out a relationship with a man. The patient also felt threatened by a demanding, older nurse supervisor. Although this patient's immediate presenting symptom was hysterical gagging, she also had phobic and obsessive–compulsive traits; her personality pattern, however, most nearly fitted that of the hysterical personality.

An only child, the patient's past history revealed many personality resources and adaptive strengths, including the ability to develop enduring friendships. In latency, her parents had divorced after a marriage stormy with physical and verbal fighting. The principal traumas for the patient appeared to have been in the oedipal period. There were overdetermining factors regarding things oral and anal: early feeding problems, struggle with the mother about food, the mother angrily trying to cram homework papers into the patient's mouth on one occasion, and a tonsillectomy without anesthesia as a small child. The patient had been given laxatives and enemas, and she feared assault from both ends. Her father was an artist and fencer. In childhood, she had had a disturbing fantasy, later repressed, of his raping her anally.

The patient was taken into traditional psychoanalysis, and over a period of about three years she worked through anxieties about her relationships with men and women and became entirely free of symptoms. She was able to experience sexual feelings directly in appropriate situations and angry feelings in situations calling for anger without, in either case, being overwhelmed by anxiety or anxiety-induced symptoms. She has remained free of symptoms for many years and is married and the mother of two children.

One of the chief problems in the course of a somewhat stormy transference neurosis was not only the interweaving of attempts to fence or fight with the analyst and seduce him, but the patient's use of the transference relationship as a resistance to working out any real-life relationship with men, even though to do so had been her purpose in entering analysis. For example, she would say, "Oh, I know we can't get married now. I know your rules. But after analysis. . . ." This attitude required repeated interpretation of her defense against the real-life relationship with a suitable man.

There are defenses against defenses and reversals against reversals, and these days when many patients in analysis or analytically oriented psychotherapy know something of analytic theory, they are also quick to interpret their reactions to the therapist as transference reactions, and they seek to *dismiss* them on that account. When the patient dismisses a reaction to the therapist as transference, interpretation must be upward rather than downward: that is, the therapist must remind the patient that to call the reaction to the therapist "transference" is to avert anxiety about real and immediate feelings toward the therapist. After adequate working through, the underlying true transference feelings can become apparent and interpretable.

The student nurse went through just this sequence of getting to the underlying transference feelings. As erotic feelings toward the analyst began to develop, she was quick to discount them as transference feelings. She seemed never, however, to doubt the validity of whatever negative feelings occurred in the course of treatment. But in time it became easy to demonstrate to the patient the childhood paradigms for her anger. When it finally became clear to the patient that there would be no real-life romantic relationship with the analyst, she felt betrayed by him as she had felt betrayed by both of her parents. For a time she then attempted to defer working out her relationships with men on the grounds that the analyst was a perfect example of how no man could ever be trusted.

During the middle phase of the analysis these themes were worked through, with gains in her concept of self and in her repertoire of possible relationships with others. They were to repeat themselves later when, with improvement, the theme of completing the treatment contract occurred.

During the final phase of the analysis the transference theme of needing the analyst for a real relationship intensified, and the content of the patient's associations became heavily oral. Thoughts of food and intellectual imbibing were common. She went through rapidly shifting periods of a sort of sweet verbal sucking at me and wishing to prolong a kind of dreamy hanging on to the analytic nipple, and bitter, biting comments at me as thought I were an ungiving dried-up breast. There were fantasies of suckling at my penis. Sometimes, too, there was a kind of spitting back of unwanted interpretations as if thrusting away an intrusive nipple, an overfeeding mother.

These periods were experienced with less of a peremptory and needy quality as the termination point approached. She reproached herself for these wishes, but in a mild manner, and exhorted herself to become independent of analysis and the analyst. She expressed realistic satisfaction with the progress she had made, sadness that fantastic goals had not been achieved, and nostalgia that analysis could not become a way of life.

## CONCLUSIONS

If characterologic substrata are to be worked with to any worthwhile extent, it may be important *not* to attempt to relieve the symptom or presenting complaint promptly, since it is the patient's disturbance that is at first the prime motivation for continuing treatment. Premature interpretations, however correct, of the meaning of a symptom may strengthen the defenses and drive the patient from treatment, and to the extent that such premature interpretations also may produce some immediate symptom relief they deprive the patient of motivation for more fundamental working-through.

Perhaps because of changes in our society, including more widespread understanding of some kinds of symptoms as stress reactions as well as more liberal and informed attitudes toward sexuality, the kinds of hysterical symptoms have shifted over the years. The acute, naive, symbolizing conversion symptom is rarely seen nowadays except in the lower socioeconomic and less educated groups and among religious groups that are both constrictive and intensely emotional. But the hysterical character or histrionic personality has continued to be prominent. This too will undoubtedly change in manifestation with the times.

In a sense, the hysterical style *is* the symptom. Nowadays it is often very close to being the presenting symptom itself. More often, though, the presenting symptom is still a result of some immediate effect of the patient's cognitive and behavioral style. Not infrequently the patient comes to treatment acutely depressed or acutely anxious *and* with a more global complaint of an ungratifying, distressing life that the patient has begun to see falls into repetitive patterns despite conscious attempts to avert them.

It is small wonder that the patient can by voluntary effort alone so slightly modify her or his behavior when we consider the cumulative conditioning of a lifetime, the more or less fixed forms of imprint-like learning in the early years of psychosexual maturation, and underlying gender-identity confusion. Similarly, it may seem folly for the therapist to attempt to help the patient toward a massive reordering of thinking style. Indeed, massive reordering cannot be an immediate goal and gratification for either therapist or patient in the day-to-day work of psychotherapy.

Instead, gratifications for the therapist lie in the easy use of curiosity, in understanding, and in the craftsmanship of finding and freeing from automaticity what might be called patients' learned reflexes—reactions just below consciousness that can be made conscious with the help of the therapist. Apart from any symptom relief there is also gratification for the patient in the process of therapy itself, in satisfying her or his curiosity, in the enjoyment of self-understanding, and in increased self-esteem.

An essential part of the craftsmanship in therapy is to communicate within the cognitive style of the patient with full respect for the patient's feelings and values. The hysterical thinking style is not inferior as far as it goes, but the hysterical style needs the complementary advantages of detailed, linear, "left-hemisphere thinking" as well. In a sense, the hysteric does need to learn how to think and what to connect in thinking, just as the obsessive–compulsive needs to learn how to feel and what to connect in feeling. The therapist has to start from where the patient is, not from where the therapist or others think the patient should be; and if this is not done the patient will shut off cooperative disclosure and therapy will be thwarted. Therapy is a special threat to the patient when her or his thinking style is considered the symptom because the style is identified with the self, and to change the style, as it were, threatens annihilation of the self rather than removal of an ego-alien symptom.

No one wants to lose a sense of self, yet that is, in fact, what a change of cognitive style threatens. Because losing something can be so threatening, it is useful and indeed more accurate for both the therapist and the patient to be aware that analyzing and understanding a conflict or a complex does not necessarily mean giving it up or losing it, but rather being able through understanding to make the involved forces work for the person instead of working unconsciously to her or his detriment. A sense of mastery can replace the threat of loss.

Irrespective of a voiced wish for sudden "cure," people do not like a sudden leaving of familiar experience. A patient once said to me, "A vicious circle is a kind of structure—and if it's a familiar one it can become a kind of home—like a project or a cause or a good workout. . . . I guess I can always count on my neurosis." Faced with change, people often need a transitional object and time for the transitional experience. They need a psychologic bridge from the old to the new. And sometimes they need a companion and a chance to try out the new on a small scale and retreat again and again to familiar psychologic territory before separation from the old and before individuation into a newly extended self. Sometimes, almost as a rule, new ways of reacting involve resuming old interrupted ways of reacting.

Reformation in thought and feeling, and an affirmative yielding to change, or at least a passive acceptance of change, precede new actions. Just to take the steps and make the choices of what to talk about without direction from the therapist seems frightening to many patients. Thus, early in treatment I may have to tell the patient: "I think you will find that you can trust your thoughts to lead us to whatever we need to know. I hope to demonstrate that to you. In this sort of work we can't always tell in advance what may be most important to know. And, anyway, it's not up to either you or me to decide in advance. We just have to accept what comes and let it fit itself into the picture. In time, something will begin to repeat and connect, and if you just talk frankly about whatever comes to mind while you're here, sooner or later the important things will become clear to us." Dogma or authoritative direction provides instant familiarity or a kind of portable comforting something. But in the end, dogma is the enemy of human freedom, flexibility, change, and growth. And it is death to the intellect.

In conclusion, I would like to emphasize that while one obviously must fit the treatment to the patient, it is generally helpful to adopt the attitude that, so far as possible, the patient must be a coequal investigator with the therapist. The therapist, generally, should avoid giving advice and should arouse the patient's own powers of initiative. The therapist should be wary of overidentifying with the patient. The therapist should give the patient ample opportunity to tell her or his own story unimpeded by interruptions, and the therapist should not be hasty to interpret. In fact, the therapist will be most effective in focusing on the patient's difficulties in full disclosure and waiting to interpret the patient's dilemmas of contradictory and conflicted feelings.

And most effective of all are the interpretations of transference that can meaningfully be made only in waiting for dilemmas to be felt in the damned-either-way responses the patient unconsciously tends to evoke in the therapist. Under these conditions, the abreactive effect is greatest. The patient does the maximum and optimal mastering work for himself, and the transference manifestations and the transference neurosis become the most illuminating. Therapeutic interventions become both easier and more cogent.

Under the conditions of waiting for the damned-either-way response, the therapist can best find the roles he or she is playing in the patient's projections. The therapist can best demonstrate to the patient that the patient is actively reliving her or his past in the treatment and in present-day conflicts of id, ego, superego, and external reality. Figuratively, the therapist holds the string at the juncture of the real world and the labyrinthine world of the patient's unconscious and past. The therapist allows the patient to unwind that Ariadnean string regressively throughout its long length into earliest childhood. And when the patient comes forward again the therapist gives back the string and map of the patient's personal labyrinth. Generally, no effort should be made to force the pace of the regressive unwinding. The patient needs to explore in her or his own time and pace in order to master. And the patient's feeling forced to yield to the therapist does not usually bring a sense of inner freedom. Only when the patient is stuck does the therapist need to clear the way a little with interpretation or give a little push with an inquiry.

When an attractive young hysterical female patient suddenly turns over on the couch and says, "But that's enough about me, Doctor; let's talk about you," the male analyst has an opportunity to interpret. The patient has a right to keep the analytic situation and the analyst free for fantasy, and it is the analyst's responsibility to guard that right. He should interpret her wish to know about him as a fear of having him know about her and a fear of knowing more about herself. Thus to the patient he might well say, "I think you'll agree that my life doesn't belong in your treatment. But perhaps you're anxious about having us *both* know *your* thoughts."

The therapeutic situation offers ample opportunity for mobilizing scopophilic-exhibitionistic anxiety for both the patient and the therapist, especially with hysterical patients. Nowhere else in life does anyone tell another *all* of his thoughts. Years of work in supervising psychiatrists-in-training convinces me that one of the sources of the beginning therapist's anxieties is an inhibited scopophilia. The doctor's need to act—to advise, to prescribe, to do something, to tell about herself or himself—is often a kind of exhibitionistic and narcissistic defense against anxieties associated with quiet and thorough reflective observation. The ability to defer action in favor of benign curiosity is, however, a necessary prerequisite for real diagnostic understanding in depth.

Finally, in all of the therapist's interventions with the patient the therapist must bear in mind that the patient too has a difficult task and is in a situation of particular vulnerability to intensifications of shame and guilt. Whatever is said to the patient, the therapist should phrase tactfully in a way to cause the least injury to self-esteem while doing the necessary therapeutic work. Hopefully, the patient can get to the point of realizing that hiding is unnecessary and of discovering a wish no longer to hide.


## REFERENCES

Abse, W. D. (1974). Hysterical conversion and dissociative syndromes and the hysterical character. In *American Handbook of Psychiatry*, vol. 3, ed. S. Arieti and E. B. Brody. New York: Basic Books.

Allen, D. W. (1974). *The Fear of Looking: Scopophilic-Exhibitionistic Conflicts*. Charlottesville: University Press of Virginia.

Allen, D. W., and Houston, M. (1959). The management of hysteroid acting-out patients in a training clinic. *Psychiatry* 22:41–49.

Callaway, E. (1975). Psychiatry today. *The Western Journal of Medicine* 122:349–354.

Freud, S. (1912). Recommendations to physicians practising psychoanalysis. *Standard Edition* 12:109–120.

———(1913). On beginning the treatment. *Standard Edition* 12:121–144.

Galin, D. (1974). Implications for psychiatry of left and right cerebral specialization. *Archives of General Psychiatry* 31:572–583.

Giovacchini, P. (1975). *Psychoanalysis of Character Disorders*. New York: Jason Aronson.

Jones, E. (1953). *The Life and Work of Sigmund Freud*. Vol. 1. New York: Basic Books.

Kernberg, O. (1970). Factors in the psychoanalytic treatment of narcissistic personalities. *Journal of the American Psychoanalytic Association* 18:51–85.

———(1974). Further contributions to the treatment of narcissistic personalities. *International Journal of Psycho-Analysis* 55:215-240.

Kohut, H. (1971). *The Analysis of the Self*. New York: International Universities Press.

Orr, D. W. (1961). Lionel Blitzsten, the teacher. In *N. Lionel Blitzsten, M.D.: Psychoanalyst, Teacher, Friend 1893–1952*. New York: International Universities Press (private distribution only).

Schneck, J. M. (1963). Historical notes: William Osler, S. Weir Mitchell, and the origin of the "rest cure." *American Journal of Psychiatry* 119:894–895.

Shapiro, D. (1965). *Neurotic Styles*. New York: Basic Books.

Veith, I. (1970). *Hysteria: The History of a Disease*. Chicago: University of Chicago Press.

CHAPTER 5

# Psychic Structure
# and the Processes of Change

MARDI J. HOROWITZ, M.D.

H ysterical personality is described in terms of behavioral traits, and these patterns in turn are based on a person's style of information processing and his or her person schemas. Modification of character requires change in ways of thinking and change of schemas as well as the learning of new behavioral repertoires. This chapter examines hysterical personality in terms of the processes of such change.

Cognitive style and meaning structures are individual, and the delineation of patterns and changes requires individual description within such a typology as hysterical personality. The patient to be described in this chapter changed during psychoanalysis, and the story of this change allows us to examine the matrix of her past history, current maladaptive interpersonal behavioral patterns, and transference enactments in the therapy situation. If the cognitive process and structure of a person with a hysterical personality is understood thoroughly enough through examination of the extensive information available from a psychoanalysis, then the clarity gained should allow eventual development of interventions that produce change in briefer forms of treatment.

The central issues are those described in earlier chapters. In terms of cognitive style, there is a need to examine the use of repression and denial and to understand how these defenses are accomplished in terms of control processes and how they are

This chapter is based in part on a paper from the *International Review of Psycho-Analysis* 1977, vol. 4, pp. 23–49, and is used with their permission.

modified with character change. In terms of self schemas, the development of a pseudofeminine or pseudomasculine self and the evolution of a more mature self-image are central. In terms of relationships, the focus would be on change from stereotyped reenactments to new forms of intimacy based on current real attributes of self and other.

The purpose of this chapter, then, is the analysis of change in a person with hysterical personality during the course of a psychoanalysis. The extensive information gained in this form of treatment is used to examine the patterns of a person with this typology as these patterns are highlighted by their change. This analysis of the changes and the change process adds the cognitive and object-relations points of view to classic psychodynamics (Horowitz 1988a, 1988b).

The strategy of approach involves a series of steps. First, the current life problems of a person with a hysterical personality are described. To give an overview of the outcome, the state of these problems at the onset and at the end of treatment are compared. Then background history enlarges the picture. The story continues by describing the history of the psychoanalysis. Then the changes in the person are formulated.

## A REPRESENTATIVE CASE

### Presenting Complaints and Identifying Information

Ms. Smith was 25 when she came for psychiatric treatment. Slender and well-formed, she had striking black hair and a pale, attractive face. During the first few interviews she dressed in a glamorous fashion, although not quite within any current style. Her manner was poised and sophisticated, but this seemed strained, as if it were a facade. Behind many evocative social gestures and conversational gambits she seemed uneasy and tense. Labile emotional expressions, unintentional "seductiveness," and covert cues to elicit rescue were observed.

She said she felt depressed and unsure about how to continue her life. She had come at the suggestion of a mental health professional who had seen her in consultation because of her frequent and hard-to-dispel deflated, apathetic, and sad states of mind. After making these statements, she feigned excessive uncertainty about why she had come as an attempt to elicit reassurance, advice, and direction.

She identified the immediate precipitant of her sad states of low self-esteem as a recent separation from a lover, but her depressed feelings were not simply reactive grief within a mourning process. She recognized that this separation was part of a recurrent pattern of failure to develop enduring attachments to either men or women. She felt defective, unlovable, and incapable of love or friendship. In addition to an inability to be relaxed and intimate, she felt severe sexual inhibitions.

When her psychoanalysis began, Ms. Smith was entering a final year of internship before obtaining a credential as a dietitian. This apprenticeship was progressing poorly. Some days instead of going to work, she stayed in bed at the boardinghouse where she lived. She sometimes felt too dizzy, lightheaded, and apathetic to get up in the morning, and was uncertain of whether her illness was physical or psychological. Phobias, dissociative episodes, lightheadedness, dizzy spells, and various genitourinary and gastrointestinal symptoms occurred episodically, but doctors found nothing physically amiss. At times, she felt a state of elation and entered into almost frantic activity, but dejection quickly recurred.

During evaluation, she reported another motive for treatment and reason for depression. Her older sister had recently had her second baby. Even if Ms. Smith were to be cured of sexual inhibitions and her inability to love, she could not marry and bear children in time to "catch up."

Most of the complaints present at the onset of analysis were relieved by the time analysis was completed. To provide an overview, the state of various signs and symptoms is listed for both time periods in Table 5–1. The plan to prepare this chapter was discussed with the patient more than a year after termination. The symptomatic improvements present when treatment terminated had persisted. She had advanced in a rewarding career and felt successful. She was unmarried but was able to relate tenderly and sexually to men. She felt that "analysis was the best thing [she] had ever done and that it was astounding in view of how [she] was before and after." She found that problems came up in everyday life but she was coping well with them. In a later follow-up letter she reported marriage and parenthood.

## Patient's Background

Ms. Smith described her mother as rigid and moralistic. Other family members found the mother devoted but joyless and often depressed. Deeply involved with an orthodox church, she was con-

## Table 5–1

### Signs and Symptoms at Onset
### and Termination of Treatment

| Reported as Initial Complaints or Present Early in Analysis | State at Termination of Analysis |
|---|---|
| 1. Frequently depressed in mood with episodes of giddy elation | 1. Specifically sad at times, happy at times, able to avoid excessive excitements |
| 2. Anorgasmic | 2. Much improved |
| 3. Unable to love men | 3. Able to love men, sustain sensuous states, later able to marry and have a child |
| 4. Friendless | 4. Makes and keeps friends |
| 5. Dull, listless, and apathetic states of mind were a problem | 5. Capable of sustained action |
| 6. Episodic dizziness, anxiety attacks, and physical complaints | 6. Episodic physical symptoms generally absent (potential for recurrence when under stress) |
| 7. Low self-esteem | 7. Self-esteem markedly improved |
| 8. Phobically avoidant states and specific phobias occasionally present | 8. Phobias absent |

cerned throughout life with social propriety, especially in sexual matters. Her origin as the child of lower middle-class parents meant that her marriage to Mr. Smith, son of a once-prominent Chicago family, indicated upward mobility. She was initially as proud of the match as she was later ashamed by Mr. Smith's eventual vocational and social failures.

Ms. Smith's mother was trained in a semi-professional skill. After her first child, a daughter, was born, she stayed home as housewife and mother. Ms. Smith was born two years later, to be followed in two more years by a third daughter. This third child had chronic illnesses. Her own problems and the infirmities of her youngest baby kept the mother from returning to work, although the family income was meager. During this period the mother may have also had a depression. The patient turned to her father for mothering, with inconsistent results. (The frequency of this situation in the background of persons who develop hysterical personalities was discussed by Blacker and Tupin in Chapter 2.) Later, she also turned to her older sister for mothering, and this too had good as well as frustrating aspects. When the children entered school, their mother returned to work at a large military base where, because of her great productivity, efficiency, and self-effacing nature, she rapidly attained a semi-executive level of responsibility. Her success there provided a central gratification in her life, although she also felt used by the male military officers who took credit for her work.

The patient's older sister was lively and spunky throughout her early growth period. She began promiscuous sexual activities early in adolescence while continuing average work in school. The patient, the second child, was quieter, more intelligent and well-behaved, and more successful in school. The youngest sister was sickly, less intelligent than the other two, and received a great deal of nursing care from their mother.

The mother also had, as a regular activity, the task of reviewing magazines for obscene content so that they might be banned by the church. She hid these magazines in her lingerie drawer, an open secret in the family. The proud moralistic stance of the mother seems to have been brittle for she sometimes wept uncontrollably over conflicts within the family. At such times, she felt helpless and complained of being unappreciated. She also felt insecure in public. For example, when the need arose to return a purchase to a department store, she would have the two older girls, adolescents at the time, do it for her.

Mr. Smith was unusual. All of his daughters regarded him as a failure and a sexual pervert, but also knew him to be intelligent, artistically gifted, and capable of enthusiasm. One of his greatest eccentricities was nudism. He insisted on his own nudity around the house, including eating breakfast while naked. He assumed the function of waking each daughter, and undressed, would lie on their beds, above the covers, until they arose. During early adolescence, this so embarrassed and upset the patient that she begged her mother to make him stop. Her mother would cry and claim that she was helpless.

In Ms. Smith's recollections, her father most often appeared as selfish and immature. But he was also recollected later in the analysis as affectionate, lively, and endearing. He drew well and would amuse the children with cartoons. He sometimes took the patient for car rides, thrilling her by high-speed turns. However, even ideal images of her father had their disappointing side. When he was obviously and repeatedly cheated by mechanics and used-car dealers, his aura of expertise with cars dissolved.

Mr. Smith had graduated from a major university with honors in art history. He then found an unusually good job as assistant curator of an art museum but was let go at the end of one year. After a sequence of further false starts, he became a pigment tester for a line of paints, going from factory to factory to assure quality. The salary was low; he was regarded as a failure by more successful friends and relatives, and he counterphobically flaunted his blue collar status at social and family gatherings.

While the father overtly chided his oldest daughter for her sexual behavior, he was covertly interested and teased her for the details of sexual encounters. Later, when Ms. Smith was in college, he wanted to visit her in order to flirt with her roommate. There were other episodes of his flirtations with women, such as waitresses. These were pathetic longings without romantic action or real intent. He demonstrated an almost ludricrous pseudomasculinity. (This pseudosexuality is similar to that discussed by Blacker and Tupin in Chapter 2.) While he ridiculed the church's obscenity committee, he surreptitiously read the pornographic material from his wife's drawer. At times he left his fly unzipped in public. Like his flirtatiousness, these exhibitionistic traits were limited, for he was never apprehended in a flagrant act. Together, the parents set a familial standard of both denial and rationalization of such behaviors.

Anger, anxiety, and guilt over erotic events characterized Ms. Smith's childhood. A few repetitive memories from the analysis illustrate these events. Striptease was a perennially favorite game of the oldest sister, and the three girls often played it together. When Ms. Smith was about 4 or 5 years old, her older sister encouraged her to strip before a group of boys 9–13 years old. Upon removing her panties she was roundly laughed at. Some years later, a boy she had especially admired from afar asked her to his room. He showed her an obscene photograph, and she rushed out.

Ms. Smith commenced menstruation when she was 9 years old. She was surprised at the blood, having had no educative preparation for menarche. Her sister, who was 11, was quite supportive, although her own periods had not yet begun. When the mother came home she assumed the menses to be painful and put the patient to bed. Her older sister began menstruation shortly thereafter. Unlike the patient, her breasts and pubic hair began to grow. The patient assumed her own breasts would never grow, and her sister encouraged her in this belief.

This older sister went on to sexual activities that the parents deplored but did not stop. The patient remained a quiet and withdrawn adolescent, devoted to religion and books. She daydreamed about boys but was afraid of them. She went to the earliest mass to avoid the shame of being seen with her family, since she felt the congregation looked down on them as social inferiors. In church, she imagined herself recognized as especially good and spiritual and relished the eventual damnation of her older sister. It would be she, Ms. Smith, who would be rescued by an ideal lover, she who would marry and have children she would love and raise properly.

Ms. Smith was sent to a religious finishing school and boarded there. She felt miserably homesick, but was only allowed to come home on occasional weekends. She was disappointed that her spiritual goodness was not recognized by her peers and teachers. The socially prominent girls, who told stories of their various sexual adventures with boys, were better groomed and dressed, and more appealing to teachers.

All three sisters had little social poise. Role models at home made ideal identifications difficult. The older sister learned by experience. Her early sexual exploits suggested a pseudofeminine role, but she was able to gradually learn a more appropriate gender identity during adolescent sexuality. She matured into an interesting and vivacious person. She dated a series of men, then married one whom the patient felt to be outstanding. This marriage proved sound, and the sister continued to develop into a warm and compassionate woman. Meanwhile, the younger sister was plagued by difficulties. She lived at home after graduation from high school, held marginal jobs, and had an impoverished social life.

While drastically limited in social activities, Ms. Smith did well academically in private school and was accepted into a good college. Wealth in the father's family, withheld from him personally, provided a trust fund for her education and later life. Her mother suggested that she major in economics, since it could lead to a glamorous life in the world of finance. Not knowing what else to do, she followed this suggestion. During the first years she felt insecure and somewhat fraudulent when she got good grades. Neither of the other sisters was able to complete college, and Ms. Smith could not stabilize her feelings of superiority or knowledgeability.

Dramatically, one day in church shortly after her twentieth birthday, she decided that her restraint from sexual activity was wasted. With a sense of anger, but no particular plan, she consumed more alcohol than usual to reduce her inhibitions and allowed herself to be seduced by a man she admired who was president of her church group. She then fantasied they were engaged. When he married someone else, she was surprised and dismayed.

On completion of college she obtained an unusually good position in a banking corporation, where, in addition to other advantages, her job had the romantic component of travel. She did satisfactory work but felt that she was only pretending to be capable. Contacts with co-workers frightened her. She gradually assumed a facade of poise and glamour, and entered into two affairs. In the first, she was clearly used and then dropped. In the second, she seemed to find the love she sought. Although she supported the young man financially, he appeared to be "on the way up." Again, despite the fact that nothing had been said, she assumed they were engaged. When he walked out on her, she felt bitter and depressed.

At this point of crisis, Ms. Smith was determined to reorganize herself. She recognized her continued lack of pleasure in sexual encounters; she felt fraudulent at work. She decided to change her position and actively to learn about sex. She selected nutrition as a field and entered graduate school with the aim of becoming a dietitian in a large medical center. She did not seek out particular men but entered into whatever affairs happenstance provided; they were uniformly unsatisfying and brief.

Attractive, personable, and successful young men were too overwhelming for her. Instead she tended to meet either older men or younger men who were ineligible for marriage. Courtship rituals with their slow explorations were also too anxiety provoking. Undressing together, especially slowly, was particularly threatening. She preferred to circumvent these rituals and tests, to get into bed as quickly as possible, feeling that the relationship would be more friendly and "less frantic" after intercourse.

The men she became involved with fell into two distinct groups in a personal hierarchy. One set of men was successful financially but less physically attractive or much older than she. Another set of men were younger and as good looking as she was, but were ineligible because of some other feature, and hence tolerable.

In the affairs with younger men she generally felt herself at first too interested and later a used and abused person. She would submit rapidly to intercourse, then expect to be taken out, especially to good restaurants, and shown off as a desirable companion. Instead, she would be driven directly home. Sometimes she would lend the lover money, clean his apartment, or perform some submissive task. She was unable to reveal, much less assert or insist upon, her own desires and need for dignity. Her one aggressive move was to reveal her lack of sexual pleasure with them, usually at some later point in the relationship. This challenge sometimes made men increase their efforts to get her to achieve a climax. They were never successful.

Older, or "lower status" men would fall in love with her, treat her tenderly, give her gifts. Then the glamorous, free, uninhibited swinger role that she initially played in every affair would rapidly deteriorate. She began to feel apathetic and deadened in the presence of these men. The only remaining excitement was in deciding when and how she would reveal her feelings and stop seeing them. To avoid hurting them, she would continue the affair; the men attempted to be more interesting, but these attempts would ultimately fail.

Ms. Smith would eventually challenge each man's virility by revelations of his inability to give her sufficient sexual satisfaction. Every affair ended in disaster. Either she was hurt, or she hurt some man. Her hopes for marriage and children grew dim. Sexual freedom and sensual pleasure did not come with sexual experience. Her graduate work entered the phase of internship, which began to go poorly as her inability to get along easily with other people interfered with her performance.

When a final affair that had seemed unusually promising for marriage collapsed, she felt painfully depressed and aware of a lack of progress in any area of her life. Someone she knew had been greatly helped by psychotherapy, and she decided to consult the same therapist. The extent of her difficulties, their complex basis in her personality structure, together with her strong motivation and intelligence, prompted a referral for consideration of psychoanalysis.

## Initial Clinical Observations and Formulations

The first interviews followed a pattern similar to Ms. Smith's relationships with men. Initially, she appeared as glamorous, animated, talkative, and provocative. Under the facade of an overmodulated and seemingly poised and vivacious state of mind shimmered signs of tension, fear, and despair. She changed topics readily, became passive, and wanted direction. Her statements contained vague descriptors such as "it," "you know," and "something." She was easily distracted, responded with rapid shifts in state of mind, was seductive without awareness, sought attention, and delivered her history in a global and impressionistic, rather than detailed, manner. She often trailed off in the middle of a topic, saying, "I don't know."

Initial formulations were drawn after the first few interviews. She felt exploited in relationships with sadistic men. Her goal was not gratification of masochistic aims so much as it was to make a prepayment of suffering that would magically entitle her to the later gratification of being rescued. The idealized father figure who would rescue her was either the same man, now transformed into positive aims by his guilt at having injured her, or another man aroused by her despair.

In relationships with some men she viewed as inferior to herself, she was able to ward off experience of a defective self-image. For example, an older lover would rhapsodize to her about her youthful beauty. She would then reject him for being of an inappropriate age for her. She would, however, be racked by guilt for having hurt him. She used the failure of men to arouse her as proof that she could not be excited and thus would never lose control and perform acts that were taboo (symbolically incestuous). In this role position, the power and danger of men were reversed into a pathetic, ridiculous impotence. She was not defective, but strong beyond their weak efforts, a heroine destined for some more romantic lover, as in a fairy tale.

In the history of her sparse relationships with women there was also a pattern. She was as pseudodaughterly with women as she was pseudosexual with men. Initially, she was compliant and overhelpful. When women came to rely on her, she would then either withdraw out of anger at not getting enough in return or wrest power from them in the form of job responsibilities or the approval of superiors (usually male). If and when she won a victory, she would give up because she felt unable to carry it off to some point of completion. In general, she was afraid of continued attachment to any competent, effective, active person of either sex.

These patterns with men and women seemed to be an unconscious attempt to reconstruct her earlier family situation in adult life, much as it was schematically organized in her mind during early development. She had not given up the hope of union with her father or the hope of a nurturing and caretaking rescue by an idealized father-mother.

Ms. Smith's main defenses were repression and denial. The

mental contents warded off by these maneuvers were related to sexual strivings, aggressive impulses, and the threat of desertion and isolation. Anxiety, fear, depression, and guilt were activated by the particular aims and object connections of these themes. But the detailed dynamics were not evident at this early period. Because of her neurotic character structure, her strong motivation, and her intelligence, analysis was considered the treatment of choice.

The analysis is described first in sequence. Later, the treatment process is reconstructed in terms of modifications of cognitive style and object relationships.

## First Year

As mentioned previously, Ms. Smith presented herself as vivacious, earnest, intelligent, and compliant during the evaluation hours. She asked many questions, asked for direction, and requested little favors such as telephone usage, carfare, and time changes. Then, after a decision for a trial of analysis, her grooming became much less meticulous, her demeanor more childlike and anxious, her periods of silence became more frequent, and she wanted to be instructed or prodded on how to continue.

She used this initial series of hours to test the analyst's response to provocation. When he was neither too reactive to attention-getting devices nor too responsive to demands for support, she began talking of current difficulties at work and in a new love affair. This most recent affair was begun impulsively, coinciding with the onset of treatment, and it was seen later as a defensive maneuver to prevent a positive transference. She had read about analysis and felt she was expected to fall in love with her therapist. She thought this preposterous, an indication of the eccentric ideas the therapist probably held and the last thing that would ever happen, however much the analyst might try to evoke such feelings.

In any topical context she continued to test the analyst to see if he would respond erotically when she was provocative, comfort her when she was upset, or pursue her when she was distant. This pattern was repetitive, at increasingly clearer levels of awareness, throughout most of the treatment period. After weeks of these episodes, she entered the room late and distraught. Obviously shaken, she stood dramatically against the door and announced that she had come only to say goodbye, that she could not go on with analysis because, among other things, she could not tolerate lying on the couch.

She agreed to talk this over and spent several sessions sitting in a chair. The constant neutrality and "coolness" of the analyst reassured her, but she complained bitterly that she needed tranquilizers and directive counseling from a "real person." She continued analysis and resumed use of the couch, but the occurrence of sad, apathetic, and hopeless states of mind increased. She spent mornings in bed and avoided her internship duties. She then had to take a leave of absence from school to avert being officially dropped, began three affairs at once, and risked pregnancy. She had stopped birth control pills because of side effects but was too frightened of gynecologists to obtain a diaphragm.

During the analytic hours she demanded and pleaded for help. She found it hard to verbalize her ideas and feelings and wanted the analyst to disclose his personal weaknesses so that she would feel comfortable enough to reveal hers. She reported many other kinds of treatment in which therapists were more revealing, kinder, more giving, faster, and better. She admitted that she consciously withheld information about current happenings. The analyst's response to these various maneuvers was to clarify what she was saying, largely by repetition. For example, with transference issues he might say, "You want me to do something more active to help you," or "You don't think you can stand it if I just keep listening and tell you what I think is going on." With outside issues, the analyst attempted to clarify patterns of interaction and cause and effect. Again, the style involved short repetitions of what she had said and occasional requests for more detail.

Some additional flavor of the analytic process may be provided by a process note of a typical hour, five months into treatment.

*Process note.* She arrived on time (she had frequently been late). Although she spoke in her usual disjointed way, with trailing off, frequent "I don't knows," and unconnected phrases, she seemed to express a guarded enthusiasm. She described an observation she had made about herself at the end of the previous hour. She noticed that she had rushed out of the room without looking at me at the end of the hour and that she felt nervous at the time. It was as I had said previously: she was scared when she felt intimate, telling of her feelings during the hours. She had also felt humiliated when I said the hour was up and had wanted to get out before I noticed her feelings.

That night she had a dream. She was in my office and was giving permission for some sort of operation. Then I changed into her employer who, in the dream, was cast as a doctor discussing something with another doctor. He was going to operate on her eye with a laser beam, without knowing how she felt about it. She emphasized, by repetition, the importance of her fear that the doctors did not know how frightened she was.

Her associations to laser beams were of superhuman power, Superman and his X-ray vision, and "something that might get into" her and "destroy" her. Doctors were persons who were impersonal, powerful, greedy, and did what they wanted. My only comment concerned one element in the dream that had to do with the dangers of vision; now that she felt committed to the analysis she was afraid of insight, of the light analysis might shed on her problems.

She admitted that she was frightened of the analysis now that it seemed possible to her. She added associations to a memory of being in a doctor's office with her mother. It was a regular appointment of her mother's, and there was a fat woman who was there frequently. Ms. Smith used to fantasy that the fat woman came to get sexual pleasure, that she was excited by and enjoyed examinations. I asked what kind of examinations, and she said the doctor was a gynecologist.

She went on to say that she sometimes fantasies that she is her mother and imagines having operations that would be unpleasant and painful. I said she spoke of these painful operations as if they had a delicious quality. She was startled, paused, then said this reminded her that she had recently gone to the dentist. He injected Novocain into her gums, which became numb, and she felt good. Then she realized her tooth would actually be pulled and she became nervous and cried. He was kind and she felt very close to him. She always feels very close to doctors after some such procedure. She usually tells herself this is because the anxiety is over. But maybe it is because there is a sexual component to the relationship. She then saw this as one of my ideas and denied it.

The next topic was a story about her not wanting a new male friend to know she had sexual feelings toward him because he was married. I said that she was afraid of knowing, herself, that she had sexual feelings. She was silent, then blurted out that she had planned before the hour to say what she had said up to this point but didn't want to go any further. I said she was frightened of the idea of letting her thoughts come spontaneously. While that was what she was saying, she seemed startled to hear me say it and interpreted the remark as if it were a directive that she must free associate. She wondered how long it usually took analytic patients to learn to free associate. She liked the idea that it was taking her an unusually long time and that she was a difficult patient because that would show that she had great personal integrity.

In subsequent hours Ms. Smith revealed indirect sexual fantasies of the analyst in dreams and daydreams, but denied their implications. She developed a phobia of walking on the street near the office, with a specific theme of fear of being seen by the analyst. This phobia generalized to a fear of riding buses because people might look at her and feel disgust, knowing that she was going to see an analyst whom she, they would presume, loved madly and foolishly.

She continued to insist that she badly needed sexual advice, support, and warmth, but was not getting it. Her wishes that she be counseled in sexual technique closely paralleled her most frequent masturbation fantasy, in which she imagined a woman lying on an examining table. A nurse told her that the doctor was examining the woman and that the procedure was done for medical reasons, was quite safe, and had nothing to do with sex. It was implied that later the doctor would gradually and carefully explain all kinds of details about sexual intercourse. The doctor, in the visual images of the fantasy, was scarcely present and the woman was only vaguely herself.

In spite of her demands to be given more, she reacted in an almost startled manner to many statements by the analyst. She episodically insisted that his clarifications were forcing her to go too far. The analyst and psychoanalysis were alternately boring and weird, orthodox and decadent, pushing her too fast and not helping at all. Nonetheless, toward the end of the year, she was working rather hard on clarifying many important life patterns and getting a first approximation of their meanings. A turning point, perhaps equal in importance to her not leaving analysis when frightened, was her rejection of a marriage proposal made by a wealthy, attractive young man who would have taken her away to another country. The proposal reenacted one of her favorite fantasies, and her reluctance to accept it signaled recognition of the deep-seated and thus far unresolved nature of her characterological problems.

She began to accept confrontations and clarifications about her global denials, childlike establishment of simple rules (a form of rationalization), and abrupt cessation of topics. As her life patterns became clear, they seemed very sad to her and she became depressed.

A one-month vacation by the analyst deepened this depression. Ms. Smith stated she had made the wrong choice when she decided to continue analysis and might "go crazy" during the free interval.

She berated the returning analyst for deserting her. At the same time she began to bring up pertinent memories from childhood in which she had experienced similar feelings from maternal deprivations. Her envy of her older sister, who was able to "get away" from the family, and of her younger sister, who received special care within the family, also emerged. Her angry wishes that this older sister be punished for her sexual activities were associated with her hitherto unconscious guilt over her own sexual acts. The wish to be like her sick younger sister and deserve special and continuous attention also emerged and was connected to similar feelings of yearning for attention from the analyst. Her wishes emerged clearly in a dream: she had gone crazy, and the analyst was thus forced to take care of her "properly" by bringing her to live in his home-sanitorium. The scene was of a white-columned mansion, surrounded by tranquil lawns, with therapy conducted beside a swimming pool. Special among a group of woman patients, she would lie along the diving board as if asleep and receive tender care.

## Second Year

The anniversary of her first year in analysis led to a renewed period of depression. Ms. Smith had heard that special patients finished in one year and she was disappointed. She reacted by setting a termination date one year hence. She found it intolerable to think of analysis lasting any longer than that. She made increased efforts at self-observation and at free association. Guarded enthusiasm about understanding herself and gaining control of her behavior led to an increasingly evident transference neurosis in which she tried to ward off sexual interest, anxiety, and guilt.

Various arousing and traumatic childhood memories were reported, such as her fearful fascination as she was allowed to watch her father shave off his pubic hair. She expected the analyst to be enthused by such revelations because they would prove the validity of his eccentric psychoanalytic theories. While she discounted the meaning of such memories, she both feared and expected that they would lead to fervid cooperation on analytic work, lyrical excitement, and then a carried-away sexual transport of both parties during the treatment hour.

Trying out these ideas in relatively clear language without such results gave her an increased sense of safety. With a lessened fear of intimacy, and also as a resistance to the transference, she became closer to one of two concurrent male friends. Her exploitation and rescue fantasies were clarified. While trying out greater freedom, she developed anxiety attacks when with her male friend or en route to the treatment hours.

Once again preoccupied with the analysis and analyst, she decided to give up her male friends until she was cured of her sexual inhibitions. She masturbated more and began work on her recurrent masturbation fantasies. She recognized her inhibitions against representing men, penises, or vaginas even in her private fantasies. Then the woman nurse figure became a primary sexual object. Although she was afraid of becoming a homosexual, she threatened the analyst by stating her intentions to experiment with homosexuality if he did not hurry and cure her inhibitions with men. Her main homosexual fantasies were a wish to stare at large breasts, and sexualized wishes for nurturance at the breast.

When the threat of homosexuality did not evoke a nonanalytic response from the therapist, and while under pressure from the clarification and interpretation of the transference meanings of these threats, she again carried her testing of the analytic situation to an extreme. She engaged in behavior that carried the risk of being assaulted by men. She started several new affairs, and then threatened suicide during the depression that resulted when these impulsive relationships ended badly.

The analyst responded with tactful and limited interpretations, avoiding interventions of rescue or rejection that she tried to provoke. She seemed to develop an increased sense of the analyst as a safe and stable person; there was reduction in her use of denial and repression, and turbulent acting out also diminished. Sexual fantasies about the analyst were spoken of clearly and linked to childhood memories of relationships with her father. The emotional responses were more fully developed and were experienced as tolerable levels of anxiety, depression, and guilt, rather than as emotional storms.

### Third Year

The third year could be summarized as a working-through of various constellations of ideas and feelings toward Ms. Smith's father and mother as repeated in transference neuroses. While interpretation of resistances remained a prominent technique, her responses were different. Instead of denial and repression, she changed her defensive operations. She used dreams, free associations, and recollections well, accepted and helped with reconstructions, and experienced and reported bodily sensations and feeling states as they fluctuated during the hour. Instead of global depressions, she felt sad and disappointed about specific facets of her life.

In general, she moved from a passive to an active stance. She had been working as a secretary after dropping out of her graduate training. She was now able to get a paramedical job on the basis of her partial training as a dietitian and reapply to school.

With continued work on her defective body image, avoidance of ideas about sex, inhibitions of arousal, and fear of altered consciousness during intercourse, she began to have more pleasure during sexual activities with men. Her first orgasm occurred during mutual masturbation; she then had an orgasm during intercourse. There were still difficulties, however, and fuller erotic experiences were not achieved until after a termination date was set some time later.

With increased freedom in heterosexual activities and fantasies, her free-floating anxiety attacks changed into phobic forms. For example, after experimenting with fellatio for the first time she feared that an ordinary facial pimple was a syphilitic canker. Her aggressive and castrating impulses toward men also emerged into clear representational expression. She wanted to control the man's penis, or at least govern in an exaggerated way when it would or would not enter her body. She feared that without such control her body would be hurt.

This fear of being hurt was reasonable in view of her childlike body image. As she was able to think and communicate more clearly, she could reveal that her self-image did not include a vaginal opening. During intercourse she had been numb in the pelvic area, although genital feelings were possible when she was alone and masturbated. Now she was able to explore herself and use words to label genital parts. The "nonexistent area" in her body image went through stages; first of cloacal chaos in which her vagina and rectum were imagined as coalesced, and then a sense of a separate, inadequate but discrete vagina about two inches in maximum length.

Not surprisingly, pregnancy fantasies emerged in dreams, then in daydreams and reverie. Her masturbation fantasies evolved in a series of increasingly mature forms. First, she imagined herself as a vague child-woman, then as a man, being the one in control and telling a virgin about both pelvic examinations and the sex act. Next, repeating the homosexual phase of the previous year, she imagined herself as a woman doing things to another woman, and, finally, herself as a woman being fondled by a very gentle, reassuring man.

This work led to intensification of the sexualized transference neurosis. She became frightened by her emotional experiences during therapy hours. She fantasied that she would cry so much she could never stop, or else that the analyst would be so moved that the love affair would at last become irresistible. Alternate exhibitionistic and voyeuristic impulses were clarified and related to her phobias and to various recalled experiences with both parents.

## Fourth Year

A mixture of yearning, frustration, hostility, and disgust toward her mother had emerged episodically throughout Ms. Smith's analysis, and at this point poignant emotional memories about her occupied center stage. Entwined with these memories were her envy of both sisters, the jealousy and the thwarted competitive urges toward her older sister, and resentment for the attentive ministrations received by the younger sister. She worked through several patterns of relationships between herself and other women, both historically and in the present, as well as those mirrored currently in the analytic situation.

In one of these configurations she was the poor, passive, helpless victim of the hostility and lack of concern from her mother, the analyst, or an older woman. At other times, she remained a hapless victim, but the other person was not so much an aggressor as simply insufficient. An idealized masculine rescuer was, in a life script on the order of that described by Berne (1961), supposed to find and care for her at this point. When she was a child of about 4 or 5 her father did fulfill this role, taking her for car rides to cheer her up. Her ideal version of him was later displaced by disillusionment but remained as a configuration of hope for another hero.

In another configuration, she at last unleashed the destructive reactions to her disappointments. To her great surprise, embarrassment, anxiety, guilt, and pleasure, she was able to lash out verbally at the analyst. She had fantasies of shooting him and of blowing up his car, and feared visiting her parents because she would expose their hypocrisies and denials. Once again, the analysis was a dangerous provocation and could be responsible for any mayhem she might commit.

As she was able to tolerate the experience of strong feelings without a sense of losing control, the various representations of herself in relation to members of her family were described, reviewed, and reconsidered with increasing clarity. Using her adult mind, she was able to compare memories and fantasies with one another. Compartmentalization of good and bad images of each important person was reduced, and she had feelings of "realization" about people. For example, she was deeply moved by being able to remember her father as having both good and bad qualities. He was interesting, sincere, aesthetic, even powerful at times, while also neurotic, infantile, perverse, seductive, and unreliable.

Her self-representations had also changed as therapy progressed, but now these changes were more clearly delineated. There was a period of conscious alteration in her sense of her body and her identity. She had fantasies and dreams of the analyst's wife, a woman she had never heard of or seen, but presumed existed. The wife was imagined variously as her sisters, mother, and ideal self. First, the wife was imagined as an idealized and flamboyant mistress-type named "Titsy." Ms. Smith also fantasied the wife as sickly or fat, and herself as a yearned-for substitute. Then the wife image in dreams changed to a mature, attractive, concerned woman who spoke kindly to her. In one of the patient's dreams she had come to the analyst's home. Uneasy about how appropriate the visit might be, she was told by the wife that it was all right, and they then talked sociably together. Ms. Smith identified in a comparatively deliberate way with these idealized projections. She allowed herself to continue complaining about her own mother, to feel sad that her mother would never change, and again, to fantasy being the child of the analyst and his wife.

During this period, Ms. Smith changed her style of grooming and dress to one that seemed somehow to "fit" her personality. She experienced guilt at entering a different status, one higher than her mother, especially as she was now able to meet and get to know professional men. Finally, she had feelings of "reality" about her mother, was able to accept her parents' limitations, and to give up some of her own feelings of contemptuous superiority. During the first part of the analysis she had been remote from her parents. During the third year, she had visited them and returned disappointed. In view of her own altered impressions of them and her feelings of control, she had expected a magical change in them that would make them capable of more intimate relationships with her. Now, when she visited them again, she felt that she could accept them as they were. She no longer felt the need to accuse them, nor was she disappointed by the limitations still imposed on her relationship with them.

Her sexual fantasies continued to shift, and she felt more open toward both the physical and emotional components of relating to men. She also began to have experiences of "reality" that were simply keen perceptions with knowledge of what was going on. She felt as if her body parts and those of her sexual partner were real, and this surprised her. She recognized a residual fear of enthusiasm in sex and linked this to her fear of enthusiasm in the analysis. Resistance was generally absent, and major interpretive efforts seemed unnecessary as the work progressed unfettered.

She felt in control of her life, effective, able to think and feel and to work out her own solutions to everyday life problems. Ideas of transience, life ending in death, aging, and menopause occurred and filled her with sadness. Then she discussed ideas of terminating the analysis. After several emergences and avoidances of this idea, a termination date six months ahead was agreed upon. She then experienced this date-setting as an unfair trick and as a loss of interest on the part of the analyst.

The ending was ill-timed, she felt, because, while her symptoms were gone and her life was in control, she had neither married and had a child nor embarked securely on her profession. A series of transference repetitions occurred in which the analyst was compared to the uncaring mother. Gratified by his fine performance in curing her, the analyst now no longer cared what she might or might not do, and planned to get rid of her before giving everything. On the other hand, he was also like the tricky, eccentric father. The termination was a way to confront her with her residual problems, or perhaps a device that would lead to a postanalytic love tryst. These reactions were readily translated into words and understanding, with toleration and working through of related emotions and memories.

At the end, she felt a little sad that she had lost some interest in the analysis, and was very grateful for the results of the work. She had occasional fears of relapse, but according to the follow-up mentioned earlier, these fears were unfounded.

## THE PROCESSES OF CHANGE

Clinical inferences about Ms. Smith can now be reviewed in terms of basic patterns both before and at the end of treatment. Changes will be considered first in terms of the classic psychoanalytic points of view (Rapaport and Gill 1958), then in terms of a cognitive-pschodynamic point of view (Horowitz 1986, 1987, 1988). Discussing the six metapsychological points of view one by one leads to such redundancy that they have been combined into three compatible pairs: the developmental and adaptational, the structural and topographic, and the economic and dynamic points of view.

### Development and Adaptation

In the hierarchical model of metapsychology suggested by Gedo and Goldberg (1973) and Gedo (1988), Ms. Smith would be seen as beginning the analysis in that stage of development in which the main hazards are disturbances in self-integration in relation to moral anxiety over incestuous and aggressive object-related strivings. Her principal defenses, repression and denial, developed because of both a cognitive preparedness for such modes at the developmental stage and the family practice of utilizing these defenses in communication.

Her characterological development was also colored by an ambivalent attachment to her mother. She yearned for maternal care as might be exemplified by cuddling and warm empathic interest. She got less than she wanted and was reactively angry but did not surrender hope of affectionate rapprochement.

During childhood development, Ms. Smith had successfully differentiated herself from her mother, and she had a gender identification as female. But precursors of adult female sexuality, such as flirtatiousness and display, were warded off. A self schema as an attractive female was not integrated into a supraordinate self-schematization (Horowitz 1991). Instead she felt partially defective. Her childlike and defective self schema was not revised because everyday forms of sexual self-images and representations were warded off. In general, this was done to avoid the threat of guilt and anxiety over sexual excitement and fear of sexual assault if she were to be provocative. With analysis, these warding-off maneuvers were interpreted, clarified, and counteracted by intentional acts of thought and behavior. The childlike and defective self schemas were reprocessed in terms of conscious experience of current self-images and representations. She was gradually able to integrate female genitalia into her self schemas, leading to increased confidence in her capacity for sexual relations.

In addition to this progression toward completion of the genital phase of psychosexual development, Ms. Smith had persistent conflicts unresolved in the oral phase as outlined in earlier chapters and suggested by Marmor (1953), Easser and Lesser (1965), and Zetzel (1970). Strong yearnings to be nurtured, literally and symbolically, were associated unconsciously with a magical belief that someone always suffered when such desires were present. Expectations of others being attuned to her emotional expressions were distorted in the direction of expecting that others would be repressively oblivious, like her mother, or intrusively undermodulated, like her father.

Either she would suck dry and deplete her mother, as her mother virtually told her she had done, or she would be deliberately neglected as unworthy of her mother's concern. These oral-aggressive components of this constellation and feelings extended into a blurred anal–sadistic dimension in which she wanted to let go of her feelings but feared a disastrous loss of control. Emotions had to be tightly inhibited (Shengold 1988). If she knew she was angry with her mother or any other nurturative-frustrating figure, then she would lose control and have a destructive temper tantrum. The fear of loss of sphincter control also colored her sexual experiments, since she had explicit fearful fantasies of bowel or bladder mishaps if enthusiastic sexual responses were to occur.

Analytic work instigated the conscious processing of these variegated and blurred themes. Ms. Smith was able to differentiate sexual strivings from wishes to be held and comforted. Her impulsivity in sexual relationships was attenuated once she could seek what she wanted at any particular time without confusions of aim and could accept partial gratification. She came to recognize when she was enraged over frustration and how she warded off the emergence of such anger.

Her oedipal fantasies were integrated with an unusual frequency of real life events. Her father was sexually provocative in his exhibitionism, and there was a real impairment in the mother–father relationship. Any fantasy she might entertain in conscious awareness was difficult to isolate from memories of expectations of real occurrences.

Her self-object schemas at the onset of analysis concretized an internalized version of these familial patterns into a set of stereotyped roles. These roles, to be described later in detail, were imposed compulsively on every relationship. Real experiences were held at such great distance, by nonappraisal of meanings and by general denial, that these stereotypes were perpetuated rather than revised. Hence, all men were alternately tricky, exciting, and dangerously self-seeking or else they were devalued, disgusting, or depressing. During analysis these stereotypes were compared with current self and object images with appropriate and gradual revision. As a result of improved recognition of real possibilities, she developed a more appropriate and extensive repertoire of potential roles. This helped her to act differently, to understand people better, and to obtain social reinforcement for her improvement.

The overstimulating oedipal father and the hostile, withholding, "bad," pregenital mother had been warded off from conscious and emotional experience but had at the same time operated as perpetual stereotypes for "role-casting" others in her interpersonal relationships. Nonrecognition was necessary because both stereotypes led to relationships in which she was exquisitely vulnerable to reactive anxiety and guilt.

The analytic situation allowed Ms. Smith to first test the analyst by her various transference *behaviors*. When the analyst was neither excessively nice nor excessively mean, it became safe to begin to *experience* the maternal transference; just as when the analyst was neither too provocative nor too remote or "selfish," she could begin to experience the paternal transference.

With transference experience came childhood memories linked to the particular feeling state as well as acting out of the configurations in extra-analytic current relationships. The combination of childhood memories, transference experience, and a certain amount of "playing out" in real life led to greater freedom to express childlike emotions and to alter the stereotyped self-object schemas.

Maturation was evident in her surrender of both her pregenital and her oedipal demands on the world and in her simultaneous experience of less fear of retribution. These changes will be reviewed in greater detail in the final section of this chapter when revision of self and object schemas and role-relationships are discussed.

**Structural and Topographic Points of View**

In the structural point of view, one differentiates three sets of functions. One is ego or "I-like" functions; the second is id or "it-like" drives; the third is superego or functions of value and conscience-like appraisals of self from a vantage of morals, ideals, and social conventions. Topography refers to conscious, preconscious, and unconscious levels of information and information processing. Elements in the preconscious can be raised upon volition to consciousness; this is not so for unconscious elements.

Before analysis, Ms. Smith operated in a constricted way. Control processes inhibited topics and concepts that would lead to intense emotions. The functions most severely affected were attention deployment, conscious thought, memory, and fantasy. Her experience of emotion was inhibited. She feared any strong feelings and reacted to them as if they were instrusive and uncontrollable forces.

Over-generalization of schematized beliefs led her to react to her peers as if they were her parents. Taboos against sexual and aggressive strivings were primitive and led to a strong predisposition toward guilt. Like the primary impulses, ideas that would evoke guilty feelings were repressed and yet occasionally intruded into conscious awareness.

Because of the general use of repression and denial, she seldom knew exactly what she wished and could not plan effective action toward gratification. Instead, there was episodic emotional experience, especially anxiety, without clear relationship of the feelings to ideational representations.

Conscious experiences had to be avoided not only because of the guilty responses that might occur, but because thoughts were equated with actions. This posture was based on her own fears of loss of control and the religious attitude that harboring certain thoughts could be sinful. These attitudes were reexamined during analysis, and she learned to qualify differences between thought and action. As she became able to experience thought in areas of conflict, she was able to review and rework the various attitudes that contributed to conflict.

This review process had many facets, not the least of which was the development of an integrated set of her own reflected-upon values, goals, and principles. At the onset of analysis she had little sense of an authentic autonomous self. She preferred the "swinger" self-representation to the depressed, neurotic, and childlike self representation that seemed the only alternative. Either role was in conflict with values that were not integrated into her self schemas but rather functioned as introjects of mother and father. When she experienced herself as a sexually active swinger, she was vulnerable to internal experiences of an introject of her rule-bound, sin-preoccupied mother. This sense of another person reprimanding her was a form of self-criticism for being corrupt and evil. When she experienced herself as a "good" woman who worked responsibly to do her duty, then an equivalent introject associated with her father excoriated her for being a passive victim: dead, inhibited, uninteresting, and stupidly compliant. In either instance, the values seemed to have their own activity, separate from herself.

In the course of the analysis, she realized the extent to which the various value systems were components of her self schemas. She could reexamine her standards and revise attitudes that she did not feel were rational or in accord with her growing sense of adult morality. As a way of regulating life choices she began to adhere to a set of principles actively avowed by the self rather than by punishment-oriented fears.

At first, the acquisition of new skills and the modification of old habits occurred because of her positive relationship with the therapist. This relationship was based on both the therapeutic alliance, with its components of realistic hope and trust, and the positive transference with its component fantasies of love and attention. The strength of the introjected therapist, part real and part fantasy, counteracted the strength of parental introjects because he was the immediate potential source of rewards and punishments.

The power of ideas attributed to the therapist, such as the acceptability of thinking the unthinkable, gained ascendancy over equivalent ideas about criticisms attributed to parents and God. Later, as transference fantasies were relinquished, Ms. Smith tended to identify with the therapist's neutral, objective, rational, thoughtful, reality-attentive, patient, and nonjudgmental operations. Thus, she learned to conceptualize clearly where she once had been globally vague. The learning occurred both by the trial-and-error discovery that clarity helped her to feel in control and by the automatic learning that goes with valuing and identifying with another person.

## Dynamic and Economic Points of View

The dynamic point of view deals with interacting forces, especially wishes, feared consequences of wishes, and defenses or controls of impulses to prevent such threats by warding off ideas and emotions. The economic point of view deals with the intensity of these forces in terms of types of motives.

As described in previous sections, two clusters of warded-off mental contents and typical defensive operations characterized Ms. Smith's dynamics. One cluster was oedipal in configuration. The second was concerned with pregenital ambivalence centered on her mother. In the oedipal cluster of impulse–defense configurations, sexual strivings toward her father conflicted with (1) taboos against incest, (2) fear of competitive maternal retaliation, and (3) fear of loss of control and sexual assault. Secondary themes in this cluster included destructive wishes against mother and father with reactive guilt. The destructive wishes against her father included a desire to remove his masculine power and independence. The destructive wishes against her mother included a desire to take away her adult female genitalia and childbearing capacities and to assume the mother's role in the family. Destructive wishes also concerned her sisters. If she could rid the family of them, she could occupy their positions.

This complex of oedipal themes was particularly difficult to work through during childhood because she was not dealing with her own unconscious fantasy. Her father's real sexual displays added danger. If she were exhibitionistic herself or voyeuristically interested in him, then he might lose control. Her principal method of warding off these threats was inhibition of sensation, thought, and action. Total inhibition maintained emotional states within tolerable limits, but the relative strength of strivings and external stimulation exceeded her capacity for complete avoidance.

Under threat of a partial failure in repressive maneuvers, she experienced intrusive attacks of anxiety and guilt, which she saw as dangerous lapses of control, even if ideation remained unclear. To reduce the threat, secondary defenses such as displacement were instituted, resulting in the formation of symptoms such as phobias and hypochondriasis.

The change process involved revising the expression–defense configuration for this cluster of themes. The first step was confrontation, enabling her to recognize the extensiveness of denial as a defensive maneuver. Awareness led to control and altered the balance of forces between defensive and expressive aims. Conscious thought increased, and she found herself able to tolerate clarity. For example, as she tested out the analyst in the transference situation, she found him safely nonreactive to her provocations. This sense of safety, along with attention to her tendency to deny ideationally what she was doing behaviorally, led to awareness that she was acting out exhibitionistic and voyeuristic fantasies. These current behavioral strivings were then conceptualized.

Once conceptualized, the ideas and feelings could be linked associatively with childhood memories, hitherto repressed in large part, of her felt emotions and response to her father's behavior. The segregation of memory fragments decreased, allowing a coherent story to emerge.

As a further example of repression, a specific memory can be considered. At the onset of treatment, she remembered her father lying nude on her bed. The memory was not, in this sense, repressed. As the analysis progressed, she recalled and reexperienced her visual curiosity about the movement of his semi-erect penis, a detail of the memory that had been repressed. She was able to reexperience her feelings of revulsion and anger at her mother for not making her father stop behaving in this way.

The connection of the feelings for her mother with the memory of her father helped integrate the experience into a holistic framework of memory. She realized how similar these feelings were to her currently active desire to see the analyst's car, his wife, and his body. As the associational connections were worked through, the need to ward off these desires by denial and repression lessened, and she could then allow herself to dream of them without great humiliation, guilt, and anxiety. This trial of clear thinking about a subject in the comparative safety of the treatment situation trained her and convinced her of the acceptability of thinking about conflictual ideas in current everyday life. Through such processes she learned to change her previously habitual inhibitory style.

Once defensive maneuvers were less mandatory, there was a general decrease in tension, and she could direct her capacities to other efforts. As memories and fantasies could be reviewed in conscious secondary-process thought, primary-process associations and appraisals became less powerful as determinants of action plans. For example, she could get to know the qualities of a new male acquaintance by checking and rechecking her perceptions and appraisals, rather than by entering into a relationship based on primitive stereotypes.

The second main cluster of warded-off contents we have already labeled as pregenital. It included an unconscious evaluation of herself as insufficiently nurtured as a child, and led to arousal of depression and rage. These emotions were averted by repression, denial, rationalization, fantasy distortion of reality, and reaction formation. She could also use undoing, although not to the extent found in obsessional personalities. When anxiety and guilt, provoked by the first cluster of sexual themes, emerged in the analysis, she would shift the organization of her experience to the second cluster of deprivation themes. These deprivation themes evoked a mood that oscillated between resigned helplessness and a kind of angry sadness, and tended to reduce sexual excitation.

## THE COGNITIVE–PSYCHODYNAMIC POINT OF VIEW

The modification of defenses as they occur in the form of resistances is essential if transferences are to evolve, be examined and be resolved. In the following section, the focus is first on the thought, emotion, and control processes by which defenses are accomplished and on the alterations of these cognitive processes in the course of treatment. The next focus is on how modification of defensive styles permits both revision and development of person schemas of self and other, a structural change related to behavior pattern change. An emphasis on new learning will be added to the familiar concepts of insight, working through, and conflict resolution.

## Patterns of Change in Ideas and Feelings

Ms. Smith manifested many of the characteristics accorded the prototype of the hysterical personality. As discussed in earlier chapters, Shapiro (1965) has given the most authoritative and penetrating analysis of how these traits are mediated by particular cognitive styles. Along with other leading theorists of cognitive controls, Shapiro emphasizes the impressionistic distortions of incoming perceptual stimuli, the rapid and short-circuited appraisal of meanings, and the limited categories and availability of memory as central aspects of thought in the hysterical personality (see also Gardner et al. 1959, Klein et al. 1962).

For the description of shifts in the neurotic cognitive style of Ms. Smith, it is desirable to clearly describe segments of the cognitive process, from perception to decisive completion of a train of thought. Then the change in each segment can be discussed in terms of the treatment process and final outcome. To avoid excessive segmentalization, four areas for discussion have been selected: perceptual attention, representation, association, and resolution of incongruities.

## Perceptual Attention

Ms. Smith habitually deployed her attention in a global manner. Her descriptions of events were vague, impressionistic, and left the listener with little sense of the context or order of events. It is possible that this trait might have been a style of communication, but as the analyst empathized and entered deeply into the patient's experience, it seemed that vagueness extended to her perceptions as well and was not just an inhibited form of speech. Ms. Smith described events that occurred within the analytic hour in the same way, and when asked about the quality of her experience, she confirmed these inferences. At the same time, details of the environment that might relate to her current wishful and fearful expectancies were hyperattended (Fairbairn 1954, Wisdom 1961, Myerson 1969). That is, details of the environment symbolically relevant to her concerns were discovered rapidly but were not accurately appraised; they were misinterpreted due to errors contributed by her excessive use of certain person schemas (Horowitz 1991).

For example, during a period of heightened sexualized transference feelings, she had frequent illusions that men she saw walking on the street were the analyst. She recognized peripheral cues quickly but retained the illusory recognition until the men passed quite close to her. She was alert to another person's interests and could mold her self-presentation to fit. Details were disproportionate, overemphasized, and combined with generalities about facets of an interpersonal situation.

While she was quick to note the surface attitudes of another person, she seemed unaware of her own acts, of what was revealed by her facial expression or bodily gestures. She might move her head coquettishly or swing her legs, and not realize that she was doing this. Such imprecision of perception seemed to be due to a too-rapid construction of images, an overreadiness toward conclusion, and an overusage of expectancy schemas. Perceptual rechecking, which would have counteracted a rapid illusion such as seeing the analyst in the street, was seldom utilized; thus, errors of assumption and extended illusions occurred.

During analysis, the defensive reasons for not recognizing her own actions were interpreted. It was paradoxical but possible to call her vagueness of perception to her attention. The interventions led her to conscious efforts to counteract her automatic, nonconscious tendencies. She slowly learned to notice details, observe her own acts, and gather clues about her own motivational states and those of others. This learning was made possible by her increased tolerance for conscious contemplation as well as experience of her emotional responses to the incoming information.

Increased awareness led to all other changes in information processing just as, transactively, the changes in how she processed information produced a wider repertoire of schemas. These styles and changes are summarized in Table 5–2.

### Representation

Information can gain expression in lexical, image (in various sensory systems), and enactive (bodily) modes of representation (Horowitz 1988). Any person's style can be discussed in terms of his or her habitual usage of and translations among the three styles. In an "ideal" person, representation in one mode could be readily translated into other forms of representation. Such cross-modal

## Table 5–2

### Patterns and Change in Attention

Style

1. On wholes rather than details.
2. On persons' surface attitudes toward her, rather than their intentions.
3. Selective inattention to some of her own actions.
4. Dominated by stimuli relevant to active, wishful, or fearful person schemas.

Change during Treatment

Learned to attend to details, her own acts, contexts of interpersonal situations, and to clues to motives of self and other.

expression gives breadth and depth to meaning. Ms. Smith habitually used enactive and image modes for conflicted mental contents and she tended to inhibit translation of such information into words. Her enactive representations included body movements indicative of sexual interest. As mentioned in the previous section, her awareness of these expressions was quite limited. She did not know she behaved provocatively and could not label her posture, gesture, or facial expression with specific meaningful words.

Representation of images derived through perception was also affected by a particular style. As already indicated, schemas of expectancy had relative dominance over accurate perception in forming internal working models of situations.

The dynamic themes of looking and being seen, sexual interest, guilt, anxiety, and anger provided many such templates. More specifically, self-object dyads, centered on herself as waif and on an object as rescuer or aggressor, provided a prefiguration for appraisal of new information. The results were representations that composited sets of information from within and without but that were heavily slanted in favor of internal contributions.

These factors contributing to a given internal working model of an external situation were scrutinized carefully in multiple episodes of microanalysis as interpersonal encounters and fantasies were reviewed (see Horowitz 1974). The verbal nature of the analytic situation, with its prevailing demand for translation of experience into words, led to details of report beyond Ms. Smith's personal tendency to vague and global descriptions. If she were describing an emotionally difficult event, such as an encounter with a potential male friend, fragments of representation of what happened would be gradually pieced together. Reconstructive efforts fleshed out the context of the episode and sequence of interactions. These reconstructions could then be contrasted with her initially vague and perhaps distorted image representations of what happened.

Similar processes clarified the patient–analyst situation. These recurrent efforts led to changes in her ability to experience an immediate situation. In addition to clearly experiencing the inter-relations of meanings expressed in enactive and image modes, she was able to verbalize what was happening.

Free association is a somewhat different experience for each person. For Ms. Smith, the experience was composed largely of a flow of visual images. To communicate these thoughts she had to translate the images into words, and early in treatment this translation was often blocked. She might begin to speak of her images but would quickly trail off without completing a phrase. She would say "I don't know," become silent, sigh. But the steady and basically gentle pressure of the analyst listening and asking grad-ually motivated her to work toward verbal translation of these images. In many ways, fantasy images dominated her conscious experience, and even when alone she did not translate these into word meanings. The ongoing expectation of the analyst for verbal communication altered this pattern.

The images of the fantasies were generally disguised wish fulfillments. Since her wishes involved object relationships, in contrast to the self-aggrandizing role fantasies of more narcissistic patients, two people might be depicted in the image representa-tions. Remarkably, neither person might be designated as "self." If she imagined a particular man she had seen as flirting with a woman, she might leave it quite unclear as to whether she was the woman or whether she imagined watching another woman.

Her conceptualization could be even more vague. The idea of

someone losing control and hurting someone else could be visualized without any particular awareness of whether she was the person losing control or being injured. Once again, the pressure of the analytic situation contributed to the motivation to label the images as self and others.

Early in treatment the request was simply for reports. Later the analyst interpreted images in terms of what Ms. Smith wished or feared from others. Finally Ms. Smith continued to elaborate images, including translation to lexical associative meanings, until the references to self became clear. Of course, interpretations of fear of activity, and of defensive switches between activity and passivity, played an important role. The central point is that the increased translation of images and enactments into words was due not only to modification of defenses and estimations of danger but was also a process of acquired skill in thinking clearly.

While lexical representation was not excluded from her experience of thought, there was a virtual absence of some types of verbal naming. She neither spoke nor let herself think the words for genitals or bodily functions. Penis, vagina, nipple, bladder, urine, and feces were all referred to as "it." She could not imagine herself as ever being able to think specifically, much less speak, in such terms. This issue of lexical vagueness was then elaborated into transference attitudes. She expected the analyst to try to force her to say sexual words and anticipated her own resistance and the excitement of the chase.

These transference meanings were worked through along with recognition of the general defensive function of lexical avoidances. Use of the lexical system meant a fuller orchestration of thought and a sharper designation of her own role, since in grammatical construction, the subject and object are usually specified: "I want him to do it to me." The image system may clarify what "it" is; the enactive system may clarify the intensity of doing it; the verbal system states the cause and effect sequence. Enhanced verbal communication led her to specify what she felt and wanted. At the end of the analysis she felt especially pleased with her acquired ability to speak frankly, clearly, and to the point in various contexts. She even advanced her career by taking on public-speaking engagements.

To summarize, Ms. Smith accomplished repression by a series of control processes. Representation was inhibited in two main ways. One was the warding off of representation of any potentially threatening ideas as images, enactions, or words. The second form of inhibition was prevention of translation between or among modes of representation. Inhibition at the boundaries of representational systems reduced conscious awareness in this manner.

Automatic inhibitions changed during analysis as the deployment of attention was altered. Topics and concepts clarified by the analyst directed Ms. Smith's attention to the possibility of representation. Conscious efforts, motivated by alliance and by transference attitudes, were made to override automatic nonconscious inhibitory operations. As representations occurred, the situation proved safer than expected. Dreaded states of mind occurred, if at all, in the supportive context of the analytic situation (Modell 1976).

Recurrent safety, where originally danger had been signaled, modified her automatic appraisal of threat and arousal of anxiety. Repetition of conscious efforts at representation altered the automatic "programming" of thought until representation and translation became the automatic formats.

Intrusive representations, often as images, were commonplace before and during the early phases of analysis. A loss of volitional control was an aspect of this experience because the expressions occurred in spite of inhibitory efforts. These episodes were themselves interpreted as events and indicated to her that she was out of control. She feared that such experiences meant insanity, yet the idea had some appeal. The secondary gain would be the opportunity to use irrational or undercontrolled states of mind to force those who neglected her to care for her.

In the course of conscious efforts at representation of usually inhibited ideas, she gained the sense of herself as active thinker of all thoughts. She tolerated threatening ideas and the resulting emotions. Because active thought was permitted, instrusive episodes lessened. The result of the increased conscious effort at representation was a sense of increased control. These various stylistic aspects of representations and the relevant changes during analytic work are shown in Table 5–3.

## Table 5–3

### Patterns and Change in Style
### of Conscious Representation

Style

1. Enactive forms of emotional expression were readily emergent with low translation to lexical mode. A subjective sense of low control over emotion and thought was present.
2. Perceptually derived images were constructed with a bias from schemas of sexual excitation, threat, rescue, and accusation.
3. Fantasy sequences avoided clarity as to which role was filled by self.
4. General inhibition of representation of conflicted ideas and feelings was present, with occasional intrusive representations.

Change During Treatment

Achieved more fluid and complete translations into word meanings, learned to check representations by repeated perception, learned to represent ideas about bodies, increased representation of self as agent. Reduced intrusiveness led to a heightened sense of self-control.

## Associational Linkages between New and Enduring Concepts in the Appraisal of Interpersonal Situations

One can postulate that any potentially new event sets in motion a series of appraisal problems as a kind of program for thought processes (Klein 1967, Lazarus 1966, Peterfreund and Schwartz 1971). The program would continue as a conceptual tendency until the ability to fit a new event into relevant schemas was exercised (Jacobson 1954, Miller et al. 1960, Piaget 1937, Tomkins 1962). Reinterpretation of new events or revision of schemas would fit new to old and so complete the process. Until such completion, codings of the event and relevant associations would tend toward recurrent representation. These representations would be experienced as intrusive if the repetition tendency were opposed by inhibitory maneuvers (Horowitz 1970, 1988a).

At the onset of analysis, Ms. Smith tended to recurrent errors in appraisal. For example, in establishing the relationship of a new event to enduring person schemas classifications she tended to short-circuit, that is, to erroneously "recognize" the new information as if it were another instance of a long-standing interpersonal fantasy. Ever expecting a rescuer, a chance encounter with a man was appraised as if he were the rescuer and "this was it."

Associations to available memories of times when similar feelings led to major disappointment were inhibited because the need for rescue was great; the idea of not being rescued was intolerable. This type of inhibition of associational possibilities was accomplished by terminating and not translating the first glimmerings of representations that threatened to arouse negative affect.

In order to move away from threatening ideas, she would declare a train of thought completed or incapable of completion. These styles were reflected in her speech. Either she prematurely closed a topic by announcing that she knew the meanings or she declared that she didn't know. "I don't know," the virtual hallmark of communication of the hysterical character, was not only a statement of fact but an injunction against further thought, an injunction now internalized but once a family style.

The repeated avoidance of establishing a clear chain of concepts in conscious thought led to a low capacity for organizing and analyzing events in terms of cause and effect sequences. She was unable to predict her own actions or plan for interpersonal eventualities. To the extent that she recognized this impairment she suffered narcissistic injuries and also feared being out of control herself or being overwhelmed by decisiveness in others. Such fear further motivated inhibitions of thought because thinking might involve knowing her bad thoughts, knowledge would lead to peremptory action, and loss of control and powerlessness over intrusive fantasies would follow.

Because of her fears of being bad or out of control, she automatically suppressed associational lines that would amplify the meanings and implications of her own activity. If ideas were evolving that designated her as active, and if anxiety and guilt increased with such ideas, she shifted topics and associational lines to those that designated her as passive. Sometimes inhibition and shifting were insufficient and anxiety and guilt mounted.

Another operation to reduce these felt emotions was to lose her reflective self-awareness, a part of a dissociative process. In such altered states of consciousness she could not remember what she had just been thinking or perceiving. For example, after deciding to lose her virginity and acquire sexual experience, she entered impulsively into an affair. She could not, however, do so while conceptualizing herself as awake and aware. She had to be seduced while drunk. Later, although she knew intercourse had taken place, she was unsure of what it had been like. In plaintive and poignant terms during the analysis, she described herself as psychologically a virgin because she had never actively and freely engaged in sex in a tender union.

Altered states of consciousness had the additional advantages of changing the type of mental contents she experienced. Instead of erotic wishes and fears, she fantasied a kind of oceanic nurturing. The distinction between reality and fantasy was blurred, making reality less disappointing and fantasy more enjoyable. Disparate attitudes could be dissociated with ease.

To recapitulate, there are a series of cognitive options available when the person with a hysterical personality wishes to repress and avoid meanings that would activate too-intense emotions and threaten entry into an undermodulated and dreaded state of mind:

1. Inhibit representation of the ideas and feelings.

2. If option 1 fails, then inhibit translation of those ideas into other systems of representation (for example, do not let images translate into words).

3. Avoid associational connections (that is, use steps 1 and 2 to avoid ideas and feelings that would be automatically elicited by information that *has* already gained representation).

4. Conclude a train of thought by early closure or by declaration of the impossibility of any solution.

5. Change from active to passive self schemas, or vice versa, depending on the direction of greater threat.

**6.** If the above measures are inadequate, then alter state of consciousness so as to reduce reflective self-awareness.

Each of these cognitive maneuvers could be recognized as experiences. Ms. Smith was unaware of her inhibitory style when she began analysis. But each operation could be explicitly interpreted in the context of some specific mental content and emotional response. With direction of attention to usually warded-off topics and how they were warded off, she could become aware of what she was doing and try to do otherwise. A train of thought prematurely closed off could be resumed and further associations elaborated.

A complete working-through of a topic would consist of several components. Usually, interpretation of each component concept is not necessary. The therapist simply says a few words to move the patient along. These short phrases can point to transference meanings, developmental linkages, relations to current events, cognitive avoidances, or to warded-off ideas and feelings.

To illustrate the interpretation of cognitive maneuvers with Ms. Smith, a full interpretive statement will be presented. The moment illustrated is derived from working-through episodes within an erotic transference neurosis. She had developed feelings of sexual excitement during the hour but was warding off recognition of such feelings. She was aware enough to communicate bodily sensations but meanings of these self-perceptions came and went into and out of awareness. The interpretations were aimed at increased consciousness and acceptance of these and related meanings. A global interpretation is presented schematically in Table 5–4. One column shows phrases always spoken in isolation but grouped here in a series as if given as one long interpretation about a warded-off erotic transference response. In the second column is the function served by the phrase. The two cognitive interpretations were (1) that she said, "I don't know" to prevent further representation of hazardous ideas and (2) that enactive representations of erotic excitement were not translated into words.

When Ms. Smith responded to such interpretive lines with introspective effort, she reexamined her immediate experience. Was she feeling excited or afraid? If she found such information— perhaps at the periphery of conscious representation—as images or

## Table 5–4

### Interpretive Phrases and Their Functions

| Phrase | Function |
| --- | --- |
| You say "I don't know" | Specifies the current content and outcome of a control process. |
| So you won't go on thinking | Says the purpose of the control process. |
| You are feeling excited now | Labels clearly, in lexical mode, the warded-off content. |
| In your body | Calls attention to the enactive mode of representation of the warded-off content. |
| You are afraid to know that in words | Identifies the control process of inhibiting translation of enactive-to-lexical representation. This also gives a suggestion that the patient should translate enactive ideas and feelings into words and provides a model for doing so. |
| Because you think it is bad and dangerous | Continues clarification of the purpose of control processes. This is also a suggestion that the patient check to see if she does feel anxious or guilty. |
| You felt the same way toward your father | Links the role-relationship model of self-to-analyst to its developmental object schema. |
| You felt that was bad and dangerous | Explains the original threat when warding-off maneuvers were desirable. |
| The same thing happens with your male friends | Links the role-relationship model of immediate transference pattern to current life experience. |
| Even though you do not consciously want to think of sexual excitement with them as bad and dangerous | Points out the inappropriate use of an outmoded role-relationship model and its incongruity between past and current value schemas. |

bodily enactments, she tried to translate them into words, to allow associations, to stay with the topic. If she were alone, she would not behave this way. With the analyst she now felt safe enough and also pressured enough to counteract her automatic avoidances. The pressure came from the role-relationship model organized by a therapeutic alliance, since she rightly believed that she and the therapist shared a value placed on full representation and communication (Greenson 1965), and from the transference relationship. She expected the therapist to be pleased and attentive if she cooperated with his wishes.

Whatever the weight of multiple motives, her conscious efforts to represent, to know, and to speak the previously unthinkable had a gradual effect. The warded-off themes of ideas and feelings were found to be tolerable to her adult mind, although they had been appraised as intolerable by her childhood mind. Avoidance by inhibitory control processes was less necessary. She worked through warded-off memories and fantasies and also learned a new way of thinking by repeated trials of representation, and by cross-translation of image, enactive, and lexical representation.

Only partial changes in control processes occurred at any one time. Every major theme surfaced again and again, each time with additional nuances and greater clarity. During episodes of positive transference she could accept her erotic yearnings with complete understanding, as she could her anxieties and guilt feelings, her inclinations not to know, and the relevant associational networks. With each repetition there was less resistance, less interpretation necessary, and greater definition of herself as active.

The statements shown in Table 5–4 applied to periods of working through in which Ms. Smith responded to an interpretation with introspective efforts. There were many times when she experienced an interpretive activity of the analyst, even simple repetitions of her own phrases, as if the analyst were teasing or exciting her. She was being forced to attend to the weird ideas of the analyst, just as her father forced his nudity upon her. Such transference projections clouded the clarity of the immediate topic but added the immediate emotionality so essential to the therapeutic change.

Clarity about transference experiences was then necessary. The modifications of self and object schemas through transference and transference interpretation will be discussed more thoroughly in the following section, but the point to be made here is that no cognitive change could occur without work on transference phenomena. The reduction in repressive maneuvers required a combination of interpretations, trial-and-error learning, imitative learning, working through of warded-off ideas and feelings, and alteration of patterns of self and object relationships.

As inhibitory control processes were less automatic and peremptory, Ms. Smith found she could maintain conceptual time and space on a given topic. She developed increased confidence in her ability to confront conflicting topics without "runaway" emotions or thoughts, the key features of her undermodulated states of mind. Once she was able to control her thinking about a given topic she could let herself explore it more. As Weiss (1967) and Weiss et al. (1986) have pointed out, the conscious control ability of deliberate suppression makes the unconscious defensive use of repression less necessary. As ideational–emotional complexes were worked through, conflict was reduced, and there was far less tension between emergent ideas and inhibitory operations. Correspondingly, intrusive episodes occurred less frequently, her feeling of being in control was affirmed by experience, and her self-confidence allowed her to take increased risks in behavior. These various patterns and changes in the patterns of associational connections and appraisals of input are summarized in Table 5–5.

### Resolving Incongruities between Internal Working Models of Interpersonal Relationships and Enduring Schemas of Self and Others

A newly represented set of information, whether from an external event or from emergent dreams, fantasies, or memories, may not fit with enduring schemas about the self, objects, or the world. Information processing can be complete only when the discrepancy between the new concepts and the enduring attitudes is reduced. Either the new concept must be revised or the enduring attitudes changed.

This form of adaption was described by Piaget (1937) as assimilation and accommodation, and has been reviewed in detail elsewhere (Horowitz 1991). Ms. Smith had a conspicuous tendency to appraise new information so that it would fit her enduring

## Table 5–5

### Patterns and Change in Associational
### Connections and Appraisal of Input

Style

1. Erroneously and excessively perceived present situations by associations organized by desired and dreaded role-relationship models.
2. Inhibited her associations when she experienced negative affect (which was easily aroused).
3. Avoided designation of self as instigator of thoughts, feelings, or actions.
4. Inhibited threatening memories, but with concomitant tendency to intrusive representation of them, resulting in feeling a loss of conscious control.
5. Changed meaning of events by shifting schemas of self and object between active and passive roles or by losing reflective self-awareness in altered state of consciousness.
6. Poor chaining of concepts, memories, and plans into cause-and-effect sequences.

Change During Treatment

Learned to suppress and recall selectively, learned to tolerate uncertainty and continue problem-solving over time, learned to allow increased network of associations, less avoidance with less intrusion of warded-off contents, more realistic appraisals of own and others' roles with ability to model and check cause-and-effect sequences and events.

schemas when, realistically, these schemas were inappropriate and should have been modified. Failure to change these enduring schemas led to a shallow repertoire of human knowledge, as described by Shapiro (1965). She behaved inappropriately, and these actions sometimes led to startling confrontations. Suddenly, people no longer fit her mental model of them. And if *they* were not as she believed, then *she* was not as she believed. She felt either betrayed or depersonalized.

Such depersonalization experiences were sufficient triggers for anxiety attacks or shifts to alternate self schemas. For example, if she were behaving with a man in the role of glamorous swinger and the man laughed at some trifling lack of poise, she might suddenly and globally change into a state of mind organized by a self schema as a clumsy, depressed, waif-like youth. This change included her inner self-experience, her actual posture, facial expression and movement pattern, and her style of thinking and speaking. Alternately, she might be unable to prevent entry into a state organized by a role-relationship model in which she was unfairly used and then abandoned by a selfish strong other, leading to intense and undermodulated emotions such as panic, weeping, or vindictive and accusatory rage. These inappropriate reactions interfered with relationships and further demolished her sense of confidence.

During analysis she learned to review the fit between her inner object expectations and her perceptual analysis of current persons. Once she could think more clearly she could repeat the ideational route that led her to form an internal working model of a dyadic relationship between herself and another. These cognitive processes made it possible to revise her opinions of who she was, who the other was, and the intent of each. From her earlier limited repertoire of possible dyadic relationships she learned to model and try new ones. From a global assessment of another as fulfilling a shallow and projected role, she was able to move toward an understanding of individuals with particular traits. These repetitive learning experiences fleshed out her internal models and increased her range of possible interactions.

Another aspect of the therapeutic process should be mentioned here, although it is not part of the central focus. As Ms. Smith was able to modify her degree of defensiveness and her self and object schemas she was able to obtain new gratifications. Each gratification acted as a reinforcement and also provided a new learning opportunity. For example, she could enjoy new aspects of personal mastery such as public speaking with less fear of being challenged for exhibitionism or of deflation by recognition of failure.

All anticipated gratifications were not real possibilities, of course, as when she tried a new behavior because she anticipated transference gratifications. For example, she might give up some avoidances and communicate more clearly in the hope that this would please the analyst and reenact an idyllic fantasy. To some extent this hope was dashed, but it was also partially fulfilled. While the analyst did not enter into an exhilarated and excited state with her, as she had fantasied, he did share with her the intimacy of working together in the unique situation of a therapeutic alliance. While she could not reenact a fantasy union with her father-as-mother or father-as-lover, she could find positive uses for an improved ability to tell and understand her own story.

The same comments apply to how she listened to the analyst's efforts to counteract her vague clarifications and interpretations. The consistency of intervention style built a model of the real therapist in the patient's mind. This model evoked analogous or mimicked behavior and eventual partial identification with a style of clarity. But the patient also invested transference meanings in the analyst's interventions. As do many hysterical personalities (Myerson 1969), and specifically as did a patient described by Rubinfine (1967), Ms. Smith also admired the analyst's statements of fact or probability as personal and phallic exhibitions and reacted as if they were sexual overtures. This was, again, a way of continuing fantasy object relationships and of avoiding serious confrontation with the meaning conveyed by the analyst. Yet the transference enjoyment also allowed her to hear and gradually respond to these meanings. Thus, each new gain provided some impulse gratification, could be used defensively, and also was used adaptively.

The patterns and changes in solving incongruities between new information and schemas are summarized in Table 5–6.

### Control Processes and Schematic Change

Control processes allow the transference situation, past memories, and current patterns of interpersonal relationship to be examined and reappraised using the tools of conscious thought. The manifestations of transference may not occur until the analytic situation and the therapist have safely passed unconsciously motivated behavioral or transference tests (Weiss et al. 1986). For example, if, when Ms. Smith exposed her neediness, the analyst was too kind or yielded to her demands for extra care, then the pregenitally based hostility within the maternal transference might never have been fully analyzed (Wallerstein 1986).

## Table 5–6

## Patterns and Change in Resolving
## Incongruities Between New Information of
## Interpersonal Situations and Enduring Schemas

Style

1. Short circuits to apparent solutions maladaptive to interpersonal dilemmas.
2. Modifies new information to fit repertoire of schemas; schemas thus tend to remain as unrevised stereotypes without depth of meanings or reality fidelity; this leads to stereotyped action plans rather than mastery of real opportunities.
3. Low level of rechecking situations for the reality appropriateness of internal working models.

Change During Treatment

Learned to recheck ideational route and inner working models of relationship situations for reality appropriateness; developed capacity to perceive and understand self and others and developed an expanded repertoire of role-relationship models; current (mature) self and object schemas become more dominant than developmentally primitive ones.

This sequence, from warding off transference based on primitive schemas to revision of schemas in the direction of maturity, can be diagramed as in Figure 5–1. The stages are (1) warding off, (2) transference tests (for example, asking for special times for appointments), (3) transference emergence, and then—granted changes in style of control processes—(4) recognition of what it *feels* like is happening as appraised in relation to what is *really* happening. This latter step leads to revision of primitive schemas of the self and others and relates to Loewald's (1960) view that transference interpretations that work have two elements: they take the patient to his or her true regressive level and they also indicate to the patient the higher integrative level to be reached.

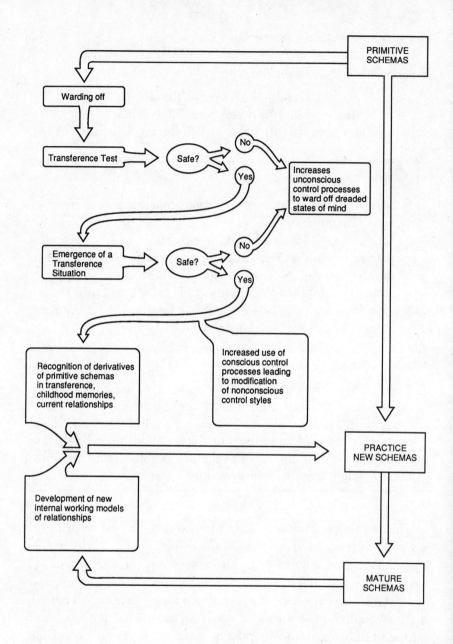

FIGURE 5–1

Schematic development as a consequence of transference
enactment, change in habitual defensive controls,
and transference resolution

## Change in Role-Relationship Models

Ms. Smith, like all persons, operated in the world by a repertoire of self and object schemas. These were organized into roles, often role dyads, and imposed by her on her interpersonal relationships (Horowitz 1979, 1991, Jacobson 1964, Kernberg 1966, Schafer 1968). At the onset of analysis there were a limited number of role-relationship models that could be fulfilled by her or by others. These roles can be abstracted and then discussed in terms of change during the analytic process.

Her basic models of self and object were derived from her childhood version of her family. A crude person schematic model of her family is shown in Figure 5–2. Each central person is given a label according to the role Ms. Smith mainly attributed to him or to her. These roles were, to a large extent, agreed upon tacitly within the family so that her inner model was congruent to the family communication and interaction pattern. In many states her father was a special exception; her mother the caretaker; her older sister the free spirit; her younger sister the defective person in a sick role; and she, the spiritually good member.

In Figure 5–2, the main attachments are also indicated as the bonds between her older sister and her father, between her father and her mother, and between her mother and the younger sister. Ms. Smith's attitudes toward these bonds and toward the persons involved are also conceptualized in the arrows radiating from herself. The basic self-attribute is isolation from attachments, with envy and yearning to establish herself in a dyad. This does not mean she did not have attachments with each member of the family but that these attachments, while pleasurable and exciting in part, were not entirely fulfilling. She felt rejected or conflicted in relation to every one of them, and this pattern, as suggested by Fairbairn (1954), led her to split aspects of reaction to each family member. That is why, in Figure 5–2, antitheses are indicated, as between contempt (withdrawal) and envy with identification (approach). Emotions such as anxiety and guilt are omitted because they are reactions to the attitudes shown, for example, anxiety over sexual interest toward her father.

Each member of the family provided a source of identification for her, both in terms of what there was in them that she could imitate and what there was in her to which they chose to react. The role

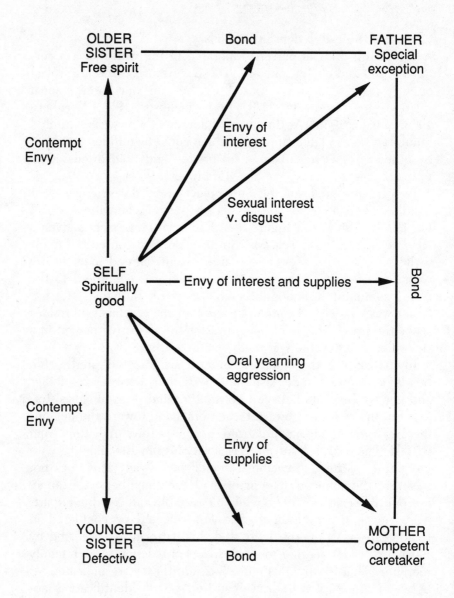

FIGURE 5–2

Family schemas

structure of the family can be examined in a way that is one step more complex than the basic model of Figure 5–2. That is, the main constructs for roles can be listed, each member of the family can be described as a personification based on these constructs, and the repertoire of self schemas of Ms. Smith based on identification with the family member can be coordinated with these attributes (see Kelly 1955, Loevinger 1973). It is much easier to see this than to describe it in linear text (see Table 5–7 on page 244).

The main person schematic constructs are goodness–badness; activity–passivity; and masculinity–femininity. The main schemas of others are listed as splits between good and bad versions of each family member. Her self schemas are shown as identifications or complementary roles in this matrix of family. Ms. Smith's parents and sisters were models for her own development as well as mirrors that reflected the development of her concept of self.

The defectiveness of her parents as models and mirrors interfered with her maturation, and the analytic process allowed both a resumption of construct development and an opportunity to resolve conflicts between constructs. The problem for analysis was to identify primitive roles in action and raise this to consciousness. This accentuation of awareness included recognition of precursors of more differentiated roles. By trial action within the analysis, the goal was to help her evolve her inner self and object models into forms more congruous with the real potentials for interpersonal relationships in her adult life, independent of her family (Loewald 1960).

This analytic task was complicated by her ability and tendency to take either role in a two-person dyad. As emphasized earlier, she could interchange active and passive roles in her inner experience of any given situation. She could be the moralist condemning a sexually active "swinger," or the swinger living more pleasurably than the moralist and more fully than the defective child–woman. This fluid propensity to change the role for self in a given role dyad is based on childhood development. Baldwin (as reviewed by Loevinger 1973) called this the dialectic of personal growth: the child learns to perceive the traits of parents; he or she then can find such patterns in the self, which in turn permits more differentiated perception of the parents, and so on in a reciprocal process. As

**Table 5-7**
**Role Structure**

| Main Person Schematic Constructs | | | Schemas of Others | | | | Self Schemas |
|---|---|---|---|---|---|---|---|
| Goodness | Activity | Gender | Mother | Father | Older Sister | Younger Sister | |
| Good | Active | Female | Competent Childbearing Caring Moralistic —vs— | | Sensuous Free Childbearing —vs— | | Sexually active swinger –vs– moralistic |
| Good | Passive | Female | | | | Deserving attention —vs— | Sick and deserving child |
| Bad | Active | Female | Manipulator Devouring —vs— | | Promiscuous Sinful | | Incestuous Devouring Rivalrous |
| Bad | Passive | Female | Depressed Depleted | | | Defective | Defective child–woman |
| Good | Active | Male | | Skillful —vs— | | | Grandiose fantasies of being skillful, effective |
| Good | Passive | Male | | Aesthetic Soulful —vs— | | | Aesthetic, Soulful Artist |
| Bad | Active | Male | | Sexually intrusive Out of control | | | Out-of-control person |
| Bad | Passive | Male | | Failure | | | Incompetent failure |

a result, almost everything found in the self is something found in significant others, as shown in Table 5–7.

Modification of habitual control purposes, processes, and outcomes, as described in the previous section, allowed schemas to be reviewed in terms of conscious derivatives. The transferences allowed here-and-now reenactments of what Knapp (1974) has called "interpersonal fantasy constellations." These could be compared with the realities of the therapeutic process and relationship. Any particular schema was labeled, known by many facets, connected with current extra-analytic relationships and with recollections of childhood.

Such reviews meant a new integration of segregated constructs. By the end of the analysis, Ms. Smith could view her parents as real people with good and bad traits rather than as split-apart good and bad introjects. Clarity in perception of these patterns engendered revision of her memory of the past and of her future expectations. She gave up the hope of finding her parents transformed into ideals, developed a sympathetic understanding of their failures, and relinquished the belief that they were deliberately causing her suffering. This increased clarity about schemas derived from relationships with her family allowed her to control her development of schemas of new people. Aware of her tendencies to externalize and project, she could check supposed similarities to see if they were borne out by real behavior. With new ways to act, her relationships became increasingly fresh and real.

### Modifications of Self Schemas

The various constructs of Table 5–7 are clustered into four main forms of self experience. Two were warded off; two were commonly experienced in an oscillatory manner. The most frequent self-experience was as passive, defective, and childlike. The second most frequent self-experience was of her ideal self. The components of this ideal were not fully integrated and consisted of the role of the sexual free spirit and that of the artistic and soulful person. Unfortunately, these ideal self experiences were unstable. They changed readily into the passive, childlike, defective self, or, in the direction of bad activity, became the warded-off self with incestuous, devouring, manipulative, and out-of-control attributes (see Figure 5–3).

The fourth self-experience was as a moralist. In the moral schema, accusations were directed against past or anticipated acts of the self or others. This state was also warded off, and might also intrude as unbidden images or fantasies. The intrusive episodes were conscious experiences of felt presences in the form of maternal or god-like introjects. These four types of self-experience are sufficient to pattern her self schemas at the onset of analysis, as diagramed in Figure 5–3. It remains to describe how they changed.

As with object schemas, changes in self schemas relied on concurrent change in thought. Reduced inhibitory controls allowed conscious comparisons between the current real facts and her enduring schemas. Discrepancies between schemas and real behaviors were recognized. Instead of revising the here-and-now information to fit her stereotypes, Ms. Smith was able in the analysis to change the schemas.

### Changes in the Sexually Free Self Schemas

Before analysis, the main manifestation of the sexually free schemas was her role of swinger. Frequent sexual liaisons revolved around a victim and aggressor dyad. She was one or the other; her partner occupied the complementary role. In the swinger role, unable to conceptualize two active persons, she invariably gave one a passive script. The aggressor took from or seduced the victim. The victim gave up or submitted. Sometimes the roles were reversed, with sadomasochistic flavorings.

The swinger role was an adaptational attempt to defy self-images as the victim of her mother's insufficient attentiveness and her father's seductions. While she imagined herself as if she were the aggressor, luring and breaking the hearts of men and arousing the envious fury of women, she also submitted to sexual usage and was ultimately discarded. Only with older or "grayer" men, or during the vain attempts of virile men to lead her to sexual climax, could she feel as if she had actively defeated them.

The possibilities of both persons being active, as is usually desirable in sexual acts, or both persons being passive, as in quiet mutuality, were too anxiety provoking. If both persons were active, this meant they would excite each other too much, reviving a prototypical danger of the patient and her father arousing each

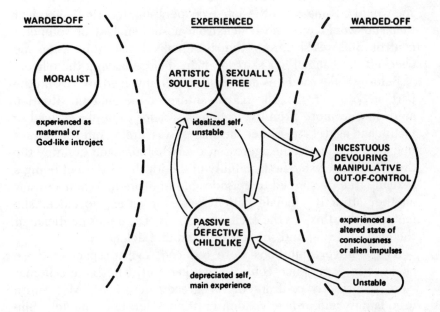

FIGURE 5–3

Experienced and warded-off self concepts

other simultaneously. It was only during the course of analysis that Ms. Smith learned a dyad in which both persons were simultaneously active. For example, later in the analysis, she felt correctly that she and the analyst were working intensively together, attempting to understand the multiple meanings of an episode of experience. At such times she would have a "reality" experience; she would be amazed at the active cooperation, feel dizzy, and fear that she would wet the couch from a sudden loss of sphincter control. She was so sure of the risk involved that on occasion she checked the back of her skirt for stains before leaving the office.

Before she learned this new dyad, which involved activity on the part of both persons, she had to interpret the analytic situation according to more primitive schemas, as, for example, a dyad of victim and aggressor. Either the analyst was forcing interpretations upon her or she was the aggressor, overwhelming and draining the drab, tired analyst. The instability of the idealized state of being a sexually free person led to episodes of humiliation. When she saw another attractive female patient leave or enter the office, she fantasied that this was the exciting mistress of a famous politician or the analyst's wife, and she felt rejected and defective.

As cognitive inhibitions were reduced, every aspect of these changes in experience could be worked out. The basic schemas were recurrently confronted. As already described, Ms. Smith used fantasy and projective identification to form new models. She softened the stereotype of swinger into a womanly, tender, sensuous set of traits. She daydreamed and dreamed of mutually active role-relationships in an idealized projection of the analyst and his wife. After these fantasy trials proved safe, she gradually experimented in reality. The inevitable disappointments did not deter her because she could now tolerate and work them through consciously. Instead of globally imitating her ideal role models, she was able to discretely act out some idealized traits. She was no longer an actress faking a part and ready for the humiliating experience of being unmasked.

In Figure 5–3, the ideal self also contains aesthetic and soulful qualities. These traits were not fully integrated with the concept of sexual freedom and sensuality. Because sexuality was dangerous, it was isolated from other ideals. Even the aesthetic and soulful ideals, however, were unstable. She was unable to work either on artistic or career-oriented tasks, and so her self-image could not be compared with these ideals without deflation. Since she could not bolster her self esteem with memory or anticipation of real accomplishments, she could only daydream. Even that seemed, at times, so hopeless as to lead to depression and a shift to a self-as-defective position.

In the course of the analysis, ideals were confronted. She could decide again, as an adult now, which ideal she preferred. She could equilibrate goals to realistic appraisals of possibilities, thus changing adolescent grandiose fantasies into achievable expectations. She was able to dissociate artistic enterprises from her father's behavior. For example, she reviewed memories in which her father had given her a set of oil paints, a bottle of turpentine, and some canvas boards and expected her to teach herself to paint landscapes and portraits. She had tried and performed only at a mediocre and frustrating level. Since she had shared her father's ideas that she ought to learn by osmosis or spontaneous talent, she had explained this failure as her own incompetence. Clear review of these ideals allowed her to reevaluate the memories. As an adult, she knew that training and practice were necessary to any skill. She then planned to take courses in technique. In executing this plan, she developed an interest in color mixing and perspective and found the step-by-step learning to be exhilarating.

These real and gratifying accomplishments provided the necessary memories for a stable idealized self-image, and she was able to separate ideas of her own artistic interests and qualities from those ideas about her father and those ideas her father had about her. Then she was able to praise or to criticize her own work and to do so from a semirealistic basis. She could admit failure in a given effort without feeling worthless.

### Changes in the Moralistic Self Schemas

At the onset of analysis, Ms. Smith was unaware that she felt guilty about her activity in general and her sexuality in particular. Her conscious thoughts dwelt on the desirability of sexual freedom. As she became aware of feeling badly about active sexual wishes, she was depressed to discover her own feelings of guilt. It seemed primitive to her and like a submission to the weird analytic ideas she expected to have forced upon her. But the ideas became clear and tolerable.

As memories and fantasies of the past were reexamined and linked to the present, she learned to dissociate sexual and aggressive aims from intrafamilial, and hence taboo, objects. Her rational thought countered the laws proclaimed in her childhood and the conditioned associations that overgeneralized them. She became the instigator of rules of behavior.

At first, this process seemed artificial and also time consuming. Faced with a given decision, she had to think through many ramifications in order to deviate from her automatically imposed inhibitions and disavowals of inhibitions. But with repetition of decisions she developed new guiding principles that illuminated new ways to arrive at automatic decisions, which were then seen as self-determined feelings rather than punitive restrictions from external sources.

With these changes, there was less discrepancy between sexual self-images and the once warded off and now modified moralistic self. Attributes from both schemas could be represented consciously without guilt or anxiety. This increased the stability of the ideal self schema and also made it unnecessary to ward off the residual aspects of the moralistic self schema. There was thus a gradual coalescence of these two schemas and of the two others still to be discussed.

## Changes in the Schemas of Self as Passive, Defective, Child

As mentioned earlier, Miss Smith typified role-relationships as a dyad between an active and a passive person. In the main version she was in the passive, waif-like role, and an active person was the rescuer. In a good outcome, because of her suffering, she would be found by an idealized parental figure, given the necessary ingredients (such as gradual sexual instruction), and then become a whole person. The bad outcome was to be subjected to abuse by a malicious or sadistic person and to obtain thereby some small attention; she would accumulate pain (that by destiny would later be traded in for gratification), and relieve the guilt accumulated from various oedipal fantasies. Since this dyad was not allowed clear conscious representation, it only organized her processing of the information of her everyday life. The dyad was not revised according to realistic appraisals. She remained a passive victim or waif, to be duped or rescued by active others.

Why could not two persons be thought of as being together but simultaneously passive in their relationship? She could not conceive of persons at rest with one another because her needs were experienced as too intense and peremptory. She also felt defective and unworthy of attention. She was incapable of relating and incompetent at work. To feel like that and be with another person who was not actively engaging her meant only that she had to feel alone, unworthy, empty, and neglected.

The treatment situation was ready-made to fit into her rescue fantasy, as exemplified by the dream of being taken to the home-sanitorium of the analyst. As she began to reveal herself and to feel that she was understood, the fantasy of waif and rescuer took over and organized her expectations about what would happen next. The analyst would recognize her needs and fill the void in a moment of lyrical union. To repeat a central point: Ms. Smith expected things that did not happen, and in the vacuum of frustration her wishes emerged as conscious desires. Because of the cognitive shifts, she could appraise them as deviant from the therapeutic contract but could also understand their import as recurring patterns.

Provided that the opportunity for conceptual clarity was also present, the transference situation allowed repeated confrontation with such everyday frustrations. Every weekend and vacation there was a separation. Unexpected separations occurred with illnesses. She could, for example, see how much she wanted the analyst to take her home, how frequently she accepted intercourse with others out of a desire only to be held and cared for, how frustrated she felt when recalling childhood memories. These real experiences evoked sadness, but the sadness was related to specific instances rather than a global self-assessment. It was tolerable to feel sad when lonely on a given night, if she did not have to go from there to endless feelings of hopelessness and despair.

As she gave up the fantasy of rescue, it was necessary to fulfill the expected functions herself. Again, cognitive processing allowed both exploration of hitherto warded-off associational connections and consideration of new and possible solutions to her motivational dilemmas. Dreams often preceded the explorations of themes in the analytic hours and may have been dreamed for the purpose of furthering the analytic process as well as for an imaginative trial of new self-images. For example, she had the intense desire to be taken to restaurants by men, and she expected this to take place after intercourse, as if, in effect, she had paid in advance. As the role schemas shifted in analysis, she began to dream of going to restaurants alone. At first, the dreams ended in anxiety. After the dreams seemed satisfactory, she attempted to act them out in real life. She had always been phobic of eating out alone. Her first step was to take food home from a hamburger stand, then to eat lunch at a busy counter-service diner, and finally to eat dinner in a good restaurant. She felt uncomfortable but successful after this series. Once she felt capable of being active on her own, she then felt entitled to be more assertive of her desires when dating men.

Part of this reality appraisal was also helpful in allowing her to recognize the improbability of realizing her rescue fantasy. At best, only children are rescued and cared for as children. In her relationships with older men she could be babied, but at a price she no longer cared to pay. If being a sick child did not lead to rescue, secondary gains were no longer present. The revision of the schemas toward more adult appraisals of herself was thus encouraged by the reduction in expectation of reward.

As the swinger schema lost its utility and necessity as a disavowal of her sense of feminine inadequacy, it was possible to consciously explore her defective body image. She was surprised to realize, when she allowed herself to imagine her own genitals, that she could not visualize herself as having a vagina and other female organs. In a way, not having a speakable word like "vagina" helped preserve her childlike status. During intercourse she did not "know" her vagina. Temporarily, as she first became more distinctly aware, the experience changed. She was then afraid she would extend her body too far and become both male and female. She wanted to control and take away the penis, or even wrestle with and control all of the male body. These explorations in reality and fantasy led to an evolving sense of body image and bodily competence. She became strongly contemptuous of men who did not shift the gears of cars with verve. She bought her own sports car, enjoyed her mastery of the stick shift, and imagined herself out-gunning the analyst in car races.

The projective identification with the analyst's wife also allowed her to elaborate and try out possible self-images in fantasy. She watched "Titsy" (her dream name for the fantasy wife) be sexy, maternal, and humane all at the same time and then tried to act that way herself. Again, the trials of conscious fantasy and acting according to new ideals seemed artificial at first, but with practice and confidence seemed natural.

As her range of experience widened, she could become aware of attitudes related to her defective body image. She feared injury by an uncontrolled penis because of her erroneous belief in a tiny or nonexistent vagina. Her pronounced scopophilia was seen not only as a libidinal impulse and as a defensive reversal of exhibitionism, but also as an intense desire to gain information about what bodies were like. Recognition of her own interest led to examination and reduction of moralistic prohibitions and exploration of her body with mirrors and her fingers. She read books on sex and experimented in erotic stimulation. Each new experience led to anxiety, but in tolerable dosages. She realized her fear of "letting go" or becoming wildly aggressive. The fear could be matched with reality. It didn't happen, and the fearful expectation was revised. As her body image evolved, she felt sexually competent. She could let her alert anxiety during intercourse wane and accumulate plateaus of erotic arousal.

### The Incestuous, Devouring, Out-of-Control Self

This final set of self-attributes was warded off and experienced as intrusive, as was the moralistic self which opposed it. At the onset of analysis, Ms. Smith was not aware of a self-experience as an incestuous, devouring, and dangerously out-of-control child. Yet the potential of such states exerted dynamic effects. Rigid inhibitory controls of schemas were fostered to avoid this state. The rigid inhibitions gave way, and recurrent father and mother transference episodes emerged. She experienced sexual wishes toward the analyst and also devouring aims.

The rule in the analytic situation of verbalizing rather than touching and the consistent neutrality of the analyst in terms of the desires he might bring into the situation made for a safer experience of such thoughts and feelings than had been possible previously. Even her feelings of rivalry toward her sisters were given a foil in the analytic situation as she envied other patients she imagined to be more interesting or more needy than herself and as she evolved various feelings for her image of the analyst's presumed wife.

As the incestuous, devouring, rivalrous feelings emerged, it was possible for her to realize that she originated these feelings—that they were not imposed on her. She was also able to realize that she was having fantasy thoughts, not taking real actions, and that there was a difference. She did not break the analytic rule against physical confrontations, did not injure the analyst or blow up his car, did not tear into the walls or stain the couch. She only fantasied that she or other patients might do this. The conceptual distance between fantasy and reality grew. Fantasy became self-generated and action was controlled. Thus, the conscious experience in the present was quite different from conscious experiences in childhood.

As she learned to experience strivings for erotic and tender attentions, she was able to further contemplate plans for obtaining gratifications. Just as the reduction in anxiety and guilt responses reduced the threat, anticipation of realistic possibilities made the experience of need less painful. She came to view the analyst as a trial object. She could experiment with various ways to contemplate herself and him. Then she could have a set of ideas, plans, and responses already partially worked out when she tried to allow herself such an open range of experience with other persons, persons who would respond to her according to their own wishes.

This course of trial feelings reduced the incestuous quality of her erotic interests. As the connections were made through associative extensions, she was able to change the object of her erotic feelings. The analyst provided a safe early displacement. Then she could allow herself to experience excitement while with her male friends. She could learn to assert her sexuality without guilt or anxiety because she was able to perceive that the relationship was mutually satisfactory, and that the associations to taboo or destructive components were inappropriate and could be deemphasized.

### Summary of Roles

By combining the main features of her relatives in the nuclear family, a series of eight roles was seen as designators for both self and object schemas. The basic elements in these roles were active and passive, good and bad, male and female. Ms. Smith had some difficulty with each role. To avoid excessive complexity, I described these roles in terms of four major and global self-experiences that were of importance at the onset of analysis. The result of changes in roles was an integrated self-experience that remained relatively consistent whether she was with someone active or passive or was herself active or passive in a given relationship.

Earlier, Table 5–7 showed the main self schemas at the onset of analysis. Change and status after the analysis can now be recorded for each of those schemas. The result is Table 5–8.

## CONCLUSIONS

This chapter has described hysterical personality in terms of the interaction between an information processing style centered on a lack of awareness and core schemas of self and others based on experiencing the self as defective, childlike, and in need of attention and rescue. These cognitive styles and structures lead to behavioral traits such as the tendency to use bodily communication of ideas and feelings rather than words or expressed images.

Each aspect of the hysterical personality can be amenable to change in the course of psychotherapy. The complex interaction of process styles and structural characteristics means that extended therapies are likely to be necessary. The work ahead is to review and describe the processes of change in such persons in sufficient detail so that with enough clarification of these processes it can be possible to insure a higher rate of good treatment outcome and to shorten treatment time by finding optimum intervention strategies.

### Implications for a Brief Therapy

The focus here has been on change processes in the extended time available in psychoanalytic treatment. What are the implications for treatment programs that must of necessity be compressed into less time and expense? While modifications of cognitive style and building new person schemas involve extended and repetitive episodes of learning and unlearning automatic patterns of information processing, some of the same principles apply to therapies

## Table 5–8
## Change in Self Schemas after Analysis

| Self Schemas | Status before Analysis | Change | Status after Analysis |
|---|---|---|---|
| Sexually active woman | "Swinger" role used to disavow inhibition and incestuous configuration | Saw defensive function and discrepancy between reality and fantasy | Felt authentically sexual, extremes of inhibition and promiscuity reduced |
| Moralist | Maternal and god-like introjects condemn her sexual and aggressive impulses; her self-attitudes are harsh but disavowed | Disavowal reduced; moralistic attitudes more clearly experienced, revised, and more realistic as patient learned to dissociate sex and aggression from familial objects | Experienced principles as self-originated and worthy of adherence |
| Passive, sick, and deserving child | Emphasized in self-images | Lessened expectancy of rescue fantasy being realized | Less prominent |
| Active, incestuous, manipulative rival | Felt vaguely evil and dangerous | Unconscious sexual and aggressive motives made conscious with reduction in viewing new persons as parent figures | Felt sexual and assertive strivings were all right |
| Defective child–woman | Felt as if incapable of intercourse, nurturing roles, and childbearing; low self-esteem | Evolved body image by learning reality of bodily structures | Felt grown-up and womanly |

aimed at working through a focal stressor event. For the hysterical personality, repetition and clarity will be especially helpful as will a relationship that avoids the pitfalls of excessive coldness or excessive rescue. Some of these brief, focused therapy techniques are summarized in Table 5–9.

An area that needs further scientific investigation is the use of new techniques in the brief therapy of persons with hysterical personality. Could such persons benefit from training courses in awareness, clarity of thought and expression, in recognition of body language? Is it possible that some of the evolutionary changes in self schemas as described for sequences of dreams and fantasies in

Table 5–9

**Summary of Treatment Interventions
for Short-term Therapy Aims in Persons
with Hysterical Personality***

| Function | Style as "Defect" | Therapeutic Counteraction |
|---|---|---|
| Perception | Global or selective inattention | Ask for details and repetitions |
| Representation | Impressionistic rather than accurate | "Abreaction" of memories and reconstruction |
| Translation of images and enactions to words | Limited | Encourage talk; provide verbal labels to designate meanings |
| Associations | Limited by inhibitions; misinterpretations based on stereotypes, deflected from reality to wishes and fears | Encourage production; clarification; differentiate reality from fantasy |
| Problem-solving | Short-circuit to rapid but often erroneous conclusions, avoidance of topic when emotions are unbearable | Keep subject open; interpretations of meaning and cause-and-effect relationship; support through safety and coherence of therapeutic alliance |

*From Horowitz (1986).

Ms. Smith could be fostered more speedily by guided-imagery techniques? Could some of her progressive trial activities, such as the series of eating-out occasions, have occurred more speedily in the context of behavior therapy, role-playing, or cognitive therapy?

Some psychoanalysts would answer these questions negatively on the grounds that every act is overdetermined, that the conflicts are too deep-seated and unconscious, that the immature development is interlocked into too many areas and one cannot change one without change in the others. Many therapists who advocate new techniques would answer positively, but they often ignore character typology in order to claim wide applicability of their methods and to promote attractively brief training for potential practitioners.

The answer will be found in efforts at psychotherapy integration associated with empirical tests. New methods should be given a trial in the context of deep clinical understanding and objective analysis of results. This eventual psychotherapy research will require a careful dissection of the person's information-processing style and schematic models of self and others. And our typological descriptions will have to grow more precise as will our rational prescription of potentially effective and potentially harmful interventions. For the hysterical typology, this trek has been underway throughout 2,000 years of clinical practice (Veith 1977). The slow but progressive clarifications brought by scientific objectivity indicate that the journey may usefully continue.

## REFERENCES

Berne, E. (1961). *Transactional Analysis in Psychotherapy*. New York: Grove.

Easser, B. R., and Lesser, S. R. (1965). Hysterical personality: a reevaluation. *Psychoanalytic Quarterly* 34:390–405.

Fairbairn, W. R. (1954). Observations on the nature of hysterical states. *British Journal of Medical Psychology* 27:105–125.

Gardner, R., Holzman, P. S., Klein, G. S., Linton, H., and Spence, D. P. (1959). Cognitive controls: a study of individual consistencies in cognitive behavior. *Psychological Issues* 1:1–186.

Gedo, J. (1988). *The Mind in Disorder: Psychoanalytic Models of Psychology*. Hillsdale, NJ: Analytic Press.

Gedo, J., and Goldberg, A. (1973). *Models of the Mind*. Chicago: The University of Chicago Press.

Greenson, R. (1965). The working alliance and the transference neurosis. *Psychoanalytic Quarterly* 34:155–181.

Horowitz, M. J. (1970).*Image Formation and Cognition*. New York: Appleton-Century-Crofts.

———(1972). Modes of representation of thought. *Journal of the American Psychoanalytic Association* 20:793–819.

———(1974). Microanalysis of working through in psychotherapy. *American Journal of Psychiatry* 131:1208–1212.

———(1977). Hysterical personality: cognitive structure and the processes of change. *International Review of Psycho-Analysis* 4:23–49.

———(1986). *Stress Response Syndromes*. 2nd ed. Northvale, NJ: Jason Aronson.

———(1987). *States of Mind: Configurational Analysis of Individual Psychology*. New York: Plenum Press.

———(1988a). *Introduction to Psychodynamics: A New Synthesis*. New York: Basic Books.

———, ed. (1988b). *Psychodynamics and Cognition*. Chicago: University of Chicago Press.

———, ed. (1991). *Person Schemas and Maladaptive Interpersonal Patterns*. Chicago: University of Chicago Press.

Jacobson, E. (1954). The self and the object world: vicissitudes of their infantile cathexis and their influence on ideational and affective development. *Psychoanalytic Study of the Child* 9:75–127. New York: International Universities Press.

———(1964). *The Self and the Object World*. New York: International Universities Press.

Kelly, G. (1955). *The Psychology of Personal Constructs*. Vol. 2. New York: Norton.

Kernberg, O. (1966). Structural derivatives of object relationships. *International Journal of Psycho-Analysis* 47:236–253.

Klein, G. S. (1967). Peremptory ideation: structure and force in motivated ideas. In *Motives and Thought: Psychoanalytic Essays in Honor of David Rapaport*, ed. R. Holt, pp. 80–128. *Psychological Issues* Monograph 18/19. New York: International Universities Press.

Klein, G. S., Gardner, R. W., and Schlesing, H. J. (1962). Tolerance for unrealistic experiences: a study of the generality of a cognitive control. *British Journal of Medical Psychology* 53:41–55.

Knapp, P. H. (1974). Segmentation and structure in psychoanalysis. *Journal of the American Psychoanalytical Association* 22:13–36.

Lazarus, R. S. (1966). *Psychological Stress and the Coping Process*. New York: McGraw-Hill.

Loevinger, J. (1973). Ego development. *Psychoanalysis and Contemporary Science* 2:77–156.

Loewald, H. W. (1960). The therapeutic action of psychoanalysis. *International Journal of Psycho-Analysis* 41:16–26.

Marmor, J. (1953). Orality in the hysterical personality. *Journal of the American Psychoanalytic Association* 1:656–675.

Miller, G. A., Galanter, E., and Pribram, K. (1960). *Plans and the Structure of Behavior*. New York: Holt, Rinehart & Winston.

Modell, A. H. (1976). Holding environment and therapeutic action of psychoanalysis. *Journal of the American Psychoanalytic Association* 24:285–307.

Myerson, P. (1969). The hysteric's experience in psychoanalysis. *International Journal of Psycho-Analysis* 50:373–384.

Peterfreund, E., and Schwartz, J. T. (1971). *Information systems and psychoanalysis: Psychological Issues*. Monograph 25/26. New York: International Universities Press.

Piaget, J. (1937). *The Construction of Reality in the Child*. New York: Basic Books, 1954.

Rapaport, D., and Gill, M. M. (1958). The points of view and assumptions of metapsychology. *International Journal of Psycho-Analysis* 40:153–162.

Rubinfine, D. (1967). Notes on a theory of reconstruction. *British Journal of Medical Psychology* 40:195–206.

Schafer, R. (1968). *Aspects of Internalization*. New York: International Universities Press.

Shapiro, D. (1965). *Neurotic Styles*. New York: Basic Books.

Shengold, L. (1988). *Halo in the Sky: Observations on Anality and Defense*. New York: Guilford Press.

Tomkins, S. (1962). *Affect, Imagery, Consciousness*. New York: Springer.

Veith, I. (1977). Two thousand years of hysteria. In *Hysterical Personality*, ed. M. J. Horowitz. Northvale NJ: Jason Aronson.

Wallerstein, R. S. (1986). *Forty-two Lives in Treatment: A Study of Psychoanalysis and Psychotherapy*. New York: Guilford Press.

Weiss, J. (1967). The integration of defenses. *International Journal of Psycho-Analysis* 48:520–524.

Weiss, J., Sampson, H., and the Mount Zion Psychotherapy Research Group. (1986). *Psychoanalytic Process: Theory, Clinical Observation, and Empirical Research*. New York: Guilford Press.

Wisdom, J. O. (1961). A methodological approach to the problem of hysteria. *International Journal of Psycho-Analysis* 42:224–237.

Zetzel, E. (1970). Therapeutic alliance in the analysis of hysteria. In *Incapacity for Emotional Growth*, ed. E. Zetzel, pp. 182–196. London: Hogarth.

————(1971). The emergence of new themes: a contribution to the psychoanalytic theory of therapy. *International Journal of Psycho-Analysis* 52:520–524.

# Index

263